BEHIND A CONVICT'S EYES

Doing Time in a Modern Prison

K. C. CARCERAL

EDITED BY

THOMAS J. BERNARD
Pennsylvania State University

LEANNE FIFTAL ALARID
University of Missouri, Kansas City

BRUCE BIKLE
California State University, Sacramento

ALENE BIKLE

WADSWORTH
CENGAGE Learning™

Australia • Brazil • Japan • Korea • Mexico • Singapore • Spain • United Kingdom • United States

WADSWORTH
CENGAGE Learning™

Behind a Convict's Eyes: Doing Time in a Modern Prison
K. C. Carceral

Senior Executive Editor: Sabra Horne

Editorial Assistant: Paul Massicotte

Marketing Manager: Dory Schaeffer

Marketing Assistance: Neena Chandra

Advertising Project Manager:
Stacey Purviance

Project Manager, Editorial Production:
Matt Ballantyne

Print/Media Buyer: Doreen Suruki

Permissions Editor: Joohee Lee

Production Service: Shepherd, Inc.

Copy Editor: Jean Pascual

Cover Designer: Yvo Riezebos

Cover Images: Copyright © 2003
Elizabeth Etienne/Index Stock

Compositor: Shepherd, Inc.

For product information and technology assistance, contact us at
Cengage Learning Customer & Sales Support, 1-800-354-9706.

For permission to use material from this text or product, submit all requests online at
www.cengage.com/permissions.
Further permissions questions can be emailed to
permissionrequest@cengage.com.

Library of Congress Control Number: 2003109626

ISBN-13: 978-0-534-63517-6

ISBN-10: 0-534-63517-2

Wadsworth
10 Davis Drive
Belmont, CA 94002-3098
USA

Cengage Learning is a leading provider of customized learning solutions with office locations around the globe, including Singapore, the United Kingdom, Australia, Mexico, Brazil, and Japan. Locate your local office at:
www.cengage.com/global.

Cengage Learning products are represented in Canada by Nelson Education, Ltd.

To learn more about Wadsworth, visit
www.cengage.com/wadsworth.

Purchase any of our products at your local college store or at our preferred online store
www.ichapters.com.

Printed in Canada
4 5 6 7 8 9 10 12 11 10 09

BEHIND A CONVICT'S EYES

Contents

DEDICATION   VII

ACKNOWLEDGEMENTS   VIII

FOREWORD   X

PRELUDE ON ESCAPISM: "REALITY IS
WHAT YOU MAKE IT"   XV

I   IN THE BEGINNING   1

Editors' Introduction to Part I   1

1   HE'S ONE OF OURS NOW   5

2   A & E   15

3   PRISON-PROPER   23

4 HOW I GOT MY REP   29

Editors' Discussion of Part I   36

II PRISON LIFE   39

Editors' Introduction to Part II   39

5 CONTROL   43

6 TIME   51

7 POLITICS   59

8 ECONOMICS   67

9 THE CHRISTMAS CHICKEN CAPER   75

10 THIRD WORLD MEDICAL   89

11 SEX   102

12 THE BARBERSHOP SEX SCANDAL   111

Editors' Discussion of Part II   121

III THE DISEASE OF VIOLENCE   127

Editors' Introduction to Part III   127

13 RACISM AND HATRED   131

14 SEGREGATION   140

15   RETALIATION   152

16   GANGS   164

Editors' Discussion of Part III   169

IV   CONCLUSIONS   175

**17   CORRECTIONAL POLICY AND PRISON
CROWDING   177**

Editors' Discussion of Part IV   183

**APPENDIX A: A THEORY OF THE TOXIC-SHAMED
CRIMINAL   190**

Editors' Discussion of Appendix A   205

**APPENDIX B: GLOSSARY OF PRISON-PROPER
TERMS   210**

Dedication

This book is dedicated to all those I have hurt. In my desire to change my life and knowing that I can never replace what I have taken, I am truly sorry for the pain I caused. I hope you have found a peaceful productive life and have come to know the peace within that I have found. Forgiving myself has been tough but I have been able to do it. Forgetting is something I never will.

Acknowledgements

I want to acknowledge the help of many of my fellow prisoners with whom I have done time, who have showed me respect, and who were honest enough to help me travel the road I have been on for the past twenty years. I hope all of you are honest enough with yourselves to grow and live a crime-free life. Only you can choose to do this. I realize as the system has changed, more and more of us have lost faith in obtaining a meaningful life and have accepted the life that we have. Even I have lost hope of living a productive life other than what I am doing.

This material would have never been possible except for those fast fingers of Sister Ann, who volunteered to type this manuscript. I will never forget her encouragement, comments, and zest for life. I realize it has not been an easy task since I am not the most elegant writer. God knows, none of this would have been completed except for her hard work. Thank you.

"Jimmy-H" who took the time inside these walls to proofread my writing. "Marlo-W" who encouraged me and became a close friend after fifteen years. I could not have done it without both of your help. Finally, I would like to thank my mother and Sister Mariella for their help and encouragement. Sister Mariella's life as an artist and educator has inspired mine. I would like to thank my other family members who helped and encouraged me also. Special thanks go to my oldest brother, who enjoyed adding his two cents every time we spoke about it on the telephone. His vision has helped me complete mine. Finally, thanks to Professor Thomas Bernard and the other editors of this book who helped me. Without Thomas this material would have never come alive.

I also want to thank the readers of this book. I hope as you read this and learn about my life, it will help you to understand the daily life of prison. Some parts get graphic, even distasteful, yet it is the reality of my life. I wish to offend no one.

Foreword

BY THE EDITORS

This book tells many stories about prison life. All the stories are true in the sense that everything actually happened at one time or another, in one place or another, to one inmate or another. And it is true in the larger sense that it accurately presents a great many truths about prisons, prisoners, and prison life. However, all the names and places have been changed in order to protect both the author and other people.

The author of the book is a life-sentenced inmate whom we call "K. C. Carceral." The dictionary defines the word "carceral" as meaning "of or belonging to a prison." We use this pseudonym for the author because he believes that his physical safety would be endangered if we were to disclose his true identity.

The main character in the book is a person called "Anonymous N. Inmate." The prison staff generally call this person "Mr. Inmate," while his friends call him "Anonymous." The name of this character is intended to convey that the stories told in this book represent things that happen to inmates generally, not what happened to the specific inmate who is the author of this book. It also expresses the author's view of how inmates see themselves in the context of a reality dominated by prison routines.

As editors, our goal was to take the manuscript as written by the author and make it suitable for classroom use in colleges and universities. We tried to deal with the presentation of the material but not with the content of the book. We feel this book will be useful for those who want to include the harsher realities of the prison environment in their classes and their studies of prison life. This book should be a useful supplement to classes in corrections and the criminal justice system in general, including but not limited to introduction to corrections and issues in the corrections system.

As we worked with the book, however, we did make a few changes related to content. Racism pervades prison life, and people routinely exhibit racism in their social interactions. In our view, K. C. accurately portrayed the racist climate in prisons, but we also felt that the pervasive racism would be offensive to many readers. Therefore, we edited out the racism that occurred in stories where race itself was not directly relevant. Mostly, this involved racist comments and racist characterizations that are routinely included in social interactions both among prisoners and between prisoners and staff. However, we left the racism that occurred in stories that were intended to portray the realities of race in prisons.

A similar issue, but to lesser extent, appeared with the issue of sex. As with race, prison social interactions contain pervasive and often grossly offensive references to sex and sexuality, both in relation to women and to other men. In our editing, we attempted to retain what we believe are K. C.'s accurate descriptions of the realities of prison life while attempting to be clear that these offensive descriptions are not endorsed either by the author, the editors, or the publisher.

The result, we hope, is a book that within some limits provides accurate descriptions of prisons and prison life. We do not expect that these descriptions will satisfy all readers. Some readers may see the prisons in this book as "country clubs" in which everyone has a great time while receiving "three hots and a cot" (i.e., three hot meals and bed) at the expense of the state. They may conclude that no one would be deterred by such lives of idleness and entertainment. Other readers may see the prisons in this book as hellholes of inhumanity. Their reaction may be that such conditions are utterly unacceptable in any civilized society. Perhaps a few readers may even see that both of these simpler views are contained at different times and in different places in this book's complex portrayal of prison life.

Whether you conclude that prisons are country clubs or hellholes, the real issue is whether they are effective in reducing crime. There are now over two million people in prisons and jails in the United States. Over 600,000 of these people are released back into society every year. Prisons affect us all, for better or for worse. As citizens and voters, we should have accurate information about them. That is the point of this book.

We would like to acknowledge the contributions of those who reviewed this book: Gary Cornelius, George Mason University; Michael Gilbert, University of Texas, San Antonio; Faith Lutze, Washington State University; Randall Shelden, University of Nevada, Las Vegas; Sam Torres, California State University, Long Beach.

Foreword to *Behind a Convict's Eyes* by K. C. Carceral

BY TODD R. CLEAR

Have you ever wondered what it would be like to go to prison?

About 400,000 people will be sentenced to prison this year, and another 250,000 will go back to prison having just been released from it. According to victimization surveys, about 24 million felony crimes will occur (not including drug crimes), and every one of these felons will be eligible for a prison sentence. But most of those who commit these crimes will neither be arrested for them, convicted of them, nor sent to prison for them. It can easily be seen that the people who go to prison are but a subset of those who are eligible, and many are eligible. It is worth recognizing that while comparatively few of us ever experience prison, many more of us would do so if we had been caught.

The median time served in prison is now about two and a half years. Imagine for a moment that you had been one of those people who, thirty months ago, had been caught in a criminal act, only to be convicted and later admitted to prison. What would you have missed over the last thirty months of your life? What events, what major turning points in your life, would be missing? What would that hole in your experience have meant for you, and how would things be different?

A related set of questions is just as affecting: what experiences would have taken their place? If you had been incarcerated, you would have missed out on most of the events in your free-citizen life of the last two and a half years, but those events would have been replaced with prison experiences. What might those prison experiences have been?

Only you can know what would be missing from your life if you had been locked up two and a half years ago. But the book you are holding in your hands, *Behind a Convict's Eyes,* can help you answer the prison question, because it offers a genuine, if graphic, narrative of what it means to become a prisoner. The book is written by someone who never expected to go to prison, but now doubts the likelihood he will ever be allowed to leave prison. He uses a pseudonym, K. C. Carceral, in order to avoid trouble should his fellow prisoners take issue with some of his views. His honesty and forthrightness enable him to tell a story rarely encountered by those of us in the free world.

Behind a Convict's Eyes is a new addition to the *Wadsworth Series on Contemporary Issues in Crime and Justice.* As editor of that series, I am delighted to introduce *Behind a Convict's Eyes* by K. C. Carceral. The Wadsworth Series publishes books that address important issues in crime and justice in ways that go well beyond the coverage provided by typical classroom textbooks. It is the aim of this series to deepen students' understanding of important questions facing criminology and criminal justice, and the series has over the years published some of the most important books on current topics of interest to the field. This book will join that prestigious list.

This book has two qualities that make it a valuable addition to the *Wadsworth* Series.

First, it is a powerful narrative about prison experiences that are, for the most part, invisible to most of us. Carceral describes prison life in its most important themes, and he tells how prison life works by recounting his own experiences. It is both fascinating and troubling. Of course, everything that goes on outside the walls happens in some form or another inside: sex, friendship, commerce, conflict, hope, fear, resentment, change. The prison sometimes distorts these normal human circumstances, but it cannot deny the people who live inside the human aspirations that give rise to these experiences. People who live in prison want to be respected, they want to have hope, and they want to feel safe. What could be more normal than that? The prison contorts these normal desires and makes their pursuit inside the walls a special kind of experience.

The second reason this book is special is that the sometimes jarring voice of the person behind bars, Carceral's voice, is joined by the more unemotional voice of the scientific observer of the realities of prison life. Noted criminological theorist Thomas Bernard is joined by three talented new scholars, Leanne Alarid, Bruce Bikle, and Alene Bikle, to provide the reader with analytical clarity about the significance of Carceral's accounts. The result is that a heady introspection gives cool and detached body to the prisoner's poignant narrative. This book is more than a first-person account of the prison; it is an active scrutiny of prison life, filled with practical stories and the conceptual context to make those stories meaningful.

Reading this book will change the way you think about prison. Much that is offered within its covers is less than appealing—prison life is intended to be that way. Some is humorous, and some is surprising. All of it is meant to provoke your thinking, to extend your knowledge, and to deepen your understanding of the American prison system. This year about 600,000 former felons will be released from prisons. Their experiences while locked up will have a powerful kind of impact on their hopes and fears upon release. It is hard to know what goes on in the mind of a person who has spent a couple of years behind bars and now arrives back on the streets. But this book, more than any other book on the market today, can help you understand.

I recommend it with enthusiasm.

Todd R. Clear
Editor, *Wadsworth Series on Contemporary Issues
in Crime and Justice*
New York
March 26, 2003

Prelude on Escapism: "Reality Is What You Make It"

BY K. C. CARCERAL

Before one starts reading the following chapters, I wanted to present a short prelude on escapism. The art of escapism is a reality in prison. Every prisoner, including myself, goes through it to a certain degree. The mind is a precious jewel that tries to maintain reality in an unreal society. Ways of coping with the insane become ways of mentally escaping. Anything that can take the mind from the modern-day prison reality is food utilized for the brain.

Escapism is a never-ending process. Usually the first stage for the new fish is sleeping. The surroundings are so unchanging, so boring, so plain, it is impossible to avoid it. Yet, once placed in Gladiator School, due to the noise, random acts of violence, and the sharks looking for a sleeping fish, I moved out of this stage. To help cope with the modern-day madness, there are other things a prisoner can do. One is arts and crafts. I did the arts for a great many years. Reading is another. This was something I had to learn to enjoy. Of course, there is writing. Then there is always the TV or radio. Rap seems to be the number-one social support of doing time for some of the younger generation. These are some of the positive forces.

The negative forces are just as inviting and can get the adrenaline juice flowing. Adrenaline to some prisoners is like dope to a junkie. These forces lead to the main code norm of prison, within which one spends a great deal of time; the prisoner slowly learns prison is a very, very dangerous place! I had to learn this. Fighting and arguing, moving from one crisis to another, can bring an existence from the mundane. Drugs, homemade hooch, violence, blaming others, complaining, and on and on, are all used to deal with the incarcerated reality. Reality is also playing prison politics to running a mini-canteen. Then there is racism, the perfect hate factory. Racism is mental escapism, violence is the physical. Or compulsive sex to relieve the daily anxiety. When one gets stuck in the time warp, the clock stops during incarceration. Through control, deprivation, regulations, and segregation one learns who is really in control while gaining attention along the way. Then the disease of violence, a perpetual trap, turns the mundane into a stressed-out, adrenaline-flowing existence—truly the drug for the masses. Fight or flight syndrome is how one chooses to do his time. Joining a gang is but another way to establish a pecking order and continue the cycle of violence. All of these do become ways to escape the accepted incarceration.

As you read through this, keep escapism in mind. Prison is all about a man's mind-set. If he mentally trips on enough stuff, he can forget about his imprisonment. Every prisoner goes through it and lives it as he lives his daily life in prison. After twenty years in prison I wonder sometimes if I will ever come in touch with reality again.

Editors' Note

The author of this book is "K. C. Carceral," a pseudonym for a prisoner who has been incarcerated for over twenty years. Carceral writes about events in various prisons for men that happened to him directly, that he witnessed, or that other prisoners reported happening to them. The main character in the book is named "Anonymous Numbered Inmate." Other inmates and staff in the book address this character either as "Anonymous" or as "Mr. Inmate." All of the events in the book actually happened, but all of the names of individuals and locations have been changed to protect their identities.

PART I

In the Beginning

EDITORS' INTRODUCTION TO PART I

"In prisons, those things withheld from and denied to the prisoner become
precisely what he wants most of all."—Eldridge Cleaver

Walls of concrete, surrounded by a double row of razor wire and towers
guarded by armed correctional officers. This image might be what people
typically think of when they envision a prison. What many people do not
realize is that within the federal system and within each state prison system
are numerous institutions with a range of security levels. Some variation of these
security levels includes supermax, maximum, medium, and minimum. Some
prisoners have the opportunity to earn their way down to a lower custody level
through good behavior, while others remain in the same custody level throughout their sentence. A small number of prisoners are transferred to a higher
security level for disruptive or violent behavior while behind bars. This book
concentrates primarily on maximum or high/close security prisons, which
together hold about 13 percent of all federal prisoners and 25 percent of all state
prisoners (Camp and Camp, 1997). The rest of the prisoner population is housed
in institutions of lower security level and more freedom of movement.

Prisons are smaller societies within the larger society, each with their own subcultures and social systems. Prisons are also bureaucratic organizations, devised with the intent to keep their inhabitants separate from the mainstream society. For prisons to be more fully understood, however, it is necessary to view them from the inside.

Imagine that we have gone back in time to the year 1982. Visualize for a moment what it would be like to enter a maximum-security prison for men for the first time at the age of twenty, having just been convicted of murder and faced with a life sentence. Most first-time prisoners have a vague idea of what prison is like, so to them, the prison world is foreign and unfamiliar. All prisons provide incoming prisoners with a formal rulebook detailing the directives and policies that must be followed to avoid disciplinary reports. Beyond the formal rulebook, how does a prisoner come to understand and make sense of this unknown world in order to survive? The prison world is routine, cold, and unforgiving. The chapters you are about to read are all about examples of prison experiences that the author, or other male prisoners known to the author, have experienced between 1982 and 2002.

The process of admitting new inmates to prison is known as "reception and diagnostics." As you will read in the first chapter, the admissions ritual consists of surrendering street clothes in exchange for a prison uniform, and undergoing a strip search, medical exam, and a shower. The admissions ritual is first and foremost a security measure to ensure that prisoners are not transporting illegal contraband. Secondly, officials make certain that incoming prisoners will not spread airborne diseases such as tuberculosis to other prisoners. The third reason for the way the admissions process is conducted is for the purpose of shaming and degradation. Harold Garfinkel (1956, 421) called this process a "status degradation ceremony . . . whereby the public identity of an actor is transformed into something looked on as lower in the local scheme of social types." In other words, through this degradation ceremony, there is a conscious attempt to make it clear to new prisoners that they are now in the custody and control of the department of corrections.

Pre-Prison and Prison Identities

Initiation, or rites of passage, take place during the early months of a prison sentence that inevitably transforms the true identity a person had on the streets (pre-prison identity) into a false identity he needs to become to survive in prison. This false self is known as the "prison identity" (Schmid and Jones, 1991). An identity is a self-defined master status that includes how other people define the self. A prison identity is also known in this text as a reputation. To endure life in confinement, an inmate soon realizes that he must develop the right reputation by respect earned with other prisoners (Stojkovic, 1984).

Schmid and Jones (1991, 419) argue that first-time prisoners actually "suspend their pre-prison identity for the duration of their sentence" to avoid being victimized and being viewed as weak by other prisoners. Prison is perceived to most newcomers as an artificial environment and the prison identity is thus seen as an adaptive mode/identity to that environment.

During the first few days, most first-time prisoners engage in emotional reflection, "extensive self-assessment," and "introspective analysis" with themselves, and are concerned that their identities will change—that they will become hardened to violence (Schmid and Jones, 418). Even though every prisoner has full intent on returning to his true self after he completes his sentence, change to the prison identity is unavoidable, at least temporarily, for a number of reasons.

First, each man was once an individual in the outside world, and now that he is in the system, he is an anonymous prisoner with a number. Second, prisoners share the same deprivations of freedom, lack of heterosexual relations, privacy, and goods and services as everyone else (Sykes, 1958). Third, prisoners have been effectively removed from contact with people on the outside who know them, not as convicts, but as people with pre-prison identities. Less contact with friends and family on the outside means that, for most prisoners, they lose touch with who they used to be. Finally, individuals who enter prison with legitimate pre-prison identities will experience a high degree of conflict and social rejection by other prisoners who see them as targets to be preyed upon. Prisoners who are more educated are also more likely to face initial adjustment difficulties, such as being taken advantage of or getting themselves hurt in a fight, than are prisoners with less education (Wright, 1989). The researchers found in their sample that less educated prisoners were more apt to have prior institutional experience and therefore would seem to be more familiar with the institution. Another researcher observed that prisoners who see themselves as having deviant pre-prison identities will tend to find the prison world consistent with their definitions of reality (Faine, 1973, 579).

Identity Construction

In the early part of their sentences, prisoners undergo a change to "construct" a new front; a false temporary prison identity for themselves (Schmid and Jones). The first-time prisoner is concerned about how he appears to other prisoners in terms of the way he looks, walks, talks, dresses, and others with whom he associates. The prison identity is quickly learned while incarcerated through the process of differential association (Alarid, 2001). In differential association theory, the prison identity is learned while interacting with and surrounded by others of primary importance in a process of communication and tutelage. The "excess of definitions" favorable to a prison identity that occur with great "frequency, duration, priority, and intensity" will create a greater tendency for individuals to learn these identities (Sutherland and Cressey, 1955, 78). Although differential association theory originally applied to the learning of criminal behavior, differential association theory may also be a viable explanation of the process of prison identity construction (Alarid).

Part of the prison identity construction is getting a reputation based on how a person handles himself in adjusting to the inmate world. For example, in the federal system, Dannie Martin (1993) was known as "Red Hog" because of his red hair and a fight he had over a pork chop during the beginning of his prison sentence. A "rep" follows both prisoners and staff for the duration of their time in prison.

Modes of transmission in the process of learning the prison identity include "prison argot." Prison argot, also known as prison proper, provides meaning to the value system and the social structure of the prisoner hierarchy. Prison argot is the basis for prisoner communication through verbal phrases and slang terms mixed with physical gestures to connote common perceptions, thinking, and behavior (Encinas, 2001). Prisoners also express themselves through tattoos as a way of telling a story about past relationships, important life events, and as a way of denoting gang membership (Encinas, 40).

Prison argot is defined by the racial or ethnic group that dominates the prison, both influentially and by sheer numbers. In the 1940s, prison argot was influenced by Caucasian males (Clemmer, 1940). Over time, as minority groups began to dominate the prisoner population, prison argot changed. Currently, in the southwest regions of the United States, prison argot is highly influenced by Latino groups, with roots in Mexico and Central America (Encinas, 59). In most other regions of the country, prison language has been developed by African American culture.

In sum, initial rites of passage seem to occur for all male prisoners that include prison identity construction, establishing a reputation, learning prison argot, and understanding the meaning of the prison world. The first four chapters in this section are in reference to these rites of passage and learning experiences that occur in the early part of prison sentences for men.

REFERENCES

Alarid, Leanne F. (2001). "The Process of Prisonization through Differential Association." Unpublished manuscript.

Camp, Camille Graham, and George M. Camp (1997). *The Corrections Yearbook.* South Salem, NY: Criminal Justice Institute.

Clemmer, Donald (1940). *The Prison Community.* Boston: Christopher.

Encinas, Gilbert L. (2001). *Prison Argot: A Sociolinguistic and Lexicographic Study.* Lanham, NY: University Press of America.

Faine, John R. (1973). "A Self-Consistency Approach to Prisonization." *The Sociological Quarterly* 14: 576–88.

Garfinkel, Harold (1956). "Conditions of Successful Degradation Ceremonies." *American Journal of Sociology* 61: 420–4.

Martin, Dannie, and Peter Sussman (1993). *Committing Journalism: The Prison Writings of Red Hog.* New York, Norton.

Schmid, Thomas J., and Richard S. Jones (1991). "Suspended Identity: Identity Transformation in a Maximum Security Prison." *Symbolic Interaction* 14(4): 415–32.

Stojkovic, Stan (1984). "Social Bases of Power and Control Mechanisms Among Prisoners in a Prison Organization." *Justice Quarterly* 1: 511–528.

Sutherland, Edwin, and Donald Cressey (1955). *Principles of Criminology.* Philadelphia: Lippincott.

Sykes, Gresham (1958). *The Society of Captives.* Princeton, NJ: Princeton University Press.

Wright, Kevin N. (1989). "Race and Economic Marginality in Explaining Prison Adjustment." *Journal of Research in Crime and Delinquency* 26(1): 67–89.

1

He's One of Ours Now

"Redemption is thought to exist in prison. However, in a lawless society, punishment and accountability do little; it is basically survival of the fittest."

DEAN THE MACHINE

JULY 2000

The car drove into a sally port. The tall gate closed behind us. The driver got out and a man in a blue uniform quickly searched the car. The driver returned after checking in, and my eyes coldly watched his shiny dress shoes march back to the car. After the man in the blue uniform waved towards a three-story brick tower, the large gate in front of us opened.

I had arrived at the Cold Springs Correctional Receiving Center. The building had originally been built in the 1930s or '40s as a mental hospital for the criminally insane. There wasn't much that had to be done to convert it to a prison. It was the same basic building, drab and dull; it now just housed prisoners instead of mental patients. I was one of the first convicted felons to pass through its doors, one of the many souls who would enter here via **cuffs** and **shackles.**

We came through a new entrance and into a new foyer. I was amazed at how nice it looked: carpeting, wooden desk, counter and railings, and plants: all the modernizing money could buy.

I was crossing into a new frontier. Little did I know then that my outside world stopped at the front gate, and the time warp was just beginning.

The police officers that brought me handed some papers to the man behind the counter. As he took them, he looked at me, a skinny, twenty-year-old, white male in cuffs and leg irons. I stood there, scared, probably white as a ghost.

I had heard many stories about prison but I'd never planned to end up in one. I was supposed to be something in life. My father had hoped I would graduate from heating and air-conditioning school and Mom wanted me to marry and have kids. No parent wants his child's career to be prison.

"Okay, he's one of ours now," said the man behind the counter, as if I was a new species. The police officers who brought me smiled at each other, then gave me a look. I was another notch in their belt for fighting crime in America.

⬥⬥⬥⬥

A second man dressed in blue came into the foyer and led me into the prison. I was still in cuffs and leg irons. If you have ever tried to walk with leg irons, then you will understand when I say it is an art. You see, shackles are purposely made so one cannot walk normally. Due to my inexperience, red rings indented my ankles for days after that walk.

The first norm of the prison system I learned is *the law of escorting officer in motion*. Officers tend to hurry only when a prisoner is in leg irons. Any other time, they're casual and slow moving.

⬥⬥⬥⬥

As we passed through three or four more gates, I saw a dramatic change. What stuck out the most was that almost every officer was wearing light blue shirts and navy blue pants. A few had white shirts with navy blue pants, but all the blue uniformed guards looked the same. Later I would learn to describe them in prison slang: **blue-shirts** (sergeants and under) and **white-shirts** (lieutenants and above). It became part of my new language.

By the fourth gate we went through, the years had rolled backward. The brand new, ultra-modern front foyer was gone.

The officer led me into a dingy gray room and ordered me to kneel on a long wooden bench anchored to the concrete and metal wall. My leg irons were removed. He ordered me to stand and face him so my cuffs and waist chain could be removed. I was happy to get them off—wearing them had seemed almost unbearable.

After they were off, I sat on the bench with another man. I was a newcomer and terrified. I wanted to cry but couldn't. My heart was clearing a good 160 pumps per minute. My mouth was dry and palms damp.

In the county jail, I had heard all the stories about prison: violent assaults, rapes, robberies, etc. None were ever good. Not knowing what to expect, I found that emptiness was setting in. As the days rolled on, I was getting harder. I had become one of the many **inmates.**

I am glad that my state doesn't have the most violent penal system in America. Over the years I've been in prison, the number of fights and stabbings has gone up, but I learned that if you stick to yourself, don't gamble, and always pay your bills, you could survive.

Some folks say the increase in violence in our prisons is due to the increase in violence in our culture. However, I believe there is more to this. Overcrowding is a large factor; the design of some prisons doesn't help to ease it.

Of course, I didn't know any of this as I sat on that hard wooden bench in 1982.

⇒⇐⇒⇐⇒⇐

"Inmate," I heard through my terrified daze. From where I sat, I could only see the top of a head behind a desk piled high with files.

"Come here."

I got up and walked softly to the desk. The guard behind the files was in blue like the rest. He was an older man engulfed by desk organizers, forms, and files. This was his little world. His age had probably earned him the desk job so he did not have to work in the main prison area.

I was the newcomer. I stood there but he never made eye contact; he only opened a file with pages of blank forms. I could tell he had had great experience at his job, since he did it so mechanically and inhumanly.

"First name?" he spoke down to the empty form, preparing his pen to write.

"Anonymous," I replied.

"Middle initial?"

"N.," I said softly.

"Inmate, Anonymous N." he said slowly. "Is that correct?" he asked. He emphasized the word *correct*.

"Yes."

"Age? And speak up so I can hear you!"

"Twenty," I said.

"Date of birth?"

"Nine-eleven-sixty-two."

"You're young to have a life sentence."

I didn't know if he expected an answer.

"Weight is . . . " he paused.

"One hundred sixty."

"Height?"

"Five feet, eleven inches."

"Color of eyes?"

"Blue."

"Race. White, black or other?"

"White."

The questions went on and on: social security number, tattoos, scars, birth marks, last address, residency, parents and other family members, addresses, education, hat size, T-shirt size, underwear size, regular shirt size, pant size, shoe size, last job, etc. It seemed they had asked many of the same questions at the county jail. The same questions over and over again.

I rattled off the answers and noticed my surroundings from the corner of my eye. The room was old. Insulation was falling from the pipes and the room needed cleaning. The corners were dirty, there were cigarette butts on the floor, and the walls were grayish yellow, probably from the years of cigarette smoke in the air. It smelled like an old closet.

"Now pay attention," his tone changed. "I'm going to give you a number: memorize it. This is how we'll identify you for your stay here."

I didn't know how long the number would be. "Can I write it down?"

"Just memorize it now!" He paused, looking down into his piles of forms and desk organizers. Then he spoke more softly: "It doesn't have to be difficult, son. Just memorize it."

Just as I saw a brief moment of humanity in him, it was gone. He buried himself in his desk organizers again.

"Okay," I said. I looked at the top of his head and wondered if he knew he was going bald.

He said the number, then said it again slower. It was a six-digit number, a number that I have carried since and have quoted millions upon millions of times.

"Okay," he said as he lifted the file to one of the top baskets and stood up, "Sign by the xs." He pointed at the forms.

I signed quickly, scrawling my name. He didn't care; he just wanted some kind of mark. I didn't read the forms since my head was spinning and I was so nervous. I could feel sweat trickling down the inside of my arms.

"Sit back on the bench," he pointed with his pen. "An officer will be here in a minute to get you."

<hr />

"Martin," he then said to a guy in his mid-40s sitting next to me on the bench.

"Si."

"Come up here and stand by the desk," he ordered from behind his little tower of papers, pens, files, and forms.

That 6-foot, 200-pound man did not move from the bench.

"Martin," he said louder, "Get up here!"

"Si," Martin said again but did not move.

The guard stood up and looked over his desk organizers, "Hey, bring your ass up here, Martin!"

"Si," Martin said without moving.

Suddenly the guard wasn't as frightening to me.

He looked at me, then Martin: "Martin, did you hear me?"

"Si."

"Do you speak English?" the guard asked him.

Martin looked at him with a blank face, then at me. I wondered what was going to happen next. The guard looked stunned.

"Do you understand anything?" he asked Martin again. His face was red with anger. He shook his head and puffed air through his mouth. His cheeks flared out, then drew in.

"Ha-b-l-a English, Sen-ior?" I said in broken Spanish.

Martin quickly looked at me with an unexpected glance. "No," he said in a calm voice.

The guard asked me sarcastically, "Do you speak Spanish, Inmate?"

"No, not really," I answered.

"Then maybe you should mind your own business. We can handle Mr. Martin!" he grunted.

"Si," Martin said again, following with a slight chuckle that only I heard. He looked at me. *I just learned prison norm number two: mind your own business unless asked.* The guard's face flushed again. He raised his pen and purposely dropped it on the desk as he looked at us both. He threw his legs out so his chair rolled away as he stepped to the door.

"Captain," he shouted down the hallway. "We have another one who can't speak English."

Again I heard Martin chuckle. The guard never noticed this.

It took me years to understand why Martin, who understood English, played with the guard the way he did. He had been in prison before and knew the ropes. I was a new inmate—a **"fish"**—while Martin had already graduated from the pond.

<hr/>

Eventually another guard came through the doorway and ordered me to come with him. The escorting officer and I walked down a hallway to a set of steps going under a living unit. Since I wasn't wearing leg irons, there was no hurry. I looked down the hallway, which was as long as a football field. It too was drab and dirty. At the bottom of the stairs, we entered a room with washing machines, clothes dryers, and racks of clothing, all dull gray except for the colored uniforms.

The guard ordered me to take off my clothes. He grabbed a small cardboard box and dropped it on the floor.

I really did not know the significance of this event. I was as green as the yard was long. However, it was already starting to happen to me: I was changing on the inside and outside.

I stripped for him as he stood in front of me and watched. Over the years, I've learned to tolerate this practice, but I've never been able to get used to it. As I handed him my last possessions of the **streets,** I did so carefully, piece by piece, folded and neat. However, I noticed that he shook them before he just threw them into the box. He had no compassion or pity that my identity was being taken away from me: he just impatiently tossed each thing I handed him into the box.

When all my clothes were off, I stood before him, naked. Once again the questions started.

"You want to keep your glasses?" he asked, drawing up a clipboard.

"Yes."

"Watch?"

"Yes."

"What's your name?"

"Inmate."

"Number?"

These questions just repeated what I had just answered. I wondered why he stripped me only to make me stand there butt-naked to answer questions.

Finally he told me to put my glasses and watch on a shelf. Then he told me to put my arms up.

"So I can see your pits."

I lifted my arms without a word.

"Hands out in front with your fingers spread apart."

I did as he said.

"Okay, now run your hands through your hair." He watched carefully.

"Any dentures?" he asked.

"No," I answered.

"Open your mouth and tilt your head back."

I did, looking at the pipes running across the ceiling.

"Lift your nuts." He stared at my sex organs and the insides of my legs.

"Now turn around."

I felt dirty.

"Lift up your right foot so I can see the bottom of it."

"Okay, now lift your other right foot," he chuckled, since I had lifted the wrong foot.

I found nothing funny about this.

"Good, bend over and *spread your cheeks.*"

Years later, I had noticed that many guards enjoy doing **strip searches.** They get a thrill out of having a human being naked and exposed before them so they can dehumanize them. Some actually get off on it.

Later when I was at Ridgewood Prison, which inmates called **Treejumper School** [treejumper is what they call rapists] some guards acted as bad as the rapists housed there for treatment. They stared, smiled, and made jokes. The perplexing thing is, this staff behavior is all within the law.

As I waited butt-naked, the guard finally handed me two small paper cups with liquid, a washcloth, and towel. "The shower is behind you. This cup is soap," he said, pointing, "the other is debug lotion for your hair. Use it, then rinse off. We don't want an outbreak in here."

I could finally move away from him. When I was done showering, the room suddenly felt very cold. I wanted some clothes. But I had to discard the towel in a basket before I got them.

The guard moved to massive racks of clothing where he reviewed my sizes from the clipboard he carried. Then he came towards me, slowly, clothes bunched in his hands. He was still watching me.

I got dressed as fast as I could. *Pervert*, I thought. As fast as he had stalked me when I was butt-naked, he never gave me a second glance now that I was in the recycled clothes and old blue hospital-type shoes. The clothes he gave me had been worn probably hundreds and hundreds of times by others.

"I need you to sign this for your clothing issue. Your other clothes will be delivered to your housing unit." When I finished signing, he tucked the forms back into the file on his clipboard and we went back upstairs. We walked down an empty hallway as he explained that a bag supper would be waiting for me on the receiving unit since everything was already closed for the night.

I passed through more gates marked Unit-7. Yet another blue-shirt stood tall with broad shoulders, holding a massive gate key in his hand. Sooner or later, one notices that all the main-lock keys are four times as big as a normal key. Some look like old skeleton keys. He swung the gate open and clipped the keys back on his belt, directing me toward the desk.

"I need you to sign these forms." He pulled them out of the file that the previous blue-shirt had handed him.

I had signed forms up front, forms at the laundry, and now forms on the unit. I was getting accustomed to signing so much that I ignored what I was signing. It didn't matter to me: they were going to do what they were going to do. Besides, this blue-shirt before me looked like a brick wall, an ex-M.P. who wanted me to just sign without giving him any shit.

It was not my time to become a **jailhouse lawyer,** yet.

He handed me a plastic bag containing a rule book, rolling tobacco, some matches, toothbrush, toothpaste, small bar of soap, razor, pen, writing paper, and two mailing envelopes stamped with the words *free mail*. Then he gave me a bag supper and milk.

"You signed saying we can inspect your mail and that you read that orange rule book," he pointed at the plastic bag, "and that you received all your items on intake. Now read the rule book so you know it. Your cell is down there at the end of the hallway." He pointed through yet another gate. This one was already open.

As I walked down the hallway, I slowed up so he slowed up, "This one?"

"No, four doors down."

I noticed men looking out their small traps in the cell doors at me, the new guy, just arrived. Some were probably just as scared as I was. I started to walk a little faster so again my big blue-shirt shadow did also. He never got closer than three feet nor allowed me a distance greater than five feet from him.

I entered the cell and he closed the door behind me. It was followed by a loud *clunk* as he rolled the lock to drop the dead bolt. He opened the small trap on the door and looked in.

"You should have a towel, washcloth, two sheets, blanket, and pillow case." He stared as I unrolled the bedroll to check.

"It's all here," I replied.

"Check by the toilet for toilet paper. If you need some I'll get you a roll."

"It's here."

"Okay. This is isolation. You'll probably be here three or four days until they get you processed for a unit. You'll be moved then. The nurse will call you tomorrow and your **greens** will be up the day you go . . . "

"Greens." I thought he meant food. *I hope I don't have to wait three or four days to eat.*

"Greens. Your prison clothes," he paused. "Is there anything I should know? You're kind of quiet," he said.

I shook my head no.

"You ain't suicidal or anything like that, are you?"

"No," I answered. *Just scared to death.*

"Good. I hate a crazy nut!" With that he was gone, leaving the small trap door open. I looked out a few times and saw eyes like mine, bored and scared.

When I made my bed, I realized that the mattress was only three inches thick. I also realized the sheets weren't long enough for the mattress.

Eventually I lay down, looking at the ceiling.

⋙⟨⟩⟨⟩⋙

REFLECTIONS

That was the beginning for me. At that time, I never expected the hatred that would later come. I would come to hate everyone in the prison and everything about the prison. I would hate so much it would freeze my inner soul.

Now I look back and realize I really didn't hate them. I hated what they, the system, made me: a convict.

Some people think that convicts are born that way. I don't remember being born a convict, but a convict is what I became. After over twenty years in prison, it is a skin I cannot shed. In the system, I am no longer a human with a name, but a number.

My identity as a number began with the process of assessment and evaluation, which was more commonly called **A & E.**

2

A & E

"We are going to test you to see your education level, psychological abilities, and medical problems. In this way we can determine your needs to help you."

SOCIAL WORKER SPEECH BEFORE TESTING
NOVEMBER 1982

"See, I told ya, they want to find out about a motherfucker. Just like social services."

AFRICAN AMERICAN BROTHER
A & E TESTING, 1982

"Hey, you guys, get up." The guard sounded surprised that we were asleep.

My **cellie** and I looked at him slowly, coming back to our new reality.

"You both have to go to testing in the A & E center." This was the Assessment and Evaluation Center, where we were to receive educational and psychological testing, a physical and medical examination, and an interview with a social worker.

We had been in the cell for about a week. All that had been allowed up to that point was the privilege of going back and forth to chow. So every opportunity to get out of the cell was a break.

We got up and dressed.

"Man, that's what sucks about the state. First we have nothing to do, then they come bitching because we're not up, waiting for something to do," my cellie said.

He was right. They give you nothing to do, then they expect you to be ready at a moment's notice. I would soon find this was the way all prison staff operated.

"Fuck, these dumb-ass tests," my cellie blurted out as we waited for the cell door to open. He wouldn't admit it, but he wanted to take the tests because he wanted to get out of the cell just as badly as me.

"You ever take them before?"

"Yes," he said sarcastically, "when I went through Industrial City for receiving."

"Receiving at Industrial City? I thought they said this is the receiving center."

"This is now, but they used to just run you either to Industrial City or Long Lake," he answered.

"What are the tests about?" I asked.

"To see how smart you are," he replied. "I don't need the shit, I got my G.E.D. last time I was in. When they're done tapping my brain, they'll say drug treatment."

I listened carefully. "Well, what if they've changed it?"

"They won't," he said, looking out the small barred window. "You got to learn, Anonymous. This is prison. They don't care about you. Get what you can get and do your time."

That seemed too easy. His way couldn't be right. Besides, I was going to be here for a long, long time!

"Let's go," the guard yelled at us. "Come on, hurry up now."

Thirty men shuffled into a room with desks in the testing center. The front of the room was full of professor-looking white and black dudes. We waited and waited. Then thirty more inmates shuffled in. Some guys didn't want the seat open for them, others wanted to sit with their **brothers,** and guys like me just sat down. Everyone fought for his own little turf. We staked out our claims over our desks.

I sat next to my cellie since I knew no one else. Some black guy and his buddy sat next to me. As we waited we did what prisoners do best, we talked.

"You know what these tests are for?" the black guy next to me asked his buddy.

"You know I ain't done this either," he answered.

They looked at us but didn't say anything. We were white and they were black and it was uncommon for the two races to just mix in conversation. I just started to notice this.

I shook my head no, but my cellie spoke. "I went through this shit in Industrial City," he bragged. "They just want to know how smart you are."

"What they gonna use it for?" the black guy asked.

"Giving you programs, maybe a job." My cellie sounded sarcastic.

Then the black guy's buddy spoke to him, "See, I told ya, they want to find out about a motherfucker. Just like social services."

"Yeah," his buddy replied.

"**Dog,** I am telling you," he finished, "they want to figure you out, get into your mind."

"Oh yeah," my cellie shot back to them, "they gonna' use this shit against ya."

Then the first brother spoke up. "I got my plan, I'm going to answer 'em all wrong, get schooling, and impress the board at my first hearing. Show 'em I am changing."

"Fuck that," his buddy shot back, "these people ain't gonna' do shit for you. It's just another part of life in the white man's world, brotha. Just give me my cell."

A black dude in front of us was watching us and listening.

"What about you?" the one brother asked him.

The dude shrugged his shoulders. We all were staring at him, so he answered. "I want a good job," he said nervously, "like a clerk."

"Man, they ain't gonna' give no **nigga** a job like that," the second brother in our row said. "Them jobs go to these white dudes." He gestured over toward me and my cellie.

"How do you know," the other black dude shot back, offended, "you just said you ain't been through this shit?"

"Man, I am tellin' ya, this is prison."

"All right then," the brother in front interrupted, "you do it your way and I'll do it mine." With that he turned around.

Then the black dude looked at his buddy. "Just give me my cell and all the dope I can buy. You know what I mean?"

His buddy didn't say anything.

⟫⟪⟫⟪⟫⟪

If I do well, then maybe I can get a good job. I overheard dudes behind me say if a guy does shitty, then they will send him to **Gladiator School** at Industrial City for training. I had heard a lot of rumors about that place and decided I wanted to avoid it.

"Excuse me," an administrator said as he walked into the room. "Can I have your attention?" I noticed that the guard had left the doorway and walked back to his desk. "I will be giving you an aptitude test to see your education level." He went on with the basic directions: "Don't write in the books, hold the noise down, don't copy, and do your best. When I say start, start. When you hear the buzzer, stop."

"What are these tests for?" someone interrupted.

"I just told you, they are an aptitude test," he politely answered. He started his speech again but was cut off.

"Why we got to take them?" another guy questioned.

"To help you. So we can find you a good spot," he replied as if he were addressing a child.

"Answer the question," someone shouted from behind me. "Why do we take 'em?"

The test administrator took a deep breath. I could tell that answering inmate questions wasn't what he wanted to do. "Lookit. We only have so much time. If you don't want to do it, don't. If you want to leave, leave."

"We can leave?" someone else shot back. "The guards said we had to come."

The test administrator looked directly at him. "You can leave, but when you see the **Program Review Committee** they are not going to like the fact that you did not take the test." He smiled, probably thinking that we'd stop asking questions now.

"Who is Program Review?" another person in front asked.

Clearly irritated, the administrator didn't realize he was digging himself into a hole. Or else he didn't care. "Program Review will place you in the appropriate prison for school." His voice became sarcastic. "If you don't do the test, they can only send you to Industrial City or Long Lake."

Those were known as the two worst prisons. Little did we know that half of us would go there anyway.

"So if I do this," someone fired back at him, "I can go to medium prison, to Spring River, for heating school?"

"I don't see why not," he replied. The key to his answer was "I". He may see it that way but someone else might not.

People asked a few more questions. The administrator finally snapped, "Lookit, I have to get started. If you don't want to take it, go."

The room went quiet but no one left. Most guys saw the test as just another scam by the state. Me? Well, I didn't know enough about what was going on and the test looked simple, so why not? Besides, I wanted to avoid Industrial City and I wanted a good job.

"Okay," he announced, "begin."

⌖⌖⌖⌖

So we began. At first everyone was quiet but it did not last long. A few guys whispered, then a few more. The administrator picked up his newspaper and slurped his coffee. Everyone started whispering.

I was surprised how easy the test was. They said it maxed-out at eighth grade level, but it seemed like sixth grade to me. One hour for twenty math problems? *Wow! This is great,* I thought, *I'll get that good job.*

Since I had all that extra time, I looked at the other men in the room. What I didn't know then was that most of them hadn't graduated from high school. Most hadn't had advanced classes or any vocational training. Most thought the test was hard.

The guy sitting next to me was checking his answers against mine. Hell, he was changing all his to mine. I wondered whether I should report him, or if cheating was allowed. *What if they offer both of us the same good job, and he got it?* But I was too scared to open my mouth. I learned later that was a good thing.

We broke for lunch and came back to take another test. Left for the day, came back in the morning for a new test and then another one in the afternoon. By the last one, no one asked questions anymore. Everyone just talked and answered the questions in a way they thought would suit the personal scam they would pop on the state. A guy in front just wrote in answers; he never opened a test booklet. Others freely copied.

A few of us actually tried.

The following week we took psychological tests. Even then dudes had their scams. *If I answer questions wrong, I can get free dope. If I answer them okay, they won't try to put me in the nut ward!*

After the tests, we either interviewed with an education counselor or with a psychiatrist. That is, if your test showed lunatic responses, you talked to the psychiatrist. If your test showed you were normal, you talked to the representative from clinical services.

I went to Judy, the education counselor.

"Hi, I'm Judy. You are?" Just like in intake, she asked me tons of questions: name, number, eyes, weight, height, sentence length. Finally she asked about my education.

"Did you graduate from grade school?"

"Yes." I couldn't believe there were people who hadn't.

"How far did you get in high school?" she asked, filling in blanks and checking boxes.

"I finished it."

"How far did you finish it?"

"I graduated!"

"Oh, we don't see that much." She checked off more boxes.

"I got my diploma and went to some tech school," I added.

"Oh, really, you're a smart one," she said in a childlike voice. Then she showed me my test scores. "Your scores are all eighth grade across the board, so you don't need any educational training—unless you'd like it."

"Actually, I want to find out about getting a job here. Someone told me you guys were hiring A & E clerks."

"Well, they are. I can put your name in. You're certainly smart enough."

"Otherwise, maybe school in the future," I suggested.

"Sure, with your time, you can do that." She ended the interview quickly and seemed as if she didn't want to take any time to explain things. She wrote a lot of stuff down but had few answers.

Marv was a skinny, 130-pound **dude** with reddish-blond hair who was in on burglary charges. Marv always had a scam going. He'd get pencils, thumbtacks, tape, slips of paper, requests, and as many passes as he could. Instead of seeing the educational counselor, like I did, Marv was sent to clinical to see Dr. Hanz, the psychiatrist. Marv's psychological tests must have showed that he was a lunatic.

"Hi," Dr. Hanz said as Marv came in his office. "Please sit."

Marv had known he'd be called in eventually. He had scammed on the psychological test.

"Now, you were referred to me from clinical," Dr. Hanz spoke very slowly, very clearly. He smiled, but never told Marv it was because of the obvious test results.

This guy doesn't look like a hard management case, Dr. Hanz thought to himself. So he popped the famous doctor-patient question. "How are you doing?"

"I'm tired a lot, don't feel like doing much . . . " Marv paused, then asked: "Did I do something wrong?"

Marv knew all the answers—hell, anyone with common sense did. Being tired usually meant depression. However, Dr. Hanz never thought that inmates were smart enough to know this stuff.

"Do you sleep at night?" Hanz probed deeper. *Maybe anxiety disorder.*

"Man, I'm up all night," Marv replied, "can't fall asleep at night, tired all day." *Do you sleep at night, doc? Yes, I am sure you do, but who with?*

"Are you having bad thoughts?" Hanz asked, holding out his wrists. He was asking Marv whether he thought about slitting his wrists.

"Not that I know of," Marv replied quietly, looking down at the floor. *Are you gay Doc, or is your wrist broken?*

"How about suicidal thoughts?" Hanz asked softly. *Do you want to kill yourself? Maybe isolation will help.*

"Doesn't everyone?" Marv replied. *Bingo, jackpot.*

Dr. Hanz sat up fast in his chair, not expecting this answer so quickly. He began writing in Marv's chart.

"What you writing?" Marv asked innocently.

"Oh, just a few notes, nothing important," Hanz smiled. "Just give me a minute." *Possible chemical imbalance, suicidal thoughts. Test results show possible delusional paranoia and potential for violent mood swings.*

Hanz looked up at Marv, once again smiling. "Have you considered a nighttime medication? Something to help you sleep? And maybe something during the day to calm you?"

"Well, no, not really," Marv replied, looking at his fingers. *Hell, yes, Doc, that's why I'm here.* He smiled again at Hanz. *Get me some of that shit so I can chill!*

"It might help you relax," Hanz smiled back. *Definitely an anxiety disorder.*

"If you think it would help," Marv replied. *The hell with relaxing, doc, I want to sleep a month or two of this boring-ass shit away.*

"How about something at night, 1,000 milligrams of zine?" **"Zine"** refers to psychotropic drugs like stellarzine and thorazine, which psychiatrists liked to prescribe and inmates liked to take. Hanz smiled. *He probably needs more, but I can jack it up over the month.*

"Okay, I'll try it," Marv agreed. *Bring on the dope, Doc, get me on that slow ride!*

"Also let's try something after lunch, too, like half of what you get at night." *He's probably driving his cellmate nuts.*

"Yeah," Marv said, "I'm tense. My cellie is probably tired of me." *Great, I can collect them and sell them. Get high, sell a little, and chill.*

Within a few weeks, Marv's "zine" had been jacked to 2,000 a night and 1,000 at lunch. He slept the time away. His eyes were always glazed and he looked drunk all the time. And he was selling some for cigarettes. I don't know who was scamming who: if it was the doctor, who was keeping guys drugged up in order to justify his job, or if it was the guys like Marv, who just wanted to stay **baked** most of the time.

⋙⋘⋙⋘

After educational and psychological tests, we saw A & E medical. Got a complete physical. Including coughing. Blood and urine tests. This would be the first and last real physical I got in the twenty years I've been in. Since then I've never received another.

Eventually I saw an interview social worker. By then I was sick and tired of sitting around, so I was ready for anything they offered.

"So, Anonymous, what do you want the system to do for you?" this geek behind a desk asked me.

"I was hoping for an A & E clerk job," I replied. *Maybe a release, yeah, that's it. The system can let me go!*

"Yes, we have the letter you sent. Also, the educational counselor noted your scores." He picked through my paper work. "I don't know if they're hiring."

"Well, I thought I'd try." Then I remembered what this other inmate had told me to do when the counselor came at me like this. I was still amazed at how many guys knew ahead of time what the counselors would do and say.

"I thought about Industrial City, but a dude from my county jail is up there and we were having problems, a lot of problems, at the jail. He wanted to kill me." When I said "kill me" I thought the social worker would take it as the usual prison jargon; I had learned that it meant he wanted to assault me.

The inmate was right. I was amazed how quickly the social worker responded to this lie. "Oh, really. It's good you tell us these things to help you stay out of trouble." He wrote some stuff down.

Great! No Industrial City for me!

⋙⋘⋙⋘

About a week later I saw the final person from social services.

"Name."

"Inmate, Anonymous Numbered," I replied. I was so used to giving my last name first that I just automatically gave it like that all the time.

He shot the usual questions at me: number, age, race, religion, and on and on. I sat back in the chair and answered. I've always wondered how many state forms have these questions.

"Okay, no drug problem, no alcohol problem, good education." He checked words off on a list. Then he finished, "Well, I see Industrial City as your placement."

What? What about my job here? "I had asked about a clerk's job here?"

"Yeah, I saw that," he replied quickly. "Just take it up with Program Review when you see them. Okay?"

"Yeah, but they told me to tell you."

"Okay, you did. So that'll do it; you can go now."

"Okay, but what about . . . "

"Just ask P.R.C. any questions you have." He shot this back faster than I could reply. "Okay, so we're done." *Bye, get, beat it, out of my office.*

I got up and started to leave. At the door I turned to ask another question, but he had the phone in his hand and waved me off.

That was the fastest interview I ever had. Supposedly he was interviewing me for my upcoming hearing. But he had burned through those forms too quickly. The only thing he did was give me the boot.

Out in the waiting area, about twenty more guys were all discussing their plans of attack. As I checked out with the officer I thought, *None of their plans are going to work with him. He doesn't want to hear them!*

I saw Program Review the following week. They assigned me to the receiving center to work. When I went through the hearing, I thought that what I had said had helped, but years later I learned that the Program Review Committee makes all its decisions prior to seeing a prisoner. They always follow staff recommendations and almost never honor your request. When they do honor a request, it is because they have an interest in it too.

Whenever I requested something, they would tell me to take it up with my social worker; that meant people like the person from social services who pump you through like dog meat. At A & E, they cared only about age and length of sentence. The rest was the next prison's problem.

✖━✖━✖━✖

REFLECTIONS

I was now a member of the prison system. I knew nothing about what was going on, only that I had maximum time to do, if I ever got out. What the state neglected to tell me was that to survive in this system, I would have to learn everything on my own. I came in innocent and green, to be corrupted—like everyone else. My crime really didn't matter to the guys I would do time with. Some even gave me honor, since I was a murderer.

I adjusted as best I could. As I changed over the years, the system affected me more than I ever thought it would. I quickly adjusted my beliefs and changed my habits and my personality to fit my new hell. I developed an emotionless face and learned to trust no one: even my closest friends have sold me out. I became preoccupied with surviving and avoiding violence. I focused on food, water, cigarettes, and survival: the basics of life.

No staff member taught me these lessons. I learned them to survive. Now they're a part of me.

3

Prison-Proper

"Yo-Yo, send me some of those **zoom-zooms** and **wam-wams**
down. My belly is touching my backside."

ONE HUNGRY GUY

MARCH 1993

"Hey, **lockdown,** everyone. Prisoners back to your cells now! Doors secured.
Just go, come on, move it! We have to strip you and search the unit.
Lockdown!"

ROOKIE SCREW

LOCKDOWN 1989

When I first passed through the prison gates, I expected things like being
locked down, being stripped, getting cold food, etc. But I never considered the
new language I would have to learn. I had dreamt of crazy men bearing scars
and tattoos, of bullies and striped suits, balls and chains, but never did I expect
the words I used to be totally unequipped for my new home.

I was white, middle class, and a high school graduate. Little did I know that
these were three strikes against me. I had to learn prison slang to survive. It's
part English and part posture. I call it *prison-proper.*

In our great society of America, this is the language that only the con
knows. It's spoken in the darkness of the American penal system. It's a language

of prisoners of all race and ethnic groups: blacks, whites, Asians, Hispanics, and Native Americans.

It is a language born on the streets for prisoners.

Prior to prison, I thought I understood the English language. I had spoken it all my life, starting with baby talk, going all the way to using professional, business words on my job. As a twenty year-old, I assumed I knew it all. However, after being thrown into this upside-down world where I was expected to already know all the ins-and-outs, I learned that I had problems communicating with other prisoners. Part of this problem was me; the other part was my race.

So I began to do a great deal of **ear-hustling.** I found myself paying close attention to the verbal skills others displayed. At first I was unsure what they were saying.

⸺✕⸺✕⸺✕⸺

In my early days, I did have difficulty speaking. The first thing I learned is prisoners do not speak like people from the middle class. At first, it was the smallest things.

"Ho man, you got a **square?**" A fella I never met before asked me this on the recreation field at the receiving center.

I did not call people, *ho man,* and did not know what the hell a *square* was.

"Ho man . . . white boy," the fella repeated, "You got a square?"

"Me," I looked at him. *White boy, who is he calling white boy?*

"Yeah, got a square?"

"Square."

"Yeah, a **smoke,** a cigarette?"

"Oh, yeah." As I reached into my pocket and handed him one, I added: "My mind was somewhere else."

"You kind of square to this shit, ain't ya."

Square? I ain't no dummy! I thought. "What shit?" At that point I noticed I started swearing more. *Shit, fuck, motherfucker, damn,* and *bitch* were becoming part of my everyday vocabulary.

"This here prison shit," he replied.

Eventually I was placed in **general population.** I had learned that blacks spoke differently than whites. At that time I did not know that black prisoners would have the greatest influence on how I spoke.

"Keep it real, motherfucker," an associate named Skin said. "You just a **honkie** from up state. Ain't seen a nigga but on TV." Skin smiled at me.

"Why do you call yourself **nigger** all the time?" I asked Skin. *What a question to ask!*

"Brother, under all that snow, you're a n-i-g-g-a, not nigger."

"I am snow?"

"Yes, white folks call us niggers. We call ourselves niggas."

"What the fuck is a snow?"

"Better I call you snow than honkie!" Skin smiled again. "And don't let them niggas hear you say nigga. If you say it they might get pissed cause you white. They think you being a racist. I can see your young dumb ass isn't no racist, at least not yet."

"They don't appreciate it?"

"Yeah, with your square talking ass, you fuck with their **manhood.**" Skin slid back in his chair. "Keep it real, motherfucker, you like being called H-O-N-K-I-E?" Skin's eyes bulged, then he smiled.

"No," I replied.

"That's because a nigga say it to you." Skin sat up and spoke soft again. "That's why no brother wants you to call him nigga. Unless he is your nigga then you two are cool like that."

I was getting my education from Skin. I don't think Skin knew it but I was trying to soak all of this in.

⚒═✕═✕═⚒

Then I learned about that four-letter word that men would snap over.

"Hey Tower," I asked my new friend as he stood in the cell doorway and I was on the bed. "Why did that guy want to fight in the kitchen today?"

"Who?" Tower asked.

"Those two guys on the vegetable crew."

"Oh, yeah, those two. Cause one dude called the other a **punk.**"

"Punk?"

"Yeah, punk. Don't ever say that unless you are ready to **spread your wings.**"

"Spread my wings?" *Sometimes I felt so out of place here.*

"Yeah, spread your wings, **throw down, bring the drama,** you know, fight."

"All that over the word punk?"

"Hey, Anonymous, you got a lot to learn."

"I understand."

"No, no," Tower smiled, "do you **dig** honkie?"

I laughed at him.

"Get used to it, and also to white boyee."

It took some time, but I learned the words that both prisoners and the system used.

There was no such thing as lunch or supper. It was **chow.**

There were places like **segregation** and the **hole.** "Do you want a **ticket?**" a guard asked me after he caught me loitering on the **tier.** "You'll do **adjustment time.**"

⚒═✕═✕═⚒

My education started at Cold Springs receiving center, but I was able to blend in better once I was transferred to Industrial City, which the inmates called Gladiator School. It was larger and more violent than the receiving center at Cold Springs, but that violence reduced the hassles the guards gave us.

At Cold Springs, we only had twenty five men on the living unit; but at Industrial City there were 350 men in the cellhall. Forty cells long, four tiers high, with three guards watching all those cells. One of the three guards was the desk sargeant who could never leave his/her assigned post. I could get lost in the shuffle. For most of my time there, I lived on the third tier, G tier, in the south cellhall.

Since it was so large, I was around many prisoners. They yelled from cell to cell and it was noisy all the time. The **cellhalls** became my main learning ground but I had to put a great deal of time into avoiding trouble.

In the cellhall I'd hear someone say, "Hey Bro, **bump that shit.**" Then someone else would turn the volume up on the radio.

If a black prisoner said, **"Five-0,"** or a white prisoner said **"Fire in the hole,"** they both meant that a guard was approaching.

If a man was on temporary lock-up pending a misconduct report, he would say, "They got me on **TLU** but I am **hanging tough.**" This also meant that the officers weren't going to break him.

If a person was "**jacked** for his shit," this meant that someone had stolen some of his personal property. If he was going to retaliate against the person who jacked him, he might use a **shank** or a **lock-n-sock** as a weapon.

If a man was busy doing something, he would say he was on a **mission.** If he was relaxing, he was **chillin'.**

And my all-time favorite, "Hey white boy . . . "

⟨━✕━⟩⟨━✕━⟩

Now, looking back, I believe I received a break because I spent the first year and a half at Cold Springs, which was a more confined prison for maximum-security inmates. While there, I could concentrate more on learning the language and less on my personal safety and security. In Gladiator School I had to pay attention to personal security, but by then I understood more of prison-proper.

Sure, I picked up bits here and there but there were gaps. Sometimes I never knew what was so funny or why a grown man looked as if he was going to **snap.** This was a foreign nation and in order to figure out what was going on, I had to learn its language. As I learned the language, I also noticed that physical posturing had a great importance.

Without both gestures and posture, you do not have prison-proper. I wonder if a prisoner would be able to speak if he were tied up. Especially in **ribbing.** I have seen more men shake, jump, swing their arms, and grab their groin during a ribbing session than I think at any other time. I believe this is because ribbing is like a celebration and the ribber is the master of ceremonies.

Yet there's also the serious, down-to-earth, ugly side of prison-proper. Two men can be saying the same words but through their postures the words can have different meanings. This posturing is the difference between one man's humor and the next man's anger. For when a man's face becomes blank, his arms tense, and he starts snorting like a bull, trouble can be around the corner. I remember old Hanson would be ribbing, "Oh, and by the way, kick that shit in, motherfucker." He would be laughing in, good humor. But if a gang member said this same sentence, it had a more serious meaning.

I realize that gestures and posture are nothing new to language. What was new to it was me and the knowledge that the wrong words could lead to assault. I was unequipped for this; the language codes were not nicely printed on a piece of paper hanging on my refrigerator door. Mom hadn't left me a note for this one. For example, don't ever call a man a *punk* unless you're prepared to *spread your wings*. But it's permissible to call a friend of yours a "motherfucker."

One of the most important lessons of prison-proper is that some terms are only permissible to use intraracially, or with members of your own race. For example, the term *nigga* is permissible to use for one black man to call another black man he considers a friend. This term is generally not permissible for any other race to use unless that person wants to get **checked** or assaulted. If a white man calls a back man "nigga," either they are extremely good friends or there is about to be a fight.

By the time I had been in prison for five years, I had mastered prison-proper's meaning and overtones, all its self-important, racist, vulgar, and sexual overtones.

In other words, I could **play-it-off** where the dude I was **kicking it** with thought I knew. Never hate the **player,** hate the **game.** If you follow through, if you're true to the game, the game will be true to you. Dig? I learned to lay back and chill, stay away from that **high-tech shit,** avoid the **drama** and the **artillery,** and just do my **time.** Soon I spoke prison-proper!

A detailed list of everyday prison terminology can be found in the glossary at the back of the book.

⤜⤛⤜⤛⤜

REFLECTIONS

Prison-proper is not heartwarming. It's not nice. It's a language of boasting and self-serving arrogance. The individuals who speak this language are self-centered, self-important, shame-based people. In prison, deprived of everything except the basics, they have a need to act out. This is complicated because most prisoners are selfish and lack any attachment to other people. It's complicated even more because of the character patterns that brought them to prison. These dysfunctional patterns are played out in many aspects of prisoners' narrow existences, including their spoken language.

This is the paradox of the prisoner, the prison, and its structure: its language lacks tolerance for others. Most prisoners are not tolerant people. Their minds are set and their attitudes are unchanging. Words that might have left the mainstream in this country in the 1960s and 70s have stayed with prisoners and their language over the years. And just as the prison system is slow to change, so is the language of prisoners, even though new words and phrases pop up all the time.

Prison-proper perpetuates prejudice and stereotyping based on skin color. For example, African American prisoners call whites **square Johns, crackers, peckerwoods, white boyees,** and **honkies.** After twenty years behind bars, many black prisoners still look at me with rejection and suspicion. Everything comes down to the fact that I am white.

Of course, I see this same prejudicial attitude when white prisoners look at black prisoners. Both groups justify their hatred because of ignorance and intolerance of diversity. Racial attitudes like these are all incorporated into prison-proper. Prison-proper expresses the great racial divide in America. In prison there is no racial harmony between groups; instead, there is a deep-rooted racial hatred.

Prison proper does not just have racial overtones. There are many terms that are derogatory toward women. It helps create and support an uncaring place where feminine qualities are seen as a target for predatory behavior. Many men are so worried about acting like a man that they forget or were never taught what a man is supposed to be. To most men in prison, women are **bitches** and **hos,** and were put on this planet for male pleasure. The physical body of women is seen as more important than the spiritual.

Prison proper is a hard language. Men threaten one another daily. A man disrespects you, and in return you threaten him. Someone cuts in line in front of you, so you must threaten him. Many bluff daily, but few want to spread their wings. To save face, and thus your future existence in prison, you have to fight. Kindness is weakness, gentleness is weakness, care is weakness, sadness is weakness, and love is weakness. *After twenty years of living like this, I truly need a hug!*

Of course you have those daily conversations, like what's on the lunch menu, what's on the news, are you going to the store (or to work, or school), and whether the recreation field is open. This is a society within a society. Sure, prisoners are concerned with the news, but it is just that we are separated from society so well that it is like hearing about a foreign country. Men have family outside the walls, but since they are apart from them, it is not a family at all. This is all incorporated into a language shared by these fences and walls.

As the years rolled by I got so accustomed to speaking prison-proper that I had to learn to shut it off during my visits. I remember one day my mother saying to me, ". . . you're cussing a great deal." I realized then that my language suited for prison was odd to her. Many times I would say things that I would have to explain. Eventually, I learned to turn off prison-proper and speak English appropriately again.

4

How I Got My Rep

"Before anything occurs in your sentence you have to get a rep."

KID

MAY 1983

"Damn right. Get your rep for not being a snitch and you're good to go. He made it sound like I was getting my angel wings."

D. TOWER

JANUARY 1983

When I was young and dumb I would just open my mouth. I did not realize how easy trouble could start.

After I was fired from my A & E clerk's job, I got program reviewed to the kitchen. I started on floors, and then I was eventually moved to better pay as head of sanitation. I worked with Dibble, who was head of the vegetation crew. I thought he was my friend.

"Gee, Dibs, I wish those guys would work harder." *Hell, I wished Dibble would work harder.*

I still had a work ethic with the expectation of promotional reward. It never occurred to me that men coming down to work rarely expect to work.

I hadn't caught on yet to the prison work ethic: do your job minimally without getting fired.

"Fire them," Dibble said.

"Fire them, right. Fire them and get planted." *Like I want to go to the smackdown hotel.*

"Ask for more help," Dibble tried again. *Dib was a man of few words, but he had a good point. What would be the harm of asking for maybe one more guy to help?*

So I asked Chuck, the staff worker in the office, whether I could get more help.

"I don't know, why?"

"Why not?" *I was slick!*

"Oh well, I'll see." Chuck was paging through the food service magazine.

The next day I showed up for work, 5:30 A.M., rise and shine. I waited for my two helpers and then realized that they hadn't come down with the escort.

"Hey, Harvey, where are my workers?" I asked the guard.

These two guys were drafted volunteers working for no pay. Their incentive was getting out of a cell.

"Per Chuck, they were taken off the work roster." In layman's terms, *they were fired*.

LeRoy, who worked in sanitation, was one of the two. He was one lazy guy who always hung out with Gary. I had lost help I did not really need, but Gary had lost someone he could chum with.

Everyone assumed Chuck fired him. And so while I was stacking the trays, the shit hit the fan—my fan!

"That dude is going beat your fucking ass," Gary told me while the other kitchen workers looked on.

"Whaaaat?" I made my voice louder than his. He was challenging me so I had to say something. *Don't want to look weak.*

"Motherfucker, you know what. You got LeRoy fired." He was raving.

"I, ah, I didn't get no one fired." *Denial is always the best policy.*

Well, by now everyone standing in tray line looked like they were watching tennis. I was at one end putting trays on and Gary was at the other, stacking them up. When he said something all heads turned his way, when I said something all heads turned my way.

"Fuck you didn't. Where the fuck are they?" he screamed.

Well, Gary had a good question. Where the fuck were they?

"Fuck it, man," was all I could muster. Gary was slamming trays left and right. I thought that he was going to jump me right there.

"Fuck nothing, you and Chuck got together and fired him. You couldn't stand him helping me."

So that was it. *LeRoy had been helping Gary do his job. He was supposed to be helping me, but he helped Gary.*

"Hey, come on you two. Stop the fucking argument," said Rob, the staff cook.

"No, no way. I know Chuck fired him, and I know Anonymous told on him not doing any cleaning." *Now Gary had just told on LeRoy.*

Then Gary turned to me. "Dibble said you wanted him fired."

I gave Dibble a sharp look. *You were the one who said fire them,* I said with my eyes.

"Well, you told me you wished they'd do more," Dibble threw back.

Now every kitchen worker was listening in and every one of them started making comments about what was happening.

Little-D, who was working on spinach. "I know LeRoy from the streets. LeRoy won't take that shit. He is gonna' beat your ass."

Tasty on mashed potatoes. "You're right, Gary, see how they all trying to cover up."

Dibble on sliced roast beef. "Hey, don't get me involved with this shit. I didn't have nothing to do with it."

I thought: *Sellout, sellout. Dibble just sold me out.*

Gordy on gravy. Silence is golden. Gordy did not speak.

Freeze on the tray straps. "**Freeze me,** dog, I ain't got no more conversation for ya."

Tower on dessert. "Y'all better lay off my boy, y'know. Ain't no one hear him snitch."

Hallelujah. Tower had jumped on my ship. Even so, my ship was sinking fast.

Rob the staffcook came in. "Ain't no one said fire anyone. Anonymous, get the trays on straight." Then he grabbed the mashed potato scoop and waved it around, pointing at people. "You guys stop it now!" That scoop of flying potatoes got everyone's attention.

"Say, man, you better watch it dog, you're gettin' mashed potatoes on me!" Little-D told him.

Rob just ignored him. "This ain't no wrestling ring. Now stop it." Another shot of mashed potatoes flew across the tray line.

By this time I turned pale. Tower was flexing his muscles, and Gary had pulled the cart of trays so damn hard Freeze had to jump to keep the trays in the back from falling. Gary stomped out and someone else ended up putting the cart in the service elevator. Dibble went off to hide. The rest headed to the smoking area to discuss the main event. I caught up with Tower.

"Man, why these motherfuckers take this shit so personally?" I picked mashed potatoes off my shirt. *Why did Rob grab the mashed potato scoop?*

"Personally. Huh, this is prison, Anonymous, everything gets petty and personal." Tower said.

"But I didn't get that man fired."

He gave me a long look. "No? Lookit, you're still a **fish.** What did you say to Chuck?"

"What? You taking their side?" *Now Tower jumps ship?*

He turned his head away and adjusted his kitchen hat. "Don't have me fuck you up. I'm trying to help and so far I'm the only one on your side."

"Yeah," there was doubt in my voice.

He pointed to the smoking area. "See that? That is their side. Now, I count seven brothers there right now. You, this over here is your side. Who's over here? Me!"

"Yeah."

"Yeah, the line is drawn." he returned sarcastically, "So what'd you tell Chuck?"

Tower was treading on my space now. I was still too green to really understand what he meant. Sides were being drawn. "I just asked Chuck for more help," I said defensively.

He grinned. "Okay. And you don't get it, do you?"

"Get what? I just asked for more help!" He was getting on my nerves. I didn't know it at that point, but he was right—I still didn't get it.

⬥━⬥━⬥━⬥

The next day I went into the office for the oven cleaner. Gary purposely came in while I was alone. To this day I forget what he said. Something about me trying to run things: the trays, the kitchen, and each other. Anyway, I ended up poking him in the back with a pen, not hard enough to really hurt him, but enough to show him what my *id* really wanted to do.

Tower shot into the office to see what was going on. As Gary left, I saw that other workers had been watching.

Once Tower had walked back out and the guard went to the other door, Gary showed up again, this time with a tray strap. He didn't say a thing. He just put the strap around both his hands and tried to wrap it around my neck. I was sitting in the chair, so I rocked back with my feet dangling. Everyone was watching through the windows. I suppose they were enjoying it.

Within seconds, I put a hand between my throat and the strap so I wasn't dying. Gary knew this, but he wasn't letting up.

"Gary, you have to stop taking this shit so personally," was all I could manage to say. *He was taking it way too personally.*

"And you have to stop running shit," he snarled. With that he was gone. But he was not finished.

⬥━⬥━⬥━⬥

That afternoon Gary and Tower got into it. By then, there were about thirty inmate workers in the kitchen and twenty of them were holding inmate court. I had to explain and reexplain my position. I didn't want to add any fuel to the fire and the only guy who really knew what I said to Chuck was Tower.

My story kept changing. By the time the third man finished his questions, I swore I only was asking for supplies. By the eighth man: I never talked to Chuck. By the thirteenth: I was not in the kitchen at all. By the seventeenth: I wasn't even assigned to the kitchen yet. I noticed that while I and my inmate court were on one side of the kitchen, Gary went into the meat cooler to steal stuff for the guards.

Tower was our new butcher. He figured it was time to give Gary a taste of his own medicine. "Gary, you know Anonymous didn't get that man fired!"

"No, he told." Gary screamed out.

"Look, I ain't going to argue with you. Your hard-headed ass is wrong. You know it, Gary."

"Fuck you. The motherfucker told," he drawled, "and I know."

"How do you know?" Tower barked at him.

"That fat, **funky**-ass Dibble told me." Gary had his witness.

"That fat, funky motherfucker would sell out his grandma if he could. You know that and I know that," Tower countered in my defense.

"Doesn't matter, he told me. Why would he lie? Hmm?"

"Yeah, and you forget it was Dibble that tried to sell us out for stealing meat?" *So pack that.* "You are so quick to forget when the scene doesn't fit your fucking needs." Tower's adrenaline was flowing.

Gary stepped toward Tower. "Whose fucking needs? This ain't no TV talk show."

"Your fucking needs, according to Gary's world. The world according to Gary." By this time they were so close they were spitting on one another.

Worse, the audience had grown to about fifteen guys outside the cooler window. They had deliberately blocked the guard's view by sweeping the floor in the corner on the far side of the kitchen. Anyone with any sense could glance around and tell something was about to happen. Yet some officials lacked sense.

I was still on the other end of the kitchen, avoiding the group; Rob was busy in the office. The officer left the kitchen at 3:15 P.M. to get the next group of workers.

As soon as he left the main kitchen, an argument erupted from the shadows by the meat cooler.

"Fuck that, Gary is right!"

"No, he ain't, Tower is."

Everyone was trying to outtalk the next man, but also trying not to make too much noise.

I heard Gordy's voice. "I know Anonymous, he wouldn't get no one fired."

"Freeze me, dog, your breath stinks!" Freeze shot back.

Yeah, Gordy, shut up, they are arguing over Tower and Gary, not me. Keep me out of it.

"I am telling you, man, the boy told," Little-D added his piece.

"Man, someone is playing a game," another voice was heard.

They were pointing fingers, arguing, and making threats. These are the times when a man has no idea what will happen next.

It got so bad that everyone forgot that Gary and Tower were in the meat cooler. Suddenly the cooler door flew open and Gary fell out, stumbling to the floor. All attention went back to Gary and Tower.

"Hey, come on now, let's not get the staff cook out here," the boil cook warned.

Then Tower dumped a bunch of pieces of roast beef on Gary as he was getting up. "There, steal that shit for the guards. You'll steal for them but not for us!"

There was silence as everyone watched Gary walk to the smoking area. I saw him staring at me. He pulled his lips back so his teeth showed, then lit a cigarette. He stared me down while conversation started up again.

Tower stepped back into the cooler and I headed to the coffee machine where I could better scope out the area.

"Man, dog, all this arguing and we missed it." Sounded like Freeze.

"Damn," someone else agreed.

The guard came back with the other kitchen workers and as fast as the crowd had gathered, it dispersed. I drank my coffee, wondering why everyone was taking this shit so personally.

Dudes asked Gary what happened. Then they asked Tower. However, both were in their convict roles. Gary didn't want to admit to how bad it looked falling out of the cooler, and Tower was allowing him to save some face.

"Look, motherfucker, I slipped coming out," Gary finally told the men who had any informal authority among the inmates. "We was arguing and I slipped. Nothing more." Gary looked like a volcano ready to blow. So no one pushed him further.

Tower gave him his space and cosigned his statement. "He slipped."

Bob came out of the office, oblivious to what had happened. "Tray line, tray line. Gary, here's your count."

"Okay." He grabbed the paper.

"You should have picked it up before now," Bob scolded.

"I was tied up."

Bob looked at Gary and then at everyone standing around. "What? What? What did I do?" With that, everyone took their places on tray line. I started putting trays on the conveyor.

"What? What?" He looked at all the silent faces. "What's wrong?"

No one talked. Bob could see the tension in the air.

Two days later I was still ducking and diving the crowd, still a little worried. Gary was giving me the cold shoulder and Chuck was back to work as staff cook.

"Hey, Chuck, why'd you fire LeRoy?" Gary asked politely.

Chuck smiled. "Security called me. He's on the transfer list. They said pull him. The other guy too. Going to Industrial City."

Word got around quick! "Hey, Anonymous. Did you hear?" Tower asked me.

"Hear what?" I replied warily.

"Why those guys were out of the kitchen?"

I blew my breath out. "Man, Tower, don't even start. I am tired of the shit. I've been ducking and diving, playing it cool."

"Yeah, I know. You're playing it cool. No sense getting another rumble going!"

"Yeah, well, these motherfuckers take shit too personally. I just want it to go away."

"It did."

"What?" *How could all my problems just go away?*

"They were out of the kitchen because they're being transferred."

"Really? Does Gary know?" I had a lot of energy all of a sudden.

"Yep, Freeze told me he was in the office while Gary and Chuck were talking about it."

I paused. "Well, that dirty no good—and Dibble. I should go talk to both of them."

"Yeah, well, be cool. Don't say shit until you have Gary behind the eight ball. You got your **rep** now for not snitching." *Tower was mentoring me.*

"What if Gary doesn't step out?"

"That's not your worry," he explained. "Now just every time someone says something to you about it, say they left because of the transfer. Then say you ain't no snitch."

I was happy to agree with him.

"Damn right. Get your rep for not being a snitch and you're good to go." Old Tower made it sound like I was getting my angel wings. Like I was getting a blessing. Like I was now in some small way part of a family.

At that time I did not understand it, but in the kitchen, it was very important. Not being a **snitch** meant I could be trusted.

"So what really happened between you and Gary in the cooler?" I asked Tower casually.

"None ya," he fired back before I finished the question.

"None ya? None ya what?"

"You are so green. None ya fucking business," he teased.

"Fuck you, man. Am I ever going to be the teacher instead of the grasshopper?"

"Yeah, someday you will." He chuckled. "I stuck up for you in the cooler! I'm glad I did. Anonymous, you ain't no **con** yet, but you're all right."

"Yeah," I looked at him gratefully.

"Now enjoy your rep for the moment!" *Was this what it was all about? A rep? People taking this shit too personally? I wasn't a snitch? Hell, this was a mixed up world I lived in!*

⋙⋘⋙⋘⋙⋘

REFLECTIONS

When a man is sent to prison with a long sentence to serve, there eventually comes a time or situation when he gets his reputation. It comes as natural as a bird spreading wings. A rep will either make you or break you in prison. I thought back at the receiving center that I was going to be "broke."

A rep is like a rite of passage, one that is incorporated from the inmate world to the convict world. Your rep is a large part of your life. I believe it is like this due to the fact that men in prison take stuff so personal. Of those who have known me in the past, my rep has always preceded me. Especially when it comes to knowing a man for ten or fifteen years.

Some reps are started before a man enters prison. For example, a rapist is judged by his crime. A rapist's rep usually starts at the courthouse and follows him to prison.

On the other hand, I earned my rep as not being a snitch and will always maintain that rep until I move on. A man also can earn a rep as gang leader, fighter, manipulator, snake, or a quiet person. A person can have multiple reps. The worst rep to have is a snitch. Especially in tougher prisons, snitches get verbally and physically assaulted.

All men have to develop a rep. There are certain actions and moods one has to project. As I learned, your true rep comes from the prisoners who are around at the time, similar to the role that Tower played for me. Tower was one of the coolest dudes I did time with when I first started because he aided me in getting a good rep in the kitchen. Tower was instrumental in passing prison knowledge to me, like a mentor.

As the younger crowd moves in, reputation seems less important. Yet it still exists.

EDITORS' DISCUSSION OF PART I

Back in 1958, Sykes commented that "life in the maximum security prison is depriving or frustrating in the extreme" (p. 146). Not much has changed about the concept of imprisonment since the penitentiary idea was first conceived by the Quakers in 1790. One persisting theme is the meaning of prisons as "total institutions" in a democratic society (Goffman, 1961). Prisons are designed to meet the needs of the institution, the general public, and the prisoners in that order. For example, in Chapter 1, new prisoners were batch processed in a ritualistic and formalized manner. Prisoners were issued identical uniforms and processed in large groups. A department of corrections number was one of the few unique characteristics that described an individual. Prisoners and staff addressed each other by last name only, or by labels such as "officer," "boss," or "inmate." Prisoners quickly learned that overt individualistic behavior attracted negative staff attention. Inmates thus surrendered to more subtle forms of distinction, such as nicknames and tattoos.

In addition, prisoners had little choice in their routines as they must adhere to the institutional schedule for mundane activities such as eating, working, attending class, and sleeping. Goffman (1961) called this "mortification," or the demonstration to prisoners that the officers are in control. Despite the author having no criminal record, being young and inexperienced, he quickly learned how to gauge his new surroundings and appeared, reluctantly, to relinquish control. The concept of minimizing individualism and putting the needs of the institution first is part of the punishment—a considerable deprivation for lawbreakers in a democratic society. Beaumont and de Tocqueville (1964) observed the irony that the United States affords its citizens with some of the most extended liberties of all countries in the world, yet at the same time, U.S. correctional and sentencing policy reflects some of the most repressive examples worldwide.

Initial Classification

One of the practices that fulfills a strong institutional need is the initial categorization of prisoners. This process is called "classification" and is performed for three main reasons: (1) to protect the general public; (2) for safer prison environments; and (3) to ascertain treatment and rehabilitative needs (Harer and Langan, 2001). Classification assumes that all prisons are not created equal. In other words, prisons have various custody levels that refer to the amount of security necessary to keep a prisoner confined. The lower the custody level, the more freedom and privileges the prisoner has. During classification, objective and subjective measures are used to decide what facility within the system will best accommodate each individual in the most cost-effective manner (Harer and Langan).

To that end, custody and security are two important features of the classification process. Security refers to the risk that an inmate poses to society at large. All else being equal, a murderer would be considered more dangerous than a car thief. Custody, on the other hand, is how the inmate "gets along" in the prison environment—largely a result of behavior while incarcerated. Low-security inmates (such as the car thief) who fight, engage in misbehavior, are disruptive, attempt to escape, or who otherwise are considered troublesome, may find themselves in a higher security facility with less privileges and freedoms. High-security criminals (such as a murderer) who have no enemies, are not active in gangs, and who have exemplary records of institutional conduct may be able to earn their way to a less secure prison environment.

Classification is a central part of the admission and evaluation process. Batteries of tests attempt to determine eligibility for programs and work assignments while incarcerated. Since most self-improvement programs in prison have limited space and accommodations, another goal of classification is to send inmates to the prison unit that will meet most of their needs in the most cost-effective way (Harer and Langan). Some correctional systems are better at the A & E process than others because they have focused on classification and program needs as a principal management tool or because they have a wide array of programs to offer inmates.

Since about 1980, correctional systems have significantly improved their classification process to better differentiate the risks and needs of each prisoner. More precise classification that separates prisoners who exhibit predatory behavior from prisoners who may become victims can result in a reduction of prison violence. Also, blending some of the younger prisoners with older, more mature prisoners can suppress volatile predatory behavior of youthful inmates (Gaes, 1994).

However, sheer numbers of new inmates coming into almost every state's correctional system have blunted the effect of even the best designed and managed system. Suffice it to say that the intake and diagnostic process of most institutions remain mechanical and impersonal.

Once prisoners complete the A & E process, they will be transferred to another facility that meets their classification (and hopefully program) needs. Placement is dependent upon bed space, or the availability to house the prisoner. In many crowded systems, inmates are transferred to a facility with a space, rather than the optimal assignment based on the A & E process. Sound prison policy begins with a valid and reliable classification instrument, along with the bed space to send each prisoner to the most appropriate unit. This maximizes public safety, prisoner and worker safety, and allows prisoners to begin the self-improvement process.

QUESTIONS FOR FURTHER STUDY

1. What is the purpose of incarceration?
2. How can we use the intake phase to better meet custody and treatment needs?
3. What kinds of intake programs and services would be most helpful to prisoners?
4. What advice would you give to a good friend or relative who was facing a 5 to 10 year prison term on how to handle himself during the first few months of incarceration?
5. When prison budgets are reduced, what programs or items should be reduced or eliminated, and why?

REFERENCES

Beaumont, G., and Alexis de Tocqueville (1964). *On the Penitentiary System in the United States and Its Application in France.* Carbondale, IL: Southern Illinois University Press.

Gaes, Gerald (1994). "Prison Crowding Research Reexamined." *The Prison Journal* 74: 329–63.

Goffman, Erving (1961). *Asylums: Essays on the Social Situation of Mental Patients and Other Inmates.* Garden City, NY: Anchor Books.

Harer, Miles D., and Neal P. Langan (2001). "Gender Differences in Predictors of Prison Violence: Assessing the Predictive Validity of a Risk Classification System." *Crime and Delinquency* 47(4): 513–36.

Sykes, Gresham (1958). *The Society of Captives: A Study of a Maximum Security Prison.* Princeton NJ: Princeton University Press.

PART II

Prison Life

EDITORS' INTRODUCTION TO PART II

In an attempt to make doing time in prison less monotonous, many prisoners attempt to escape their reality through self-improvement and "programming." This means that they become involved in programs and activities that pass the time, such as working a job, education, drawing, reading, writing, legal research on their case, religious activities, and other treatment programs for self-improvement. Prisoners who program keep to themselves and are known as "squares" or "square johns" (Irwin, 1980). Squares are not viewed by other prisoners as "convicts," but for the most part, they are left alone.

Other prisoners decide to do their time a different way by "getting into the life." This choice is seen as a way to use prison connections to do easier time and reduce the deprivations of incarceration. Getting into the life can either be temporary or permanent. A permanent way of getting into the life can include joining a prison gang (gangs are discussed in the next section). This section of chapters addresses activities that a prisoner can become temporarily involved in, such as prison politics, the prisoner economy of illegal goods and services, and sex.

The Prisoner Economy

The prisoner economic system is an integral component of every prison. It is a system based on bargaining and exchange of goods and services that is not approved by prison administrators, but to a certain degree is allowed to continue to maintain stability within the prison (Kalinich and Stojkovic, 1985). The prisoner economic system is also known as the "sub rosa" economic system and the "contraband" system (Kalinich, 1980; Williams and Fish, 1974). The purpose of this system is to decrease the deprivations of prison. Prisoners assume roles and establish connections through their prison work assignments that allow them to obtain goods and services that are otherwise unavailable to them (Gleason, 1978). For example, all prisoner uniforms are routinely washed and dried. However, if a prisoner wants his uniform ironed and starched he must "buy" this service through another prisoner who works in the laundry. He may trade a pressed uniform for yeast that he steals from his prison kitchen assignment. The laundry worker can use this yeast to make homemade alcohol, or he can trade the yeast to a third prisoner for another product or service. In this way, no money is exchanged, but each prisoner is able to provide goods or services using state supplies (Gleason).

Previous research found that while dangerous weapons and illegal drugs were automatically confiscated, other types of contraband (gambling material, kitchen food, homemade alcohol, extra supplies) were considered more of a "nuisance" than a direct problem (Guenther, 1975; Kalinich). One study found that some forms of contraband were allowed to exist, at certain times, with open approval (Kalinich and Stojkovic). An example that you will read about of this "approval" is during the holiday season, in Chapter 9 entitled: "The Christmas Chicken Caper." Bear in mind that enforcement of prison contraband varies from prison to prison, and that some forms of contraband that are "overlooked" in one prison may be taken very seriously in another prison. The extent to which the prisoner economy exists is largely dependent on the knowledge and attitudes of the prison administration.

Sex in Prison

Another deprivation that is felt when sentenced to prison is the lack of heterosexual relationships (Sykes, 1958). Sexual desire does not simply disappear during incarceration, as it is a normal human function. Most male prisoners adapt through sexual abstinence and masturbation, but from time to time, some prisoners engage in consensual sex with another male prisoner. In women's prisons, consensual sex with another prisoner was more common than consensual sex with correctional officers, and this is also believed to be true in prisons for men (Alarid, 2000).

It is difficult to estimate the number of male prisoners who have experimented with consensual sex because sex in American culture, particularly sex with other men, is seen as repulsive and immoral. After many years of not having sex, some male prisoners will consent to sex with another man, but imagine that they are actually having sex with a woman. The best estimates available suggest that between 12 percent and up to 65 percent of all prisoners had participated in consensual sexual activity when incarcerated (Nacci and Kane, 1983; Tewksbury, 1989). Even the terms used in "prison-proper" for these sexual roles serve to protect the psyche of men in prison. Sexual experiences of being "turned on by another man" may be so damaging to a prisoner's self-esteem and definitions of masculinity, that they actually become violent toward other men. Gilligan (1996) called this type of violence a "homosexual panic" whereby prisoners attempt to prove through violence that they are still men.

Research on sex in prison clearly focuses on coerced sex much more often than consensual sex because coerced sex (harassment, coercion, rape) is related to violence and is thus seen as an institutional problem. One study of seven prisons for men found that 21 percent of male prisoners had experienced one or more episodes of pressure to have sex or actual forced sexual contact, and at least 7 percent of men had been raped at their current facility (Struckman-Johnson and Struckman-Johnson, 2000). The chapters you will be reading on sex in prison are primarily about consensual sexual relations, both prisoner–prisoner and between prisoners and staff. Bear in mind that staff–prisoner sexual relations are rare, but they do occur from time to time. When staff are found to have engaged in sexual relations with a prisoner, or relations of any kind other than that of a professional work-related nature, the staff member is fired and the prisoner is usually transferred to another prison unit.

REFERENCES

Alarid, Leanne F. (2000). "Sexual Assault and Coercion Among Incarcerated Women Prisoners: Excerpts From Prison Letters." *The Prison Journal* 80 (4): 391–406.

Gilligan, James (1996). *Violence: Reflections on a National Epidemic.* New York: Vintage Books.

Gleason, Sandra E. (1978). "Hustling: The 'Inside' Economy of a Prison." *Federal Probation* 42 (June): 32–40.

Guenther, A.L. (1975). "Compensation in a Total Institution: The Forms and Functions of Contraband." *Crime and Delinquency* 21: 243–254.

Irwin, John (1980). *Prisons in Turmoil.* Boston: Little, Brown, and Company.

Kalinich, David B. (1980). *Power, Stability, and Contraband: The Inmate Economy.* Prospect Heights, IL: Waveland Press.

Kalinich, David B. and Stan Stojkovic (1985). "Contraband: The Basis for Legitimate Power in a Prison Social System." *Criminal Justice and Behavior* 12 (4): 435–451.

Nacci, Peter L. and Thomas R. Kane (1983). "The Incidence of Sex and Sexual Aggression in Federal Prisons." *Federal Probation* 47(4): 31–36.

Struckman-Johnson, Cindy and David Struckman-Johnson (2000). "Sexual Coercion Rates in Seven Midwestern Prison Facilities for Men." *The Prison Journal* 80 (4): 379–390.

Sykes, Gresham (1958). *The Society of Captives.* Princeton, NJ: Princeton University Press.

Tewksbury, Richard (1989). "Measures of Sexual Behavior in an Ohio Prison." *Sociology and Social Research* 74(1): 34–39.

Williams, Virgil L. and Mary Fish (1974). *Convicts, Codes, and Contraband: The Prison Life of Men and Women.* Cambridge, MA: Ballinger.

5

Control

"I run this unit and don't you forget it."

SERGEANT POT

SUMMER 1982

"You know, this place really sucks!"

MAC, THE HOBBY CLERK

MAY 1984

"Mr. Inmate, could you come here for a moment?" Sergeant Pot said to me while I was standing in the hallway.

He and Officer Minks, his sidekick, were at the desk. No one else was around. Pot had chosen his time well. I approached the bars that separated the officer area from the living area and the exiting door on the other side.

"Come through the gate and sit here."

I sat down and wondered what was coming.

"Officer Minks tells me you have a view to express about the incident yesterday that resulted in inmate Washington going to segregation," he said formally.

I raised an eyebrow but didn't show any emotion. The chess game had begun.

"He told me you and Skin, I believe that is his nickname, were discussing your opinion of the events in the dayroom." He carefully pronounced each vowel of each word. Then he stared at me.

My mind raced back to where Officer Minks had been when Skin and I were talking about the incident with Washington. I remember that as soon as we saw him come over, we talked about something else. *He must have been standing in the hallway listening before we saw him.*

On the unit Minks always tried to play the cool officer role, telling us he hated the unfairness of the system and he disliked Pot. Now he had informed on me to his commander, Pot. *No matter what, staff will always back staff!*

"Well, yes, I had my concerns," I tripped over my words. *Busted. If I told him what I really said, he'd lock my butt in seg.* I could see checkmate coming.

He gave me a look. "Officer Minks expressed to me you had more than concerns." *The secret police know all.*

"Well, you know," I squirmed. *I ain't doing too good here. Got to think of something to say.*

"I know," he interrupted me. "Yes, in fact I do know. Officer Minks told me that you accused me of being a racial bigot. You said that I ride the black men on the unit. You said that I am quite the asshole." He looked at Minks, then me.

Pot cleared his throat. "I believe that is disrespect, disruptive conduct, and planning a riot to assault staff."

I was stunned. *Checkmate! Holy cow, what have I got myself into now? This fucker's going to burn me!*

"You're turning awful white, Mr. Inmate," Pot said with a small smile. *See, I know everything that goes on around here.*

"Yeah, well, not in those exact words," I quietly responded, looking at Minks. He stared at me. *Oops. Pot knows I'm lying now.*

"Add to that lying," Pot stated.

"Yeah, well . . . " I said again. *Minks, you rotten, no good dirty bastard, two-faced cop, sit back there in the dayroom and complain about Pot, then tell him what I said. Fuck you!*

Officer Minks leaned back against the wall and crossed his arms. "I know what was said."

"Mr. Inmate, I am not going to lock you in segregation. This is your warning," Pot said coldly.

I now felt two inches tall in that chair. *Look, Daddy Pot, my legs almost touch the floor.* It was very quiet. I guess Pot was waiting for me to react or thank him. I did neither.

"Now Mr. Inmate. Mr. Inmate, may I call you Anonymous?"

Call me Anonymous. Oh sure, Dick, we are all on a first name basis here. You call me Anonymous, I will call you Dick, and we all know Dave! Fuck you. "Sure, I don't mind." *Fuck you.*

"Okay," he said. *Sure, I will call you Anonymous, but don't you forget that I will always be Sergeant Pot to you!* "How much time do you have to do?" He paused.

"Life sentence," I replied just as if he really did not know. *I knew damn well he did. He has a face card.*

"How long have you been locked up?" *Are you feeling uncomfortable again? Is your ass puckering? Yes, I will take you down memory lane.*

"About a year." *Come on, asshole, what is the point?* All guards ask the same stupid shit, like they think prisoners forget what they are locked up for.

"You have a year in on life. Now, you and I can do that time **together** or apart. I really don't care." *New inmates, they have to be trained to keep their mouths shut.*

"Now, the type of talk Officer Minks told me about will not be tolerated as long as I am sergeant." *Inmate, you better catch on to who is boss.* "You can do your stay here or in seg. You do have a nice job right now. I don't think you want to lose that over a misunderstanding about what happened to another inmate."

"Yeah," I replied. *Checked, checked, and double-checked. I think this is what everyone called being in Pot's pot with the water hot!*

The chess game was just about over. Pot adjusted his glasses. *I am God here, and don't you forget it.* "Now, you do not know these black inmates like I do. I have been a correctional officer for about ten years now. You have one year in. I knew Skin over in the other prison. I knew most of these other guys. I would strongly suggest you do your time with your own kind. It will make your life easier in the end."

He looked down at his belt, adjusted it, then looked through me. "I run this unit, and don't you forget it. This is my world and no, I repeat, no prisoner is going to change that. Not you, not Washington, not any of these black guys with their complaining." *I am the one, the top dog.* "What do you have to say?"

"I understand where you are coming from." *You are the h-e-a-d c-r-a-n-k in charge!*

"Now I am not saying don't talk to these guys." He moved into his kinder, gentler, fatherly role. "Just watch what you say to them. Don't take their side unless you know mine."

"Aahu," I replied. I didn't realize the impression I was giving.

"Do you have a problem with that?" he snapped.

He had caught me off guard. "Ah, well, well, I get along with Skin okay. And I do have to live and work with these guys . . . "

He sighed. "I am not saying don't talk to them. Play some table games together. Just don't get caught up with them."

I nodded.

"Okay then. Mr. Inmate, I am glad we had this talk." *See how easy that was to sell your soul to Sergeant Pot!*

My legs hit the floor. *Hmm, Daddy Pot likes me.*

"You can go now. Just remember what I said."

I went back to my cell.

Pot knew the rules and he enforced them. He had broken prison life down to me on its most basic level. Even though I only had a year in by then, his tutoring that day was one of the most memorable lessons I've had. He was the keeper and I was the kept. He was the master and I was the slave. I have never forgotten that.

Over the years staff has talked down to me, yelled at me, sworn at me, made rude gestures like pointing, waving me off with a hand, grabbing my body, pounding their hands while speaking—all of which I have considered disruptive and disrespectful towards me.

Yet I never again allowed anyone else to make me feel two inches tall. Pot had begun turning me into a con.

Years later I watched an informal group control tactic carried out by three correctional officers. By then I was well into my con life and was ready for it.

At that time, Sergeant Nat, Officer Ralphy-Ralph, and Officer Harris all worked the cellhall tiers at Industrial City.

These fine upstanding correctional officers got tired of writing misconduct reports for the loitering that was going on. Loitering brought a minor ticket: no temporary cell lock-in, no seg, only loss of recreation. The officers wanted more done but the captains of the **kangaroo court** weren't listening. On hearing day the captains kept taking recreation away. Nothing more.

So the officers put their meager brains together and figured out if they wrote up a person for disobeying orders, disrespect, and disruptive conduct, the captains would do more. This came to be known as the "Day of the 3Ds."

"Come on, let's go," Harris yelled out from the catwalk on the front side of the cellhall. It was class exchange and people were walking in and out of the cellhall.

The plan was working pretty well. The problem was that no one told new guys about it. Remember, the codes didn't hang on the refrigerator door. Most of the new guys came from the north cellhall, where they could still loiter.

"Come on, let's go," Harris yelled to Tony, my new neighbor. Tony had just moved from the north cellhall.

Tony knew Harris was talking to him, but ignored him.

"Hey, you dumb fuck," Harris yelled out, "You in front of cell G-16. I know you can hear me."

When a few other prisoners heard Harris say, *dumb fuck,* they opened their cell doors to see who he was yelling at.

"What! Who you calling dumb fuck?"

Harris had told him to move on while he stood on the tier. *There's the first D—disobeying orders.* "You. I'm telling you to move on."

"Well, fuck you too." Tony had seen the others watching. He could not let that go in front of the other men. A man has got to save face.

That's the second D—disrespect, Harris smiled to himself. "You other men close your cell doors."

"What, you don't want them to hear you call me a dumb fuck?"

Well, that makes disruptive conduct, Harris thought. "Hey, why are you getting their attention? That's disruptive conduct, you know."

"Whatever," Tony shouted and slammed his cell door.

That's it. Had to slam the door. Harris walked over to the intercom on the catwalk. *1-Adam-12, 1-Adam-12, one for lockup*! "Hey, Nat," he spoke into the box, "Tell Ralph to lock-in cell 24 on G tier. He's loitering."

"10-4," came over the intercom.

The first tier was let out. Then the second. Ralph passed my cell and stopped in front of Tony's cell. The tumblers rolled shut on his door as he slammed the large key in and out of the lock.

"Hey, why you locking my door, man?" Tony yelled at Ralph.

"I don't know, I was just told to lock your cell," Ralph smiled. *Loitering, you idiot. Are you that dumb?*

"Hey, but . . ." Tony started.

It was too late. Ralph marched down the tier and it was **ringout.** Tony sat back on his bed, pissed that he was locked in.

Three days later Tony got a pass to go pick up his ticket from the hearings officer. It was a major, not a minor, so he had a choice: take it the fast way by having it heard right there in front of the captain, or take it full due process. Well, since Harris had called him a *dumb fuck,* he felt he was innocent of all charges and so he took it the long way. Full due process.

When he came back to his cell and was locked back in, he yelled down to a dude a couple of cells away. "Hey, John. That fucker on the **catwalk** wrote me a ticket for loitering. But the ticket doesn't even have loitering on it. It's got disobeying orders, disrespect, and disruptive conduct."

"Haw-haaaw, you got the 3Ds!"

"Three what?" Tony asked.

"The 3Ds for loitering."

"Yeah, but I can beat it," he argued, insulted by John's laughter.

"No, you can't," someone else yelled out.

"Who is that, who is that?" Tony yelled.

No one answered.

"Don't worry about him," John replied, "Worry about your ticket."

"I can beat this shit. I was loitering! He doesn't even say that rule. Then writes me up for the three others. He called me a dumb fuck."

I lay back in my cell and chuckled. *He'll learn. It's all about who's in control.*

John went over to his cell and read the ticket. "How are you going to beat this ticket, Tony? You 'disobeyed his order to move. You said fuck you.' That's disrespect. You 'caused others to look on' while you were running your mouth and 'slammed your cell door,' that's disruptive conduct."

"I'm telling you. In the north cellhall, that's loitering. They can't do this."

"Tony, you ain't in Kansas anymore," John said.

Well, Tony went to his full due process hearing with three witnesses saying Harris called him a dumb fuck.

"You know," the captain said after hearing them, "you still disrespected the officer when you said 'fuck you.' "

"But I was only loitering. He called me a dumb fuck," Tony shot back. He was certain the captain would have to do something about that. *They just cannot make a loitering ticket into the 3Ds.*

But the captain did. Three days in the box. So Tony became one of the victims of the 3Ds.

If the guards started to dislike you, they could turn into some of the pettiest people. Bed is improperly made, talking in an area where it didn't really matter, wearing a shower cap outside, shoes untied, improperly standing in line, shoes off on the rec field, showering too long, having coffee in a powdered drink container, having a cardboard box, hanging a clothes line, having tape on your wall, damaging personal property like a broken pen, having your hair combed the wrong way, improperly shaking hands, not walking fast enough, shirt not tucked in, and on and on. They would come up with anything and everything.

Life would get harder for some guys. Other guys like me would lay low and obey the ten or fifteen petty rules that some officers loved to enforce.

⊂⊃⊂⊃⊂⊃

REFLECTIONS

After just about one day in captivity, I learned that no matter what the state might provide a man, it takes more away.

Besides missing the most important things like family and friends, your work and your home, you miss being able to sleep when you want, cook when you want, and shop for the groceries you want. You miss going outside and taking a walk when you want.

Then you start missing stuff that never mattered before, or that you never even thought about before: privacy on the toilet or in the shower, adjusting the thermostat, choosing your own desk, getting a brighter light bulb.

One day your pen doesn't write properly, you have no stapler, the dust blows around and you don't have any cleaning supplies. You can't get a paper clip or sharpen a pencil. You wonder how you ever took this stuff for granted as you try your best to reclaim the smallest, even the insignificant, things in your days and nights.

Then it sinks in: you've been deprived of everything, including control.

I have heard many prison philosophers expound on this:

Control is a state of mind.

Since the state pushes and we pull, who is really in control?

If you never give them your mind, they never have control.

Freedom is in your mind, my brother, not in your surroundings, say the prison philosophers. But then men in twenty-four-hour seg tell me that freedom is being in the yard. Men in the yard will say that freedom is not in the yard, it's out there on the streets.

The control a guard has over a prisoner is like a master–servant relationship. No matter how innocent you are, no matter how correct you are, no matter how justified you are, in the end you are the slave at your master's bidding.

As their careers progress, officers become accustomed to giving orders. Even guards who are relaxed and laid back and like to joke with the inmates remind you who is in charge. Everyone wants to be a **boss.** Mix this with the staff's power to control and deprive and you run into some very sadistic guards working for the state.

Naturally this affects the prison population. Every day in prison is unsatisfactory. If a prisoner is in twenty-four-hour segregation, he wants to be out in population. If he has no job, he wants one. If his job pays $10 a month, he is jealous of the guy who gets $20. If he is in a maximum-security prison, he wants to be in a medium. If he can stay in the dayroom until 10:00 P.M., he wants to be there until 1:00 A.M. If he is given a tray, he wants the chow hall. If he has the chow hall, he wants a tray. If the food is too spicy, he wants it bland. If too bland, he wants it spicy. There is nothing positive about life.

Even the roughest, toughest, law-breakers—the axe murderers, the rapists, the hardcore social rejects, the boasters and braggarts—those who were once the social bullies—are reduced to constant whining and complaining. Men like these do not operate well in an environment that takes control away from them. They begin to feel vulnerable and end up full of bitterness.

A man will try to mask his feelings of vulnerability by acting out. However, a prisoner is allowed to react only in a certain way.

Rules and regulations are designed to correct his unwanted behavior, and the state employs an army of guards to help maintain control. In most cases, the more violent the prison, the less petty the rule enforcement. This is because officers working in a more violent prison have more serious things to worry about (likely possibly being assaulted).

However, control and deprivation is still sanctioned by an overabundance of rules. The state-disciplinary code manual has about sixty rules, including one that permits each institution to create more. Those sixty rules quickly become 600. At Ridgewood prison, I was given an administrative rulebook and a loose-leaf binder. The binder held an additional 100 pages of rules created by Ridgewood for Ridgewood.

A man is told that these rules will help him become a productive member of society, no matter how petty they seem. How? I still don't know, but I do know there are so many rules it is impossible to obey them all.

Add to this the fact that a man's day in prison is not spent with counselors, social workers, doctors and nurses, or even support staff like food service personnel, barbers, maintenance men, or teachers. A man's day is mostly spent around guards who are there to constantly remind him of the rules.

In this situation, misbehaving becomes a way to get attention. Even though the disciplinary system is based on negative behavior, it nonetheless is attention. Many men spend their lives looking for the parent they never had. They find it in the parent–child, guard–prisoner, master–servant relationship: the prison disciplinary system.

I call this *negative attention via segregation*. First, an officer corrects your behavior and writes you a misconduct report. Argument and attention. Then a sergeant or captain asks you for a statement. Reason and attention. Next you are hauled off to the hole, that is, talked to, cuffed, and given a personal escort. Physical threats and attention. You fill out forms and talk to the officers at your disciplinary hearing. A staff member, usually a guard, helps you represent yourself at your hearing. Finally, you have a hearing and can present witnesses. Your case goes to the prison disciplinary committee and you get still more attention.

Believe it or not, I found that going to segregation on a misconduct report gets you more attention than seeing social workers, teachers, or going to church. The part of the hole that I enjoyed was that people talked to me. Sure, they took all my property, but the hole was a change from the usual routine. Hell, it was great to get a little peace and quiet.

As you will see in an upcoming chapter, isolation sucks. To fulfill your attention needs you have to go inside yourself. You start chatting with yourself. Shit doesn't faze you. Then once you're out of the box, you're considered a disciplinary problem and guards begin to ride you. But you have learned to live inside yourself and so you have isolated yourself from others. More social deprivation.

And you just wanted attention.

The problem is that negative attention reinforces negativity. This is the great paradox of prison. You get the attention but the more you are isolated and deprived, the more stress and hatred you develop. But no one cares, and you hide this paradox from outsiders and from yourself. No wonder people in prison return to seg, and people on parole return to prison.

6

Time

"This is the freeze zone and they have froze me like a dog."

FREEZE

JANUARY 2000

"Our mission here is to help rehabilitate the offender over an extended period of time, at taxpayer cost, yet we seem to still have an 85 percent recidivisim rate."

WARDEN AT ORIENTATION

OCTOBER 1998

❦

Dennis used his old wind-up alarm to wake up every morning. His alarm rang just before his cellmate came back into the cell. "Today is my day!" his cellie exclaimed.

"You get that job in the laundry?" Dennis asked.

"No, no, they haven't called me back over there. But it is my day. My day!"

"Your day," Dennis repeated as he dressed. "What's your day? You win at the football pool? Exercised? Got money in the mail? What?" Dennis grumbled as he spoke. Mornings were no longer easy for him. He would get out of bed at times just downright angry.

"Come on, Grandpa," his cellie said back. Grandpa was a name he called Dennis because he was older. "What day is important to every man?"

"I don't know. I'm going outside with Anonymous for coffee at the table in the rec yard. I don't know and I hate it when you don't explain yourself."

"Dennis, it is my birthday!" his cellie exclaimed. "Let's you and me talk for a while."

"Your birthday? Well, happy birthday," Dennis said, gathering his stuff. "You know I go to the yard every morning to have coffee with Anonymous."

"Aren't you even going to ask me how old I am?"

"How old are you, cellie?" Dennis paused.

"Twenty-one!"

"I got locked up at thirty-one," Dennis replied.

"Yeah, well, when's your day?"

"January."

"Do you do something special, Dennis?"

"Son, I haven't celebrated a birthday since I was thirty-one."

"No, come on, Dennis, you have to do a little something."

"My brother and my parents used to come and see me. They died about seven years after I was locked up. Then my brother stopped coming. I don't call but maybe once every other month."

Dennis really did not like this memory lane stuff, so he changed the subject. "You going to call that girl you write to or your momma?"

"I can't call my girl, phone bill's too high. Ten bucks a call."

"What about your mom?"

"Already did this morning. She gets up early. Said she forgot this year but was glad I called. Actually she forgot the last three years but I didn't say anything."

"Yeah, well I know how that goes."

"My first year they were up for visits: Christmas, my day, and other holidays. She sent cards and clothes. Now she doesn't do anything really."

"You're going home in three years, cellie, think of it that way. I ain't going nowhere."

"Yeah, then I'll catch up for everything. I hope my girl is still around. She don't act like she wants to stay, though."

"You can't recapture what you lost, cellie," Dennis continued half-heartedly. "I tried and I'm back."

"Dennis, you are so depressing sometimes!"

"It is life for me, cellie. I have to go, Anonymous is waiting."

"You dress warm. It is cooler out there."

"I ain't that old. I can handle it," Dennis snapped.

"Yeah, you talk tough!" his cellie smiled.

Dennis liked his cellie. The kid wasn't dirty or a thief, but he would never say why they put him in the old man building at Ridgewood. Every now and then a young guy showed up in here. Probably had some troubles somewhere else.

⟩⟨⟩⟨⟩⟨⟩⟨

Dennis strolled out to the recreation yard and started toward the picnic table where he and I drank coffee early almost every morning. Juice also walked out into the yard, and pulled out a cigarette to smoke but he didn't have any matches. This nineteen-year-old's philosophy was: *Why buy matches when every-one will buy them for you?*

"Hey, old man Dennis, give me a light," Juice shouted at him.

" 'Give me' died, young fellow," Dennis retorted.

"Hey old man, you're at fifty," Juice retorted, snatching Dennis's matches from his hand. "If you want to make it home don't talk to me like a punk."

"Shit on you. Give me my matches back," Dennis yelled.

Juice got in his face nice and close, "Old fart. 'Give me' died. Now give up your cigarettes too for talking **slick!**" He pulled them out of Dennis' shirt pocket.

"Hey, you fucker, give them back too."

Juice stood up. "Fuck you, you baby raper. What'd that boy say when you grabbed him like that?"

"I ain't in here for no rape case, boy. Didn't your mother teach you to respect your elders?" Dennis stared hard at Juice.

"What you are looking at I don't know, old man. I take my respect."

"You're a young punk that gives no respect. No one brought you up right." Dennis knew he was nearing that thin line between name-calling and violence.

"Maybe they did and maybe they didn't, but I'm in here, they're out there, and I don't give a fuck what an old man has to say." Juice got up to him real close again. "You call me punk again, Grandpa, and I'll kick your bitch ass."

Dennis grumbled but said nothing. He looked away. At fifty, he knew better than to push his luck.

Juice grabbed him by the shirt, "That's better!" Then he headed to another table.

There had been a few more of these exchanges before I got in on one.

✦━✦━✦━✦

I arrived at the picnic table about 8:30 A.M. The yard had opened half an hour ago. Usually we hit the yard every day, had coffee, and talked for an hour or so. Dennis would never admit it, but it was all he really had for serious conversa-tion. We had been locked up too long! I saw Dennis coming towards me across the yard.

"So what took you so long?" I asked.

"My cellie was telling me about his birthday. He's down about it."

"It comes, it goes."

"He's just got a little more than three years in," Dennis replied. **Old cons** always measure someone by the number of years they have in. "He's down because his mom forgot. Phone bills too high at his girl's place."

"Ain't been down long enough! He'll learn," I said harshly.

We talked for a while and then Juice came our way. I knew him a little from the building I lived in. He told Dennis he wanted another cigarette.

"I don't want no more shit out of you," Juice commanded.

"Here," Dennis answered coldly, "smoke it but stop asking me for cigarettes."

"Fuck you, old man. We went through this already," Juice replied.

They exchanged a few more words before Juice walked away.

"Dudes just can't do their own time anymore," I commented as I sipped more coffee.

"That fucker is always asking and taking shit. He already took my matches," Dennis said angrily.

I could see he was pissed. "It isn't the same, Dennis. You can't check young men like it used to be. You get no honor trying to talk things out."

"When I was young doing my time, we at least respected older men. These young guys don't have any respect at all," he said.

"True. It seems like they are reluctant to get along. Like everyone instantly threatens a guy's life or they want to instantly fight over this state stuff."

Dennis cut in. "I ain't going to tell on no one but I watch these guys. They want to fight and steal and if that don't work, they snitch."

"They have no patience."

"Yeah," Dennis agreed, "they don't wait their turn."

He took a sip of coffee. "That fucking Juice, I never would've talked that way. I would love to put Juice over my knee. When I was younger, I might have ended up in a fight with him. That fucker. What do I do now? I am fifty years old and can't play the young man's game."

"You ever think we're just getting older, Dennis? I'm tired of doing this shit and I am sick of motherfuckers helping the police. I am sick and tired of these dysfunctional cranks I'm doing time with." I was on a roll and Dennis knew it. "I meet their fucked-up side. They say I would make them do stuff, or it's everyone else's fault, or I run this, you don't. Self-centered bastards never think of anyone but themselves. I've never seen so many selfish motherfuckers in my life. It's the ones who say they aren't selfish that are selfish. Everyone I've met has something wrong mentally."

I was tired. I was tired of talking about it.

Dennis smiled at me. "Even me, too?"

I winked back, "Yea, you too, Dennis. But I can talk to you. When we have our arguments we get it out and move on. These other guys are too locked into themselves to care. They are so dumb they don't know any better."

Dennis tried to calm me down. "Hey, I was the one who was mad at Juice. You're mad at everyone."

I agreed with him and said that was why I hung with so few men. "I am mad. No matter how I work for the better, the Board doesn't care," I said.

"You think you have a right to parole?"

"No, Dennis, it ain't the parole. For me, hope is a thing of the past. It's sanity I need. If they're never going to let me go, I understand. Just don't keep a carrot dangled in front of me."

<hr/>

For Dennis, time had stopped years ago.

"I got my auto book in the mail yesterday. Got a '57 Chevy in it." He put his new magazine on the table. "I owned a '57. Paid two thousand for it. When

I get out I'm going to get me another one. Every man needs a fast car to pick up the ladies!" Dennis liked cars and his mood always picked up when we talked about them.

I was about to remind him that he was fifty now but decided not to. "Man, those babies cost a lot more now."

"I only paid two grand for mine. I bet I could get one running for three and a half, maybe four."

"Shit, running? Hell, that's too cheap," I argued.

"A new car costs five. Maybe a good one costs ten grand."

"Dennis, a mini-van cost thirty grand!"

He wasn't impressed. "Vans always cost more."

"Yeah, but Dennis, two grand was years ago. Like cheese don't cost fifty cents a pound no more," I argued. It wasn't the first time I knew he was wrong. "You're talking prices when you were out twenty years ago."

"I know this place just up north where the cars are cheap. Very cheap."

"But, Dennis, it ain't like that no more."

"I am telling you up north, you can get a car cheap!" he was irritated. "You just don't know where to shop!"

"And you know a hell of a lot of places up north where everything's thousands of dollars cheaper."

"Well, I know these places because I worked on cars all my life. Have you ever seen a 454? 350? Even a 327?" He was shouting those engine numbers out. "You know the timing on a Chevy small block? How to realign drum brakes? Change a distributor cap? I do."

"Well, maybe, Dennis, I don't know." I did know that all those little parts Dennis ran off, distributor cap, drum brakes; cars don't even have some of that stuff anymore.

He was growing old in prison but he had his dream and it wasn't for me to take it away.

Bob stopped to talk. He was a friend I met in Gladiator School. Dennis knew him too.

"What you old farts talking about today?" he asked with a smile.

"Cars, we're talking cars," Dennis said.

"Are they leaving you here?" I asked.

"Nah. First they send me here, then I get here and they say I got too much time, so I got to go to Gladiator School for a while. I'll be out of here next week."

Bob completed his AA degree while in prison on a previous time for rape. Bob was now twenty-eight years old and liked drinking and getting high. He was a real dope fiend in prison.

"You shouldn't have come back," Dennis said grumpily.

"It's not like you think it is out there anymore, Dennis. Things change. I just didn't change with it," Bob said.

"You did eight and a half years flat. Got out and came back in six weeks. Now you got twenty-eight years!" Dennis wouldn't look at Bob.

"I ain't saying I didn't fuck up, Dennis."

I changed the subject. "How's mom and pops?" I asked. I remembered that Bob's parents were still together.

"Mom still talks to me, Pops don't anymore," Bob frowned.

"He is pissed you're back."

"I am back. He is a drunk and Mom still puts up with it. They had high hopes for me."

"How's your girlfriend and your baby?" I asked next.

"Man, she don't want much to do with me either!"

Dennis interrupted. "I have to go. See you tomorrow, Anonymous."

"Bright and early, coffee hot!"

After he left, Bob asked me why Dennis was so angry.

"He ain't pissed at you, Bob. I just think you remind him of himself. The man's fifty, spent four years in, got out, and came back in with a life sentence. Killed his wife." I lit another cigarette.

"Yeah, I suppose."

"He'll come around. So your boy, did you see him?"

"Yeah, about two months ago. He's a year old."

I was seriously surprised. "I don't know how you do it. You get out, get a girl pregnant, and after six weeks you're back. Fuck, Bob, what were you thinking?"

"Started using **coke.**"

"You partied for six weeks?"

"I threw my life away in six weeks!"

I heard my name over the rec field loud speaker: "Inmate, A.N., report to your living unit. . . ."

"I got to go. If I don't see you before you move, good luck."

<hr/>

Joe was caught in this time warp too. He was a cook, a drunk, and a liar. His life had stopped for him the day I met him at the receiving center in 1982. Now it was 1999 and he was still cycling in and out of prison.

"Joe, what you going to do this time when you get out?" I asked, hoping he wouldn't come back.

"I'm tired of doing this. I ain't going to come back."

"So how come you don't settle down with your baby's momma?"

"She wants me to but she cheated on me so I'm never taking her back."

"But you told me you cheated on her!"

"That was after she cheated on me!" Joe gave me a cold look. He gave me that look whenever I asked questions that he didn't want to answer. Or he'd answer them with a lie.

"Okay, but then what?"

"I will just find me another girl to live with."

"Aren't you getting a little old for that game? It keeps getting you locked up."

"But I like young people!"

"That's why you're always working out to keep your gut off?" I was curious.

"Man, lookit. I hang out with young people because they have no cares. Remember when you were sixteen or eighteen? People that age live a carefree life."

I got serious. "I also know it's statutory rape to sleep with someone that age!"

"Man, I don't sleep with them," he said. "I watch them and hang out. I float on their cloud. Sometimes I get them to run around in their underwear."

"You mean you're a pervert. You are a dirty old man. You play on their youth and get them to entertain you. They think you're going to sleep with them but you know you just want to watch them in their shorts!" I smiled at him to soften my words. "You're a dirty old man!" I repeated.

"Man, I like their carefree nature!"

"Joe, you're basically forty like me, got no savings, no retirement, nothing. All you do is get out, rent a place, find a job, and come back. You always start out from the beginning. What are you going to do for your retirement?"

"What the hell you going to do for yours?"

"Right. I'm thinking I'm not getting out. I don't know. But you have a chance to make something for yourself. I probably don't."

Our conversation went on but Joe was stuck on being twenty years old and not any older. Over time he went home, but I figured I'd run into him again in a few more years. A man's sentence will turn him gray, but the prison mentality will keep him believing he is young.

◄══◄══◄══►

REFLECTIONS

The day I stepped into prison, I felt like I had entered a time warp. It was 1982, but I was slingshotted back in time so fast I got whiplash. This was the beginning of what I later described as *the time warp mentality.*

The clock stops when a man is in prison. Eventually the years become just numbers on the calendar. The calendar itself becomes just a piece of paper. First you lose contact with the holidays.

Oh, they still come every year but they are not the same. A man no longer celebrates special events like he used to. There is no family get-together over Christmas. There is no spirit of Christmas. There is no Thanksgiving. Then other holidays pass without notice. Even your birthday becomes unimportant.

A man may struggle year after year, phoning, writing letters, sending cards. He may tell those around him what day it is, what special occasion it is, what memorable occasion he has coming up. Yet most men in prison don't care about someone else's special day. Without family or loved ones around, it has little meaning. No birthday cakes, no presents, not even that dreary fruitcake. There is nothing hung on the wall, no pumpkin carved, or lights to hang, nothing. It is all removed. No matter how hard one tries to hold onto the meaning of an event or holiday, it is lost.

You lose touch with routine reality next. You don't watch your children grow up. No diapers to change, no first day of school, no report cards, no teen years, no driver's license, and no graduations. You don't see your grandparents, parents, brothers, and sisters age. I've never seen my brother's son, my nephew, who has graduated from high school. Hell, I haven't seen my brother for twenty years. You rarely see prisoners grow old and die since older people are housed in separate geriatric units. The closest thing to a funeral you see is a when a stabbing victim is carried out.

As your hair turns gray, you realize that you have no future. No one helps you or tells you to plan for a rainy day. There are no taxes, no savings accounts, no 401K plans. You don't have a broker. You don't have a company pension. You are not going to get a social security check.

Eventually you focus on your immediate surroundings, and the years you've spent in prison become more important. It's all you have left in common with other prisoners.

The time warp mentality is why inmates refer to being in prison as "doing time." While all this is going on in your immediate environment, you've lost contact with the outside world. The problem is that no one prepares you for the changes you'll find out there—if you're ever released. This can be quite a problem.

Say you're released as a forty-five-year-old after twenty-five years in prison. You still have the mindset of a 20-year-old. You see that time is running again and it's running fast, not standing still like it did in prison, where time never moved. The shock, the stress, the strain of the fast pace can get you down and you can end up returning to what you know best. You can end up back with what you're most comfortable with.

Soon you're on your way back to prison. The sad thing is that you may find more comfort in prison than you did on the streets.

7

Politics

303.21, Conspiracy. If two or more inmates plan or agree to do acts that are forbidden under this chapter, all of them are guilty of an offense.

303.20, Group Resistance and Petitions. Any inmate who intentionally participates in any group activity which is not approved or is contrary to provisions of this chapter, to institution policies and procedures or to a direct verbal order from a staff member, but which does not create a serious risk of injury to person or property, is guilty of an offense. This is designed for a non-violent disturbance—for example, a sit down strike.

DEPARTMENT OF CORRECTIONS MANUAL
APRIL 1990

"Rules are made to be broken. That's why they have so many rules."

J.W., INMATE
APRIL 1985

I t all started when no one went to supper.

No one was really protesting anything that I remember. This was a test of loyalty. The organizers wanted to build solidarity and to see how many people would get involved. They told all those who were willing to skip supper to wear a colored shirt to lunch.

Now, skipping a meal was not a rule violation, so we knew that we couldn't get in trouble. At least that is the way we saw it.

No more than twenty men from the cellhall went to supper that night. But the administration feared this was a rebellion since so many of us were involved—and because the security director hadn't received any snitch letters, nor had any blue-shirts overheard prisoners' conversations. This hadn't happened in twenty years. Even the inmates who organized it were surprised that the administration didn't know ahead, since normally word is passed on to them either directly or indirectly.

They had to find the organizers. After weeks of investigation, a few people were shipped out to different institutions.

Something else happened as well. We received a memo that stated inmates would be able to sit where they desired within designated areas, while eating meals. The first thing a person learns about memos is there is always a catch. The catch here was the term "within designated areas."

One guard was known by other inmates as "Richy-Rich" as well as many other names behind his back. From the old school, he was typical of the blue-shirt's mentality. He had been a blue-shirt for about ten years. His psyche and essence were built on control. According to Richy, no inmate was smart enough to make his own decisions, especially in day-to-day living and thinking. He was a *true keeper*.

He was ex-military so he saw inmates, blue-shirts, and the administration as the chain of command. He served in the trenches and the change in seating policy was a direct challenge to him: the administration was taking away his control and affecting his trench. He saw himself as the last line of defense in prison.

He had always ruled the cellhall by writing misconduct reports. He would write and write: radio too loud, smoking on the tier, talking during count, loitering on the tier, the list went on and on. This is how prison politics works.

The morning after the memo was handed out, Richy made his way down to the front of my cell. Memos in maximum always were distributed after the cellhalls were locked for the night. This was a political tactic. The administration didn't want a bunch of inmates moving around out of their cells while they were complaining about a new rule.

Richy asked if I had read the memo. "I can't believe it. No one will know where to sit. It will be all screwed up. The warden's giving too much away. There's enough trouble in the chow halls without this. It's going to cause more mix-ups than solve anything. You all miss one meal and right away they're giving the place away. How are you going to know where to sit?" He stared at me.

He was totally wrong but I knew that if I spoke I'd be pressing his authority and I'd suffer for it. I almost smiled at him but turned the other way. I had learned who had the power, learned never to disagree with anyone in control if I wanted or needed something. It's prison politics—in this instance, *their* politics.

Richy lit a cigarette. "I'm telling you, no one there to tell inmates where to sit. It's going to cause problems."

"Yeah, I **hear ya,**" was my only comment.

He stared at me again. "You can probably do it, but you're not like the rest." He smiled and dropped his cigarette, putting it out with his shoe. He glanced at his watch. "Got to go, class exchange is coming up."

In my time in maximum security, this was the first and last policy I've seen enacted that actually helped all inmates. Forced seating had always caused problems—everything from fighting to being uncomfortable about having to sit next to a man who never showered. Inmates were happy with the change, and this infuriated the blue-shirts. Who would ever have thought an inmate could find a seat without a guard's help! Many blue-shirts saw this the same way as Richy did: a loss of control.

⋙━⋙━⋙

The dress code memo came out next. A new warden had taken over, and every new warden creates a rash of new rules, just as a reminder of who is in control.

Sometimes the prisoners will scratch at that rash until it becomes an open wound, which is what happened in this case.

The new warden was a former high-school football champ with a "tough guy" attitude. This attitude showed in a new policy that stated, "Every inmate leaving the cellhalls shall have his shirt tucked into his pants and only the top button can be undone."

When new rules are created, they have to be enforced. So on D-Day, as it soon was called by lifers, two white-shirts and three blue-shirts watched everyone leaving for chow. They stood at the cellhall exit, intimidating everyone and demanding absolute compliance. Anyone whose shirt was untucked or unbuttoned was sent back to his cell and locked in.

As each man went back to his cell, he passed right by the other inmates who were going out to chow. Stirred up by being sent back, he stirred up others. Tempers flared and led to more people being locked in. By the end of the meal, out of the 300 prisoners in the cellhall, the **keepers** had at least eighty, maybe 100, locked in.

Enforcement didn't stop there.

This situation became the white-shirts' personal war to impress their new "tough guy" boss. They often were out in the prison to make sure the blue-shirts were enforcing absolute compliance. Since most blue-shirts had Richy-Rich's control mentality, they went right along with it. For the remainder of that day and up until the lockdown, blue-shirts who saw inmates with their shirts untucked would order them to tuck them in or be locked in. Some didn't even give an order; they just called the cellhall and had an inmate locked up once he returned to his cell. He was told only that he was being placed on temporary lockup pending a report, and sure enough, he'd receive a misconduct report a couple of days later.

The tension grew until we had a chow hall riot and a lockdown was ordered. The media investigated the lockdown, and the official press releases said that the inmates were testing the new warden. I'm sure this is how the warden saw it—after all, he was the one who issued the official press releases. The press release explained his logic behind the new policy: "If an inmate looks neat, he will feel better about himself, thus becoming a better rehabilitated inmate to be released into society."

On the other hand, after the lockdown, the reason for the new dress code changed. The new logic went that it was to prevent weapons and contraband transfer: items can be hidden under a loose shirt.

This sparked a whole new round of resentment. First, the policy didn't make any sense. Most people already wore clothes at least two sizes too big, so they were baggy. Having one's shirt in or out would not stop weapons or contraband transfer. Next, when the reason for a rule is changed, inmates interpret this as the keepers thinking they're dumb, in the same way a parent tries to get a kid to do something but never has a reason why, or keeps changing the reason. Most adults take offense if treated in this manner. Prisoners are not any different.

The saddest part of the lockdown was how the administration presented it to the media. We were portrayed as rioting merely because we had to tuck in our shirts. An outsider reading about this or seeing it on TV news would probably back the prison administration.

In reality, it was the prison administration's behavior—the petty need for control—that sparked the riot.

<hr/>

Another example is the politics of manipulation. Tiny, Trace, and Steve had intertwined their lives with politics. The three had traveled from maximum to medium security.

Tiny was a big bear-shaped guy with a crewcut. Even though he had had his share of fights in maximum security, he had made it to medium with all his teeth. He was a unit worker who lived in the same building as I did. As a unit worker, he had greater access to his bosses, the blue-shirts. He was able to talk to them in out-of-the-way places as well as at the officer station. He would "politic" for their favors like a representative for votes.

I was on the yard one day when Tiny walked over. "Hey, Anonymous, what's up?" he said as he approached.

"Same-old, aim-old," I replied, the typical greeting between prisoners.

Tiny started in on how things were going in the building where we lived. "Man, these **hooks** are spreading frickin' rumors again in W-building." He assumed I had already heard because I spoke to others in that building. "Check this out. Dude got fired from his job and locked up for sending cigarettes to guys in segregation. Everyone says I told on him. I didn't snitch on anyone."

"You know how it goes, Tiny. Everyone wants to talk," I replied.

"You know how we played it. We both came from the **Walls**," he said. *We both did time in maximum.* "Dude goes and tries to sweep some shit under the door in the segregation area for his buddy, but the **police** saw him. Well, everyone is saying I set him up by letting the police know he was going to do it. When he was making his move, someone pushed his room emergency button so that one bitch guard ran down there." (The segregation rooms have buttons in them like hospital rooms in case of emergency.) "When she got into the area, dude was trying to sweep the cigarettes under the door. I'm glad he's gone. That sucker owed me money and wasn't paying. And he was always in the policemen's faces. He got what he deserved."

"Yeah, what's making everybody think you snitched?" I was careful to not infer I thought he was a snitch. If I called him a snitch I might have gotten my words back with his fists.

"I don't know. I mean, come on, you know how I take care of my business," he smiled. He knew that I knew he had been a fighter in maximum security. "They're saying this because I talk to the same female police that caught him. Don't say anything, but it's that damn Trace who started it all," he said bitterly.

In prison, a common practice is that one man will tell another something about a third, hoping word will get to the third man so he doesn't have to confront him. Tiny knew I knew Trace, so when he told me not to say anything, that wasn't what he really wanted. I believe he hoped I would tell Trace that Tiny was willing to fight about this, in hopes that Trace would stop talking about him.

"See, Trace is jealous, that's all. I talk to that female police so he wants to throw dirt on me. If I weren't so short to going home, I'd bust him up, guaranteed. Frickin' punk!" he slapped the back of one hand into the other. Tiny had made his point.

◄═✕═►✕═►✕═►

Days later Trace and I and another man were walking the outer perimeter of the recreation field. Trace started talking about what Tiny was doing now.

"Yeah, and the sucker got dude locked up for trying to pass cigs to another dude in segregation. See, Tiny is playing two sides. Dudes get hired over in W-building, and, if he doesn't like them, he starts **throwing dirt** on them to the blue-shirts." Trace was getting upset about this.

"I didn't know Tiny was one to tell," I said, not revealing any of my previous conversation with Tiny.

"Oh yeah, when I got hired he was pissed, I mean pissed. After a while he started complaining about how I was doing my job, being late, you know. What makes it worse, I didn't know he was doing it." Trace paused.

"How do you know?" I interjected.

"Because a blue-shirt told me he was. He said to lay low and away from Tiny since he was complaining about how I was doing my job. Frickin' punk!" Trace paused and switched his conversation to the other guy that he thought Tiny had reported. "Here's the scoop with dude. Tiny used to hang out by that one female blue-shirt who works our building, I forgot her name. Anyway, Tiny is always telling her stuff, always. He'd steal food out of the servery for her, you know, steal for a blue-shirt but not a prisoner," he stated harshly. "And he'd be complaining about everyone he didn't like. He acted like she liked him, but the broad used him. He started thinking he could get away with anything around her, but when she wrote him up, gave him those misconduct reports, she wasn't his friend.

"What made it worse, Tiny would say she was doing it just to make it look good and he would still talk and do stuff for her. You tell me who was using who?" His voice trailed off.

"Then he finally gets caught telling. She ran over to the segregation area when Tiny was talking to her. What does that say? He set up dude for passing cigarettes." Trace lowered his voice. "Now he's pissed at me because I'm supposedly spreading rumors that he's a snitch. Hell, everyone knows he's the one who told; how could it be any other thing? So now he wants to fight me again."

"Yeah, I heard that," I said.

"Yeah, of course, he brings it to everyone else but me. See what I am saying, the punk couldn't bring it to me. Punk is what he is. I got him in the Walls, I'll get him here, too." His voice was cold.

At this point I knew Trace was telling everyone Tiny was a snitch since Tiny was telling everyone he was going to fight him.

This goes on all the time in prison.

⊱⋅☾⋅⊰

It was not until later that I learned what was closer to the truth. Steve and I were walking the rec field about a month after Tiny was paroled. The conversation turned to Trace and Tiny. Steve told me that when he was in W-building, Tiny kept trying to **take** his canteen. "You know Tiny. I ain't going to fight his big ass. He'll tear me up. I almost got even with him, too. You know that Tiny hates Trace and likes to catch a man up with the guards."

He went on to explain that when Tiny was at the desk talking with what Steve called his "so-called girlfriend guard," another worker was passing cigarettes in the segregation area. "So I told one of the guards walking around. He went back to the desk and told Tiny's girlfriend guard. She jumped up so fast running over there to catch him, I couldn't believe it. And Tiny followed her with his dumb ass to see what was going on."

Steve was grinning. "When everyone in the building started talking about it, I told Trace that I heard Tiny tell his girlfriend guard about the cigarettes, but not to say anything because I didn't want Tiny after me. That got around real fast. Next thing everyone figured Tiny snitched."

"What did Tiny do?" I asked.

"The next day Tiny came to try to get some more shit out of me. I acted like I was cool with him and asked him why he was letting Trace tell everyone that he snitched if he was so tough?" Steve knew that Tiny's ego was too big to let that pass and that he'd have to find out what was going on. "I rubbed it in pretty good." He grinned.

"It couldn't have worked out better. Trace was telling everyone that Tiny was a punk and a snitch. And Tiny said he was going to fight him."

Steve was happy with the mess he stirred up. "It almost worked too. But when they fought, they didn't get caught. Man, if they could have gotten caught, I could have moved up to Trace's old job and got a raise and gotten Tiny off my back too," Pat said.

When the guards finally found out, Tiny left the next day on parole.

People like Steve scared me because they were the master manipulators who got others in trouble. People like that are common in prison. At least half the people I have been locked up with try games like this on a *daily* basis.

Sometimes your enemy can be your friend, and your friend, your enemy.

⋙⋘⋙⋘

REFLECTIONS

In the riots I've been through over the years, the administration has used the media this way. Inmates have no voice in the media; the administration does. Thus, the administration will perpetrate every lie necessary to maintain their control.

One thing I learned about prison is that the keepers shouldn't use intimidation and force to enforce a rule that is simply petty. Intimidation brings intimidation, and force brings force. Tempers flare, fights start, and people get hurt. Even the blue-shirts eventually saw this, and when tensions lessened and the lockdown ended, enforcement of the dress code rule changed. Guards stopped shouting orders to tuck in shirts. They asked—politely— a person in noncompliance to tuck in his shirt, which was then mostly done without incident. Prisoners with shirts out were no longer locked in. The fiasco was over.

Politics is the way of life in prison. The gossip, intimidation, manipulation, and persuasion among prisoners, and between the prisoners and the employ- ees, run the prison society.

From a simple meeting on the yard to a complex parole hearing, prison politics keep prisoners focused on their surroundings but not seeing their imprisonment. Prison politics are an invisible fence that holds everything together.

The keepers use the politics to glorify the rules and exemplify the petti- ness: to remind you who is in control. The inmates use politics to fill idle lives with things to do.

I have seen so much of this that I have burnt out on the whole thing. If people did not play games or feed into someone else's game, I believe overall, prison would be a better place. Unfortunately, if prisoners do not have their politics, they might turn on their keepers.

The social design of the prison reinforces prison politics. Big changes gen- erally come from the front offices. The administrators there are a part of the physical prison but not its reality. These are the bureaucrats gifted in making rules people are expected to follow. They may visit the inner parts of the prison but seldom, if ever, understand the people housed there.

Prisoners use the politics to get their needs and desires met. Since they have little to do, many inmates pass the day away gossiping about the next man. Telling lies about one's own life and throwing dirt on others' lives becomes a soap opera and a way of life. Mix all this together and you get prison politics: *the hottest game in town.*

8

Economics

303.40, Unauthorized Transfer of Property. Any inmate who intentionally gives,
receives, sells, buys, exchanges, barters, lends, borrows, or takes any property
from another inmate without authorization is guilty of an offense.

DEPARTMENT OF CORRECTIONS MANUAL

APRIL 1990

"See that yard? There's money to be made out there."

A. H., INMATE, 1987

Prison has two economies: the *official economy* that's created by the administration, and the *prisoner economy* that's established and blessed by the vast
number of locked-up **wannabe** merchants.

The official economy permits purchases only for certain amounts and only
at certain times and places. It makes a simple purchase a complex task with red
tape and rules. It controls each prisoner's finances through an established
account. Funds come out of his account in three ways: he can buy from the
canteen, the official government store; he can buy mail-order property; and he
can be required to pay a debt he owes the state.

The canteen is similar to a convenience store except it supplies a limited
amount of hygiene, smoking and writing items, and food—mainly junk
food like snack cakes, bars, chips, and candy—and there are restrictions on the

number of purchases. In my state, the maximum amount a prisoner can spend is $130 per month, but if his account is in the red, he cannot buy anything. If a prisoner destroys state property, the replacement or repair cost is automatically deducted from his account. Other automatic deductions are for recreation (hobby) and/or photocopy expenses.

A prisoner can send away for allowed items that aren't sold in canteen, such as sweat suits, underwear, tennis shoes, small fans, 13" TVs and radios. There are spending caps on these items also, and there are special restrictions on electronics. More red tape.

Outsiders may think that, at $130 per month, inmates have a great deal of money in their accounts. But this is the maximum amount they can spend, and most inmates don't have nearly that much income. If they work in the prison, most inmates get $25 to $30 a month, and some prisons have 30 percent to 60 percent unemployment. The only other major source of money is that which is sent from friends or families. Some of the poorest inmates live on $5 a month.

The prisoner economy gets the majority of its products from the official economy, but otherwise it is completely opposite. Its first goal is to immediately provide an item that a prisoner might otherwise have to wait weeks to get. Its second goal is to provide items the state will not let him have. The prisoner economy is greater in size and easier to access. It runs like a medieval, pre-currency economy and touches every prisoner; even though it's considered illegal, everyone uses it, and everything is for sale in prison. I mean everything.

When I came to prison, I had to adjust to not getting what I wanted when I wanted it. I had to learn to plan and budget around canteen days. I also had to learn to barter and sell.

⋙⋘⋙⋘⋙⋘

One of my first experiences with the prison economy was when I was moved from the north cellhall to the south cellhall and was getting dug in. Unfortunately, it was the north cellhall's week to go to Commissary. As a new resident of south, I wouldn't get to go this week, as I had planned, and instead would have to wait until next week. And I was almost out of tobacco.

"Hey, John," I yelled to my next door neighbor over the cellhall noise, "how you set on smokes?"

He yelled back that he had some and asked why.

"I'm almost out and I won't get to the store until next week. Over in the north cellhall, I would have gone this week."

"Do you know Mike in the bathhouse? If he thinks you're cool, he'll help you out," he replied. "I'll help you out until then."

"Okay. Good idea," I shouted back. I knew I would see Mike's buddy James at pass control on class ringout for school. James was a **runner,** and runners can walk anywhere in the joint.

The mega-blaster buzzer in the cellhall went off three times, buzzing my tier out for the afternoon. I came out of the cellhall and walked past pass control with the 200 other men.

"Hey, James, hey, over here," I called over the crowd.

So he walked out of the pass control area and followed me to hobby shop. I asked him if he could tell Mike that I was out of smokes. I wanted him to come up to hobby and bring me a can of tobacco. I knew Mike had access to everything.

"I don't know if Mike can come right away, but I'll go down there now and tell him," he said as he pretended to look over my project.

"All right, but I leave here at 1:30," I told him.

"Yeah, I know. I do work at pass control." He said this smugly.

He was right. I had forgotten that people who work at pass control learn the prison ringout schedule. They know every time there's a movement.

As I worked on my project, Mike came in the hobby shop. Like James, Mike was also a runner. Mike asked Bob, the staff hobby director, if he could talk to me. Mike's excuse was that I was making something for him. I wasn't, but that's how he could get in.

Bob was laid back and didn't mind the incoming and outgoing traffic in his shop. He was more worried about art. "If Security comes, don't stay, okay?"

Mike walked over to me. "So you need tobacco," he said to me.

"Yeah. With moving over to the south cellhall, I won't get to canteen until next week."

He put his arm into the towels he was delivering to the bathhouse and pulled out a can. "Will this do?"

"Hey, my man, how much?" I smiled at him as I hid the can.

"Well, they sell for $4 and I usually charge two for one back." He was into his salesman pitch. In prison, everyone says two for one—what they mean is that you pay two back for every one that you are given. "But I like you, you're cool."

"Yeah, well come on, Mike. I can't stand two for one. Can I make you a deal?" I brought out the belts I had made that no one purchased. "I have four belts dudes ordered but never paid for."

He looked over the belts. "What do you want for one that fits?"

"Oh, it'll fit! I usually sell them for $15 to $20, but you're doing me a favor." We both were good salesmen. We had our speeches ready!

"Well, I like these two, but I want to trade for them. I only have my **store**."

"Cool," I quickly answered, "fifteen bucks, they are yours."

"Well, kill $5 for the tobacco, since I have to make a little profit, and I'll owe you $10," he said.

"Okay, what do you have to sell?" This was a loaded question, since Mike had access to everything. I was asking what he had in stock.

He looked like he was checking off his list. "Well, I have hobby stuff like pens, pencils, paper, glue, erasers, tape. Or bathhouse items: sheets, socks, towels, pants. They just got in some brand new underwear. Kitchen food. Wax. Soap. Shit from the other shops. Hell, a handgun if you really want it." With that he smiled.

I told him that I really needed paint thinner. "They won't let me buy any more through hobby." I pulled out my quart can. "And some wet/dry sandpaper, 400, 600, and 800 grit."

"Okay. I don't know if I can get a full can." He knew damn well that he could.

"Well, I really need it."

"Yeah, but I have to walk halfway around the prison to get it. What if I got caught?"

"How about a couple of matching buckles for your belts?" I pulled out some buckles and set them on the table. "Now, come on, I don't have all day!" I smiled.

"Deal!"

"That was fast!"

"Yeah. You can make these to fit James and me, right?"

I pulled out my pencil and paper. "No problem. I just need waist sizes."

Now, this deal might seem set. However, this was prison, not the corner store.

Mike swung by pass control and told James that he got him a belt. "Anonymous said he'd finish them up today if we can get him a pass."

Hell, James was getting a free belt so a pass was no problem. Mike went off to the bathhouse, and James forged a pass for me, then mixed it into the pile of about 30 other passes that the officer had to stamp for other inmates.

James brought the signed pass to me at the hobby area. "Here's your pass," he said, waving it as he came in.

"Let me see that," Bob said. "Hey, I didn't sign this."

"Yeah—yeah, Bob, but Anonymous is making us belts. Can he stay long enough to finish?" James asked.

Bob walked back to me. "Lookit," he started off seriously, "you know I don't like this type of shady shit in my shop." *Bob, you sound so much like a con.* Then Bob cut to the chase, "If you stay, I need you to fix my wallet too." Everybody had an angle, even Bob.

"Cool," I replied, "but I'll need some of the dye back there." *Hell, it was state dye, so why not?*

So James and Mike were getting belts, I got an all-afternoon pass, Bob got his wallet fixed, and I was soaking him for dye. What next?

By this time, Mike was doing his daily running with a 6 x 6 laundry cart. Since Mike delivered rags, he visited every shop and knew all the runners. His cart carried a lot of rags and a lot of contraband.

Jerry, the paint shop runner, saw Mike coming. They both were outside running around on their runners' stripes.

Mike stopped his cart and showed Jerry my empty can. "Hey, Jerry, I need a favor. I need this filled with thinner."

"A quart?" Jerry was surprised. "That's a lot. You gonna' make a bomb?"

"No, no, I need it for some business I got going in hobby."

"Well, what you gonna' do for me?"

"What do you need?"

"I tell you what. Can I get all new clothes when you're working the bathhouse counter?"

Mike agreed, but said it could take a couple of weeks. Jerry said he didn't mind waiting. Then Mike asked when he could get the thinner.

"Tomorrow?"

"I need it today if possible, really."

"Well, then I have to hurry up and run these passes to pass control." Jerry said.

"I'll handle the passes. James works up there. I'll just give them to him," Mike answered.

"Okay, I'll go clean up. I'll be behind the shop cleaning brushes in about twenty minutes."

When Mike said he'd bring the rags over and get the thinner, he remembered he needed the sandpaper too. Jerry told him to get it at wood shop.

"You can't get any?"

"We do that in the morning so I can't get it today."

"Okay, I'll go see Smoky."

"Don't forget me on my new clothes."

Then Mike went off to the wood tech shop to deliver rags. Three pieces of sandpaper wasn't much, so he swung a deal with Smoky for a pack of cigarettes as well. Caught James picking up attendance slips and gave him the passes.

"James," Mike said quietly so the guard at the end of the school hallway wouldn't hear. "Jerry's got a can of thinner outside. If I grab it, can you walk it to hobby?"

"I don't know," James replied. "I have to go past Murphy. He's a prick." Murphy was the rotunda gate officer, the **turn-key.** He ran the main gate on the right side of the rotunda and liked to hassle everyone coming through. That's all he did all day: turn a key and hassle men!

"I'll bring it up to the rotunda on the other side. I just have to check into the bathhouse first. Otherwise I'd run it up there."

"Okay," James answered, "I'll meet you over there in about ten minutes."

"Hey, do you have any cigarettes? I need a pack for Smoky."

"I got a pack up at pass control."

"Can I borrow it?"

"Yeah, sure," James assured him.

"Can you get it to him?" Mike asked, "I can't go back over that way now. I made all my deliveries for the day."

"Yeah, I'll get the thinner to Anonymous, then cut to wood tech and give the smokes to Smoky. I still have to pick up attendance slips."

They had their plan. Meanwhile, I was at hobby working on their belts and Bob's wallet. I stayed there all day. Mike got the thinner for new clothes. James would bring it to me, and then would take the cigarettes to Smoky for the sandpaper. Mike would come up at the end of the day and give me the sandpaper and get his belts.

With all the action going on, it was no wonder when Security finally came down on the runners. They caught many of them with little note pads and pens. Some runners kept a list.

⟨⟩⟨⟩⟨⟩

I went back to my tier with a can of tobacco in my art bag. A young red-haired kid saw me with it as I passed his cell.

"Hey," he called to me, "can I get some of that tobacco?"

He couldn't have been more than seventeen years old. His cell was pretty much empty except for a TV. "I don't know. I have to give some out to another dude, and I need the rest until canteen." It was a lie, but no one was getting my shit. And in prison, it's easier to lie to someone than to tell the truth. Saying you owed someone else was easier than saying no.

Big Ron stepped behind me. "What's he want?"

"Something to smoke," I said. "I just don't have it."

"Now, Red, what'd I tell you?" Big Ron said to the kid. He ignored me so I walked down the tier. "If you need anything you just come to me."

I didn't talk much with Big Ron. He ran the store for one of the gangs in the prison and was always looking for new prisoners to hook up in debt.

"Yeah, but I owe you so much, I'm trying to get you all paid off, then I'll be cool," I heard Red answer.

"Well, until then," Big Ron said, "if you need anything we just put it on your tab and you can pay us off."

Now by that time I had learned the loop. Lesser gang members and nongang members could get stuff out of the store two for one. They had everything canteen had, without the wait! The whole point was they would either take all your prison paycheck, or take just enough that you'd be looking for a smoke or a snack by the following week. And no one else would loan you anything because they knew the **gangbangers** would get their payment off the top.

Trade went on at night too, even though we were locked in. Night was when the janitors would run around the cellhall cleaning—and transporting.

"Hey, Chico," I hollered out as he went by. Chico backed up and looked in. "Hey, can you take this down to the red-haired kid?"

"Man, I ain't taking him nothing."

"Why not? He was asking me for a little something to smoke earlier. I figured I'd help him out."

"I would but the gang boys are taxing his ass. He owes them about fifty bucks. You know how they play it. If I help him out, they'll cut my action off that I got transporting their shit."

To help out Red meant I wanted to pay his bill. Unfortunately, I could not do that.

⟨⟩⟨⟩⟨⟩

REFLECTIONS

Based on the barter system, the prison economy is based mainly on canteen items like stamps or cigarettes. However, new T-shirts, sweat suits—or whatever else the state allows an inmate to have—can be traded for a debt. I have seen fellas run out of money so they trade items such as stamps for such items as coffee or cigarettes. One fella received a new pair of tennis shoes from home. He didn't want them so he sold them for food and cigarettes out of canteen. When I was making belts to sell to inmates, most would prefer to trade their canteen rather than have money deducted from their account.

A service can also be a bargaining chip. For example, some men will do another man's laundry for a price. I had my small fan cleaned once or twice a month for a couple of sodas per cleaning. Others will cook for a group if they are eating together. Many times I have allowed another man to eat a snack with me based on the expectation that he would wash the dirty dishes.

Men will pay for sex.

Some men will pay for protection, although sometimes stronger prisoners will force this on them.

Finally, prisoners will use their assigned jobs to grant favors to other prisoners. For example, my job was to wash mops and rags. I would wash and return the mops to the canteen first, and in return, I would be picked first to receive my canteen on the day I went.

Never upset a pass runner who could get you extra passes, a laundry worker who can press your clothes, or a food service worker who can give you extra food. Otherwise, you'll never eat enough, never go anywhere, and will have the worst-looking, wrinkled clothes that exist. In the prisoner economy, each of these services speaks the same as cash.

Taxes are a part of the prisoner economy just as they are a part of the U.S. economy. However, they have a whole new meaning in prison. Taxes are "compulsory contributions" on transactions that are used to run the entire political and economic system. Just as transactions in the general economy are taxed in various ways, prisoners tax their own economy through *strong-arming, theft, commissions and donations, intimidation, and manipulation.*

The most severe form of **taxation** is **strong-arming.** The majority of strong-arm victims are new to the prison and are afraid or don't want to fight. Others prey on this. The better a person knows the prison language, the prison environment and the people around him, the better he can defend himself against strong-arming.

Theft is the most common form of taxation in the prison economy. Everyone steals. When I first entered prison, stealing from the state was considered "ethical," while stealing from another prisoner was considered "unethical." However, this has changed over the years. Now the norm for stealing from other prisoners is: *Don't get caught.* If you get caught, you may get assaulted.

Most transactions come with a *commission* the seller applies to the transaction in order to make a profit. Inmate merchants often consider themselves to be like Robin Hood ("I steal from the state and give to the inmates—except what I need for expenses"). These inmates always take a commission to insure their own profits.

Donations are a unique type of tax. Prisoners have few material goods and many inmates constantly ask other inmates for donations of small items, such as cigarettes, a light, stamps, or snack food. Donating these items becomes an expense for an individual and is thus like a tax. Although donations are voluntary, saying "no" doesn't always work in prison.

9

The Christmas
Chicken Caper

"Nobody cared that we were smuggling dope, bribing the officers with food,
or stealing and transporting prison goods. Life was good."

PRISONER LIVING IN DORM B
SUMMER 1993

"Whatever it is, it smells good. Pull one out."

SERGEANT TURNER
CHRISTMAS EVE 1993

———————

Over time, I got tired of living in a cell and asked to be moved to the fifty-man dormitory. Bert, a good friend of mine, was up there. So were George and Chris, who made it their mission to toy with the second-shift guards, just as second shift had made it their mission to toy with us.

A moron sergeant led the second shift. While he was digging around in one corner of the dorm, we would be up to no good in another. We developed the game of giving the guards what they wanted in one spot while we broke the rules in another. For a while, we came together and ran second shift wild.

However, living in such close quarters, you had to be careful. If someone did something against you, everyone around knew and expected you to get even. If you did nothing, then they'd start taking advantage of you too.

In prison, dorms and double-celling result in a breakdown of civilization. Dorms tend to be more violent. Yet there were times when I felt like that dorm was the best place I stayed while doing my time.

———✂———✂———

Sergeant Derk welcomed me to the dorm. He always had a joke. His jokes made prison life a little more enjoyable by breaking up the monotony of the daily routine. He and his sidekick, Officer Harris, started right out with me.

"Anonymous, you went to college, right?"

I was putting my property away and just nodded.

"Me and Harris are having an argument. Maybe you can settle it. What's that famous state they grow potatoes in?"

"Idaho?" I replied.

"Oh, you-da-ho, well, I-da-pimp! Gotcha, gotcha," he laughed while he put one hand in his armpit to make a farting noise. "Gotcha, gotcha!"

"Fuck you, Derk. So this is what my parents' tax dollars go to."

"And his and his and his," Derk pointed to the other men in the dorm.

Then he turned serious. "We have three rules up here. No brewing **hootch.** No smoking marijuana . . ."

Harris interrupted. "And no looking at Derk's ass during standing count!" he yelled.

Derk stopped and looked at Harris. "Well, I kind of like it when they look at my ass." They walked out of the sleeping room, laughing.

"Hey, we have three rules," a high-pitched voice came from behind me.

I turned around and saw my buddy Bert.

"I see they put you through their routine, too. Square ass motherfuckers! That's Derk and Harris!" He chuckled and told me that we inmates have three rules: "party, talk slick, and jag your dick."

I settled in and started to get the hang of the place. On Friday or Saturday nights, the guys would eat a late meal together. We'd hook up our soups, chips, cheeses, and snack cakes and sit around the table, chew the fat, make jokes, and congratulate each other on how good that food tasted.

———✂———✂———

One of the official rules was no use of electronics back in the sleeping area. There weren't even any electrical outlets by the bunks. So we couldn't lie on our beds and listen to our radios, even with headphones.

One day I saw Chris and George back by my bunk. They were working on the floor heater. I had always thought that Chris was an intriguing person. It was his first time in prison, and he had a few years already in. As he got to know me, he granted me a lot of trust earlier than I expected. On the other hand, George was suspicious and didn't give his associations away very easily.

"If you need to, Chris, you can sit on my bunk," I told him. In prison there's an unwritten rule about a man sitting on another man's bunk. A bed is a man's personal space. I was in a lower bunk. George was in the lower bunk next to me, and Chris was in the one above him.

"Are you watching for Derk and Harris?" George interrupted.

"I can watch if you have something to do," I offered. The guards already knew that I did a lot of drawing and so I sat on my footlocker for long periods, using my bed as a desk.

George gave a suspicious look but agreed. "Don't let them see us. Tell us if either one starts to come back here." George gave me directions like I was green. I didn't think it was a good time to tell George that I knew how to stalk the police while the police stalked us!

"Then I can help you out," Chris said to George.

George asked for the screwdriver and Chris pulled it out from his pants leg. George started taking screws out of the heater. I wondered what they were doing, but figured I better not ask. I watched them take the cover off and look inside. They were like surgeons inspecting their patient.

Half of George's head was inside the heater. Every now and then he would look back at me, checking to see if I was paying attention to the officers. "Okay. Wire and outlet."

"You want the connectors right away?" Chris's voice was soft. A diagram of some kind was on the floor next to him.

George had two or three tools and pieces of wire on the floor. He had electrical tape on his finger.

"Keep it down," I whispered to George, "the guys up there are looking our way."

Then I couldn't see Derk's head in the observation window. "Hey, hey. I can't see Derk."

"Hide the tools," Chris ordered. "George, get out of there."

I walked to the entrance of the sleeping area to cut Derk off.

<hr>

"Hey, Derk, I was wondering if there was any way you could get a new pencil sharpener?"

He stopped. "I can call maintenance about it." He started walking again toward Chris and George.

"All right now, what are you doing?"

"Looking at these car books," Chris replied.

I sat back down on my footlocker. "What do you think of my drawing so far, Derk?"

"Hey, that's nice," he commented while his eyes cased the area. All guards naturally case. Then he asked George what was going on.

George looked guilty. "I don't know what you're talking about."

Derk pulled a dust bunny from George's hair. Apparently it was off the heater. He dropped it on the floor and started to stomp it. "Bad George, bad George, you got bunnies!" Derk laughed. "Don't you ever clean?"

George wasn't laughing. He was sweating.

Derk noticed it too. "You all right? I can call the nurse to do a general G.I.," he laughed again. George just sat there.

Answer the man. "Derk," I interrupted, "so you think you can get a new pencil sharpener for the dorm?" I looked at George and then at Derk.

"You want it for drawing, to sharpen your pencils!" Derk said this like he had just figured out rocket science.

"Yeah, that's right." *Very good, Derk. I guess prison guards do have something going for them.* "Well, actually I thought if you got a new one, then I could steal it and take it to hobby. We really need a new one down there!" I smiled at him.

"No, don't do that. There's enough stealing around here." He paused. "I can't find the damn extension cord that was up by my desk."

George shifted on his blanket. Derk's cord was underneath it, cut into pieces. "Yeah, it sucks when a person steals, I hate that." I said, looking over at George. He was still quiet. "You know, Derk, maybe second shift took it." Whenever there were problems, when things turned up missing or when the officers were fighting among themselves, second shift got the blame.

"Yeah, probably did," Derk answered, "but I'll get another one. I'll steal it out of the shift commander's office!" He thought that was pretty funny. Eventually he walked away, looking here and there around the dorm, then went back to the officer station.

"You all right, George?" I asked.

"Yeah, I just ain't accustomed to having Derk walk right back here in the middle of shit. Then he finds the dust bunny in my hair." He looked me dead in the eye, "Makes a guy nervous!"

"Yeah, you mean you were going to shit your pants!" Chris started laughing.

They quickly finished wiring Derk's extension cord into the heater. Now we had power so we could listen to music on our bunks!

※══✕══✕══✕══※

Then I had an idea. "Why don't we pull the lag bolts off the housing for the pipe that runs to the heater?" I pointed to where it ran. "It gets hot as hell with that water coming through it."

Chris looked over, "Why?"

"We can warm food on it," I smiled.

It wasn't long before those three-inch lag bolts were out of the wall.

Now we had music and an oven. And we had successfully worked right under the noses of Derk, Harris, and the twenty men moving around in the sleeping area. We were circumventing the rules, but that was our story in Dorm B: circumventing the rules.

By the time we were finished, it was almost two in the afternoon. Second shift was on the way. To get caught by second shift meant a certain 360 days in the hole for all of us, no questions asked. So we cleaned up fast and sent Chris on his way to take the tools back to wood tech.

※══✕══✕══✕══※

Time moved on. President Reagan was in office and we were having another riot, but it was small and no one got hurt. Chris, George, and I became good associates. Bert and I moved closer, from associates to friends. He and I were crossing that line of the prison code that said trust no one, befriend no one.

We were so different. I was white and he was black. I was raised in the middle class, and he came from the inner city. But we also had many personality traits that were alike: we both were control freaks, both had similar crimes, and both were trying to change.

When we'd cook and eat our weekend meal together, Bert contributed dope to smoke, Chris and George supplied most of the food, and I cooked. Mom had taught me well!

We ate great food. Knowing Kim, the kitchen runner, helped. We weren't stealing from the kitchen since we greased the guard's hand now and then. It was only stealing if we were caught smuggling food in. Once in, it was allowed.

Things happen easy when you grease everyone's hands. Once a guard gave me a $100 bill for my artwork. I gave the **C-note** to Bert to help pay for the weed we were smoking.

Sure, life had its downs in the dorm too. Many people were jealous of what we did and what we had; they just wanted in on the action. Knowing that someone would snitch eventually, we kept it a secret as long as we could.

Nobody cared that we were smuggling in dope, which was a felony, or bribing the officers with food, also a felony, or stealing and transporting prison goods, another felony. Life was good. All of these could have landed us in the seg unit, but felonies committed in prison are seldom prosecuted in the courts. While assaults and batteries, sexual assaults, and other felonies went on, the prison administration worried about how you walked, if you talked and how many rolls of toilet paper you had. The downside of this was the atmosphere of total lawlessness that was allowed.

◁▷◁▷◁▷◁

The Christmas holidays were coming, and we would be off work for four days. At that time of year, the prison goes into a general lockdown, and we would be stuck in the dorm, able only to go to rec. But we were determined to have a good time.

"Your girl's coming up, Bert?" George asked. That meant *Is she going to bring in weed?*

"Yeah. I'm going on the **corner.**"

I reminded him about the C-note I'd given him—the one that the guard had given me.

"Already gave it to my girl," said Bert.

"What C-note?" Chris asked.

"Don't worry about it, Chris." There were times when no matter how much you chummed with someone, you did not tell all.

"We gonna' get some?" George asked.

"I got a quarter coming," I said.

Bert smiled. He knew that was a lie. I had a half coming but Chris and George only needed to know a quarter. "You figure out a cost of a meal and I'll pay you in joints. Hell, I'll just cut the pile up for us," I said.

Chris and George agreed to the payment, but I knew Chris did not really smoke weed. He would sell or give his share to George.

"What about Kim?" Bert asked.

I had already figured it out. "Well, here's that deal. I'll see him at hobby and ask for a refill of spices and about getting some cooked chicken with barbecue sauce."

"Yum," Chris exclaimed. "Smoke flavoring, too?"

Kim made the most tantalizing sauce I ever ate. He had already had about ten years in to perfect it.

"Will we have enough chicken?" George wondered.

"Full nine yards," I replied. "I'll pay him off in cannabis, though. Probably a gram of weed."

"A gram! Sounds like a lot." George didn't want that pile getting any smaller if he could help it.

"Well, you get what you pay for. We're asking a lot of him," I replied.

✖━✖━✖━✖

Chris asked me about getting some yeast. He probably didn't expect an answer but I had one for him. "Not a problem. George and I already decided on that, but where are we going to hide the hootch while it is brewing?"

Chris and George grinned. "The heater!"

"Can you guys handle that?" Bert looked like he was discussing a business deal.

"Yeah, wood tech's got containers. Just got to smuggle one up here," Chris said.

"Juice?" Bert asked.

"We buy four oranges at canteen," George said. "I'll buy the lemon drink and grapefruit juice."

We went on plotting our feast. We knew the regular staff wouldn't be working over Christmas so that made it easier. Plus as the holidays came, most officers did less and less. That meant the rules would loosen. Except officers like Turner.

When I was at hobby, Kim showed up. "I need yeast," I said to him, "about four pieces of chicken, spices, and smoke flavoring! What kind of deal do you want?"

"Food and spices no problem. The yeast, harder to get." Kim's voice was quiet. He could pass for a CIA agent if he had the right clothes; he had that look. Maybe that was why he was in prison for embezzling money.

"I got a half of gram of weed for it," I bargained, tantalizing Kim. "I also need some of your barbecue sauce." I felt like I was in the grocery store.

"Half a gram's pushing it. Is it good?"

"Have I ever failed you?"

"Yeah. Last month when you promised dope but I got cigarettes instead."

"Well, besides that?"

"Well," he laughed. Kim had a memory like an elephant.

"Okay, okay," I cut him off, "so I fucked up a few times, damn."

"A few times!" he joked.

"Where'd you get such a memory?" I jested.

"Golly, Batman, I don't know."

"Can we deal?" I got serious again.

"I'll do it but I don't know if half of a gram is enough." He was driving the price up.

"Well, I might have more but the half is guaranteed."

"That's it?" he exclaimed.

"Not exactly, but I want to joint out some and get rid of it." *Ooops, now he knows I got more. There goes my edge.*

"So now I know you got more." He grinned.

I knew he'd drive up the price. "Okay, I'll give you a gram. Don't ask for more now."

I needed to get back to the yeast. "Four tablespoons at least." I watched him.

"Hell, that's a quarter cup of yeast!"

"Yeah, so?" I acted innocent.

"How much **volcano juice** you making?"

"Oh, two gallons."

"You don't need a quarter cup for that much!"

"We're trying to get it to pop in three days," I pointed out.

"Still, you need that much?"

"Don't think of it as a quarter cup, it makes it sound like so much!"

"Okay, four tablespoons. That much?"

"Come on now, Kim, I got some **lightweights** brewing the shit so I got to be sure." I urged.

"I can get three tablespoons for sure. I'll try four."

I knew Kim. Even though he had said he'd try, once he agreed, he'd do it.

"You all are having a feast, aren't you?"

I got serious again. "Yes, sir, so I need the chicken on Wednesday before holiday lockdown unless you want to do a recreation transport."

"No." He knew that was dangerous.

Then he asked me when he'd get paid. I told him we'd see him Christmas Eve at rec. Dude's girl isn't coming until then.

⊰⊱⊰⊱⊰⊱

The spices and the container for hootch were hidden away. Smoke flavoring was staying cool in the window. We were ready. On Sunday, George, Chris, and I were all out of bed early. The sleeping area was mostly empty since the other guys had gone to recreation.

"Okay, you and Anonymous each make two quarts of the lemon drink shit." George handed Chris the container.

I handed my oranges to George. He put them under his blanket. "I'll peel them."

"Don't bother. Throw the peel and everything in the jug." I said.

"W-h-a-t?" George was dragging out the word.

"Trust me," I looked George in the eye and smiled. This was no time to argue. "With all that sugar going in, the peels will help bitter-up the mix."

So he quartered the oranges. We shook them with the lemon drink, the yeast, and a whole box of sugar. We added the grapefruit juice and closed the container, but loosely, so it would breathe. Then we put it into our oven, the heater. It would keep the mix a good 90 to 100 degrees!

We guarded that heater like it was our baby and everything was working perfectly until Tuesday when second shift arrived. Sergeant Turner. *The police at the prison.*

"Man, it smells in this area," Sergeant Turner grumbled, doing his usual check.

"I don't smell nothing," George replied.

"Smells like funky fruit."

That's all it took. George heard the word fruit and you could see him start to sweat.

"I just ate an orange," Chris quickly remarked.

"Did you shower?" Turner asked George.

"Yeah."

"Well, you all clean up this area," Turner commanded like the wannabe general he wanted to be. "It stinks back here."

When I came in, I saw them both cleaning and asked them what they were doing.

"Turner smells something," George groaned.

"Yeah, and by the heater it's thick," Chris followed. "If he'd gone over there we'd be gone."

We tried to think of a spot to move it. Ceiling was no good. Can't hide it in the common area.

Suddenly I realized that wood tech was right below us. "They got any ceiling tiles in wood tech?"

"Plywood."

"A plywood ceiling?"

"Yeah, all across the shop, but what does that have to do with this?" George asked.

I pointed up. "Well, look at our ceiling. Wooden beams. That means they've got a space between our floor and the wood shop."

"Yeah," George looked up, "but how do we get through the floor here?"

"Chisels. Utility knife. A leather hand mallet."

"What about the noise?"

"Well, we'll try to cut everything instead of chipping."

"Okay, let's say we can, but what if we hit a pipe?"

"Come on, George," I answered sarcastically, "you know they don't run hot water pipes through wooden beams."

"Man, this is going to be work," Chris said.

"We could put it over by the guard's desk like we did before," George suggested.

"They know that spot. Preb always checks there," Chris reminded him.

George was looking at the floor. "You know, we can lift those tiles right up." He pointed to where the hot water pipes came through the floor. "Park a footlocker here. If anyone comes, slide it over the area we're working. Hang a blanket on a bunk. Block their view."

Our plan was set. We worked and watched for the guards. When other prisoners walked by we'd lie back and smile at them. As soon as they left we'd go back to work.

Then it was Wednesday. Turner would be working, but we didn't know if his sidekick Preb would be too. If Officer Preb was working, we all would be **pat searched.**

———◇———◇———◇———

I went to hobby to meet Kim, who showed up with the chicken. He could only get three pieces but they were breasts and I was happy. Then Chris walked in. "They're patting down."

"Man," I moaned, "Trouble. Well, I'll hide the chicken in my hobby shit."

Chris didn't like that idea. He said we should divide the pieces and put them down our pants. He also told me to take my pass back and sign back out. "It'll help distract the guards."

So I told Bob, the staff hobby director, that I had to go to the dorm to use the bathroom and I'd have the guards sign my pass. Sure enough, Turner was watching us come back. He thought he was slick but he didn't realize we could see guards standing by the entrance of the dorm. We were on the second floor so we could either drop our shit on the stairs or reshuffle it as we walked upstairs. The guards never look into the stairway as people moved around. And with two guards searching and ten guys walking in, hell, the guys coming in at the back could see where and what they were looking for.

We got lucky when we hit the stairs. Bert was going up, too. I was carrying some hobby stuff plus my pass. So I gave up all my contraband to Bert, and then made sure Turner patted me down. I had to explain my pass and put all my hobby stuff on the table for him to examine. The others would go past Preb. He never searched hard.

But Preb called me over. "I'll do you next."

Ooops, don't want him. "Well, I got this hobby stuff plus a pass for Turner to sign."

"Okay," he waved me off to Turner. "You three. Chris, Bert, George, over here." Preb didn't look happy.

"Full search today," he announced. No wonder he wasn't happy. This wasn't his style. "Pockets empty and out, shoes and socks off, shirt untucked. You know the routine."

I hoped Turner wouldn't dig too hard through my hobby stuff. He told me to put all my hobby shit on the table.

I complied, saying nothing. Turner started picking through my hobby stuff. No spot check this time. Customs was checking everything through the gate.

Then he started with some small talk, so I told him about my pass. In prison, you learn quickly that distractions confuse thoughts.

"Why'd you come back here then? You trying to run stuff up here?"

"No, I came back to use the bathroom." *The excuses and lies just roll off my lips; it's so easy.*

He was digging through my hobby stuff. Digging too deep. He inspected every item. Something wasn't right. I was worried, but didn't show it.

Then I got a break: the phone rang.

"Stay right there," Turner ordered as he ran up to the desk.

I couldn't hear much of the conversation, but then Turner looked right at me. "He's right here."

I was caught off guard. What was going on? Stuff like that raises the hair on your neck.

Turner hung up the phone and came back down the stairs. "That was hobby on the phone. He wants you back down there now." He signed my pass.

"Well, can I use the bathroom quick?"

"Yes, but hurry because he said he wants you now."

I grabbed my half-searched shit and moved on. *Lucky!* Preb finished searching the other three and I went to back to hobby wondering what was wrong.

The call from hobby was nothing: Bob wanted me to get my stuff put away since he was leaving for the holidays. But in prison you never know what will haunt you. Every time I was served a misconduct report, it always seemed to be for something that happened days ago.

When I went back to the dorm again, I found the patrol squad waiting to search the next group. And Turner finished patting me down.

❧

I walked into the sleeping area. George, Chris, and Bert were back and cool. But then Turner walked through the door and yelled, **"Shakedown."**

We thought he was going to do his normal routine, but he didn't. Instead, he headed directly to the heater by us and Preb went straight to the heater on the other side. They immediately started taking them apart.

"I got you now," Turner said as he put his tools on top of the heater.

He looked at Chris and George. "Anything you have to say?" *I am Sergeant Turner, the screw. I will take all statements now!*

As he talked, he kicked the heater lightly. He never figured we'd taken out all the security screws. The front cover fell off and hit the floor right at his feet with a terrifying bang. He was so startled that he jumped back. But Chris was standing right behind him, so then he jumped forward and shouted, "Get away from me!"

It was the funniest thing I ever saw, and everyone cracked up. Even Preb. Sweat ran down Turner's forehead. "Yeah, Turner, I wanted to tell you the screws are missing," Chris said then.

"Shut up!" Turner looked around at everyone. "And that's enough out of you too, Preb." *No one laughs at Sergeant Turner of Dorm B.* He continued to pull the end off the heater.

"Ahhh-hawww," Turner exclaimed with great excitement. "What's this?" *I got them now. No one laughs at Turner!*

Of course everyone looked innocent. But Turner had found the end of the extension cord that was wired into the heater. In his rage, he didn't think, didn't care, or maybe didn't know any better. He just reached into that heater, grabbed the cord by the end and gave it a pull! The cord didn't break clean. It frayed, leaving live wires bouncing around inside the heater.

Turner got a shock so big he jumped back again, and this time fell on his ass. The heater turned off, went back on, then off again. I figured it would never come back on.

"Aw what the fuck!" Turner was on the floor looking at the heater.

"Your radio!" Preb shouted. It was on the floor. A radio on its side sets off the alarm in central command. Preb snatched it up and Turner looked at him fast and hard. They both waited for the alarm to go off.

Luckily it didn't. I think even Turner was glad it didn't. He was not the kind of staff to want thirty other screws running in to see him holding wires from a torn-apart heater in the dorm sleeping area.

"You all right?" Preb asked.

"Yes, damn, give me my radio back. Jeez, Preb! Don't touch a thing," he told us as he and Preb went back to the desk.

⋙⋘⋙⋘

Once they left, it got noisy. Everyone else was laughing. We weren't, though. I could see it on George and Chris' faces, too. Someone had told. So far we'd got away with it, but what if Turner brought the whole crew here to shakedown the whole place? We did not need that.

Then our luck changed. Preb walked back to the area and said, "Help me fix this thing if you can."

"Why?" George shot back. "Turner fucked it up!"

"Yeah, yeah, I know," he admitted in a soft whiny sort of voice, "but he pulled the wires out so he can't call maintenance."

"Tough," said Chris. "He broke it, so let him call maintenance."

"Come on now. He's backing down now. Don't piss him off more or he'll shakedown the whole place." Preb was giving us fair warning, so eventually we did help him. We disconnected the extension cord, rehooked the original wires, and generally cleaned it up. Once it was back together, Preb flipped the circuit breaker and on it went. The heater was okay.

While we were working on it, Preb told us that they had gotten a note saying someone was screwing with the heater. It was unsigned. He also said Turner had guessed we were brewing wine from the smell.

❦❦❦

Finally it was Christmas Eve and we were going to enjoy it. I made sure that everyone was paid off. I divided the dope I had between Chris and George. We'd start cooking about six. Drag the hootch out about 9:30 when Turner and Preb would be at the desk waiting for third shift. We'd be rocking by midnight!

It was six and Chris found me in the TV room with Bert.

"Where's George?" Chris started to laugh.

"What?" Bert and I said at the same time.

Turner was on his break. It was like clockwork: when Turner took a break, people gravitated to the TV room. Sometimes the smell of weed got so strong, we had to open the windows. Even in the middle of winter!

"Your eyes," Chris laughed at us, "you better get some eye drops."

We smiled back. "So where's George?" I repeated.

"He was just in here," Chris looked out the TV room windows. "There he is."

"Okay, well, go ask him if he wants to start cooking."

We couldn't smoke any more in the TV room anyway until Turner left. He had a habit of coming into the TV area and smelling around. If he smelled weed, he'd write down everyone sitting in that general area for a **U.A.** test.

I went back to the sleeping area and opened my locker, then Bert's. Chris brought me tuna cans and lids. They fit perfectly into the heating pipe housing without being really visible.

I tossed Chris a raw onion. "Cut that up."

"Okay, but where?"

"See if someone else is cooking in the common area and do it next to him so Turner doesn't get suspicious." I deboned the chicken and mixed it with the sauce. Added half the onion with the other ingredients. Put it all into the cans we used for cooking.

Chris came around to my side of the bunk and pulled on the housing. I carefully slipped the cans into the hot heating pipe oven with a towel.

About an hour later, George smelled barbeque!

I suggested spreading baby powder around. Baby powder covers a lot of smells. But it wasn't strong enough: Preb had noticed the smell. By the time I returned from my shower, Turner was following his nose too.

When I dropped my stuff from the shower on my footlocker, Turner was right behind me. "Smells damn good back here."

"I really didn't notice," I told him.

"Yeah, right. What you guys doing?"

"I'm not doing anything," I replied.

Chris and George watched Turner asking me questions. Then he just followed his nose to the heating pipe.

"Anonymous, what is that shit inside the pipe?"

"It's my stuff," I admitted.

"Yeah, but what is it?"

"My Christmas Eve supper." I mentioned Christmas Eve hoping it would mellow him out!

"Whatever it is, it smells good. Pull one out," he commanded.

"Turner, come on" I begged.

"Pull one out," he repeated.

I reached in the housing area and pulled a can out with a towel. I popped the top so he could smell. He grabbed for it but I pulled it back.

"Hot as hell, Turner. You'll get burned," I said to him like he was a kid. By this time we had an audience. I figured my chicken rolled tortillas were gone. *Fuck.*

"Why so many cans?"

"Because you've told us that if more than one person eats, we can't use the same container!"

"So more people are involved." *I am the master detective.*

I smiled at him. *Oh, you are so slick, all right.* "I'm doing it by myself, no one else."

I figured the stuff was gone. Then Preb got up from the sleeping area desk and came over. "Hey, Turner, you got a phone call."

"Preb, you smell this before?"

Officer Preb replied: "Yeah, I told them they could do it." *I almost fainted. I could not believe this. What did you say? Preb cosigning with me?*

Turner looked at me. "Merry Christmas!" Then he walked away.

"Thanks, Preb," I said, thinking, *Gee, I should take back everything I thought about you!*

"Don't thank me, thank Chris."

"What?"

"Chris told me you guys were cooking. Hell, everyone can smell it. He told me and asked if it was cool. Just be sure it's all cleaned up and you don't cook back here again."

Now everyone in the dorm knew we had chicken cooking. Thus the gossip started, stories spread about the contraband chicken caper. *And I damn near got hauled off to the hole by Turner.*

⟨━✕━✕━✕━⟩

By that time it was 9:30 P.M.: hootch time. It wasn't hard to convince myself that I needed some homemade hootch. We slid footlockers in front of the hiding spot. Pulled out the four two-quart pitchers. I was watching for Turner.

"Chris," George whispered, "move the bunk over a little." He slid it off the loose tile, then lifted his footlocker up so no one could see. Up came the jug.

"It's starting to stink," Chris said.

Bert came back from his shower. "I smell something."

He was already throwing baby powder around. I cracked a window and the incoming air not only froze Bert in his underwear, but also blew the powder around.

"Damn, close the window! You want to freeze everyone to death?"

I closed the window while George finished pouring. He put the container back, wrapped the pitchers in towels, and covered them.

After they called 10:15 and flashed the lights, we got our stuff and went to the common area. We settled in at the table furthest from the third shift guards. Chris took a rolled tortilla up to the sergeant. Grease payment. Others donated food too. The sergeant sat at his desk, snacking and doing his puzzles.

We ate, drank, and made occasional trips to the TV room. By 12:30 in the morning, we all were intoxicated. The sergeant came over to tell us the tortilla was great. I'm sure we all looked guilty as hell. But we all smelled like after-shave so he couldn't smell the hootch.

After the holiday, U.A.s hit the dorm like wildfire. Obviously someone had sent a note to security. However, if any of us were taken out to seg, someone else would be cooking, brewing, and smoking weed. The prison economy was still booming and many prisoners were still reaping the harvest of the system. The year of 1993 was my most enjoyable Christmas lockup.

⟫━⟪⟫━⟪⟫━⟪

REFLECTIONS

At times prison can be an enjoyable place. One has to forget the stress and strain of life. If not, my hair would be grayer. The chicken caper, as it was called, provides insight to how the prisoner economy operates. It is the light side of prison life that many people outside of prison know little about. Most people think of only the violence, suffering, and daily dangers. At times we make light of our lives and do the best we can with what little we have.

10

Third World Medical

When I was sent to the **Walls** prison for cyst surgery, some old-timers told me I was going to the **death house.** At that point I didn't understand what they meant. However, once I entered the hospital section inside the prison, I found out. It really was a death house. It even smelled of death.

"You're new here?" asked Mike, the fellow in the bed next to mine.

"Yeah, I came in from the county jail where they have state prisoners on the work program.

"Oh yeah? What's wrong with you? My appendix almost burst; they have me here recovering."

"I have to have an inflamed cyst removed."

"Really, and they sent you here! I thought this place was only for major medical emergencies or for people who were dying!"

"They sent me here because they said this was the only bed available. I sat up front for three hours waiting for a bed. What are all these guys here for?"

"Some of them I know about from listening to staff talk. Dude over there has that inter-**bone** shit, I don't know how to say it. He's dying. His family is trying to get the governor, old Bullhorn—no-tolerance Bullhorn—to release him so he can die at home. I guess he only has six months to live."

"He sure seems to be in a great deal of pain."

"Yeah, and the nurses treat him like shit!"

"Noticed that. When I came in they were giving him something. Looked like he was choking and the nurse said he was playing games to get more pills or something . . ."

"The old guy over there has heart problems. They said he should have had a bypass a few years ago but you know the state. I think after a minor heart attack they took him out for surgery but he had a stroke. I was talking to him but now he ain't said much."

I looked over toward him.

"Those two have cancer; they just lay there and do nothing. Hell, they might be dead." He grinned.

"Too bad."

"Dude over there with no legs had his colon removed. I guess he got an infection from the surgery or something."

"I've seen him before," I said.

"They had his wheelchair here but they took it away."

"Maybe they were worried he would escape!" I smiled.

"Could be."

As I lay there all I saw around me was death. I noticed the worst thing about the place was not the disease, not the building, not even the stupid rules to die by. It was how the staff treated everyone. Out of three shifts of nurses, one actually offered ten minutes of her time to just sit and listen to patients who only seemed to want just a little human compassion.

<hr/>

"What are you here for?" asked the doctor. He had a thick foreign accent.

I thought this to be an odd question since he had my file and read my wristband.

"I have a cyst to be removed."

"Where is it?"

"Well, that is embarrassing for me, doc, so bear with me . . ."

"You have nothing to be embarrassed about. Where is it?"

"It's on my nuts."

"Oh, I see."

He proceeded to inspect my groin. "Does this hurt?"

"No."

"How about that?" he started squeezing my testicles.

"Yes," I said rather loudly, "I can feel it if that's what you mean."

"Good."

"How about this?" he squeezed both my testicles in his fist until I started choking.

"Yes . . ." my eyes watered. *What the fuck you trying to do to me,* I thought.

"Good."

I was at the point of telling him to leave my testicles alone when he stopped.

"When you masturbate, do you have any pain or blood?"

What kind of question is that? "I **jag** just fine, doc."

"Good. We will do surgery here shortly." He filled out a form.

With that I was led back to my bed from his office. Needless to say, I could still feel his cold hand squeezing my testicles.

"What'd the doctor say?" Mike asked.

"It wasn't what he said, it's what he did!" I lay back slowly.

"They going to remove it?"

"Yes, soon."

"Man, I would never let these people cut on me, never."

It was funny how Mike repeated what I've heard many men say. Everyone is so quick to say that they would never let the prison staff operate. *I wouldn't let them do it.* Yet the ones saying this aren't the ones needing surgery.

"They took out your appendix."

"No, I went to the local hospital."

"Oh, that's right, they were the ones who let your shit almost burst. I bet you told them then, didn't you."

"I am just saying."

"Well, it's a fucking dumb thing to say. You ain't the one that needs it and I don't see no other doctors lining up to do it. I don't have a choice now, do I?"

<hr/>

"You men just mind your own business," one nurse ordered.

"What's going on now, Mike?"

"They finally realized the old man that had the heart problems and stroke is dead."

"What?"

"He died early this morning but they didn't check on him until now."

We were all getting our lunch trays. "Really?"

"Yeah. They might have been able to save him but no one even came through this morning; they never do on Sundays."

"In this place maybe it's for the best." I watched as they lifted the old man by his chest and put him on a **gurney.** A gurney basically is a stretcher with wheels. It looked about thirty years old.

Mike dropped the bomb then. "He was forty-nine years old."

"What! I thought you said he was old." Then I realized Mike was no more than twenty.

━━✕━━✕━━✕━━

"Inmate, they want you in the surgery area," the nurse signaled me to follow her.

I laid on the table as the doctor prepared to do surgery. He gave me a local anesthetic to freeze the area. Being with the state, he used as little of the local as he could. Then he cut the area.

"Did that hurt?"

"Man, what'd you do, lance me?"

"Oh, it didn't hurt," one of the nurses replied.

I guess I wasn't the patient. I lay back on the table staring at the ceiling. He dug and cut. I could feel everything. It hurt so bad my face was sweating.

"Are you all right?" another nurse asked as she turned and looked at my face.

"I didn't know it would hurt this bad . . ."

"He's almost done."

"I will be done shortly, I have to put in three stitches. You'll be okay."

When he put the stitches in I felt all three. All I felt was pain. Man, it hurt. I could not take it. "Man, those stitches hurt."

"I am done."

Thank God! Man, it hurt. Having my cyst removed was the most painful surgery I had with the state. I never suffered so much.

Then he was so nice to show me what he pulled out. "This is what I removed," he held up the jar like a little trophy.

I looked at it, then let my head fall back on the bed.

"Hey, are you all right? Are you all right?"

"Yeah, just not used to seeing a piece of my body in a jar."

━━✕━━✕━━✕━━

Years before in Industrial City I learned how medical worked. Everyone who went to medical always exited with nonaspirin. I have a headache, nonaspirin; my eye hurts, nonaspirin; my knee is sore, nonaspirin; my ankle is swollen, nonaspirin; my eye is black and blue, nonaspirin. I have a cold, nonaspirin; my ear hurts, nonaspirin; my sinuses are stuffed, nonaspirin. I think I got a fever, nonaspirin; I must have the flu, nonaspirin; I think I have an infection, nonaspirin; I have chest pains, nonaspirin; I got high blood pressure, nonaspirin; I'm feeling dizzy and light headed, nonaspirin; I'm feeling short of breath, nonaspirin; I turned blue and felt faint in my cell, nonaspirin. I never knew nonaspirin could cure so much. In the cellhall we called it going to medical for the *nonaspirin cure*. The only medical variation was laxative juice for bowel evacuation!

━━✕━━✕━━✕━━

"Dorn Nixon, you're next," the nurse called out from the examination area. Here they had four stations set up where each nurse would inspect a man's problems and screen him for the doctor if necessary.

Dorn walked in and sat at one of the stations.

"What are you having problems with today?"

"Since yesterday my stomach area has been hurting. My throat feels funny, it can't swallow right. It ain't sore, just don't want to swallow right. And I've had a headache on the side of my head. I ain't sick though. No flu, no cold, just having this pain and feeling woozy."

"Have you been taking your diabetic shots?"

"Yes. Last night when I got my shot I gave my slip to you." A slip is required to be filled out for a medical appointment.

"Anything else?"

"No, just woozy and warm but I know I ain't sick."

The nurse checked his temperature. It was okay. Blood pressure within normal range and heartbeat okay. "I'm going to give you some nonaspirin."

"I got some of that stuff last night from the nurse when I got my shot. I'm having problems. I think I should see the doctor or someone. I know this ain't right. I shouldn't be feeling dazed and shit."

"The doctor doesn't come in today. Come back tomorrow if it keeps up."

Dorn went back to his cell. He stayed in the rest of the day. After night lockdown he was feeling even worse. He waited for the guard to do a round. "Officer," Dorn yelled as the guard zoomed by.

"Yeah?" the officer asked as he stepped back in front of the cell.

Dorn was sitting in his chair looking at the floor. He looked up at the guard. "I ain't feeling too good. I feel numbish."

"You haven't been smoking none of that funny shit, have you?"

"No, no, not that. I went to see medical this morning and they gave me nonaspirin but it ain't that."

"You aren't having chest pains, are you?"

"No, but above my stomach, the pain isn't right. I got pain on my right side and feel like I am going into a diabetic coma but it ain't a diabetic coma. My blood sugar is fine."

The officer shined his flashlight on him and could see he was sweating. "I'll call medical but you can't go anywhere unless it is an emergency. It's after lockdown."

Dorn waited for about an hour, then climbed into his bunk.

✂━✂━✂

"Nixon," Officer Ralph yelled, "you have a medical pass." He stood out in front of his cell.

Nixon lay in his bed and didn't move. Officer Ralph could see his eyes were open but he didn't move.

"Nixon, boy you gone deaf on me?" Officer Ralph increased his volume. "Get up to go on your pass." He placed the pass on the bars and walked on to hand out the rest of the passes he had.

At the desk the desk officer noticed Nixon didn't go to class that morning and hadn't gone the day before either. The officer called the pass control area that monitored prisoner's attendance to report Nixon's absence. About half an hour later medical called. Nixon hadn't come on his pass and he hadn't come down for his diabetic shot that morning. The desk officer asked Ralph if he gave him his pass. Ralph assured him he did. He decided it was time to go check on him. Refusing a pass was also a misconduct report.

"I got him now," Ralph said to the desk officer. Ralph flew up the stairs and down the tier. "Nixon!" Ralph called in front of his cell.

Nixon lay there with his eyes open but did not move. This struck Ralph as odd since he hadn't moved since he came around before. He was literally in the same position lying on top of his bed, staring at the ceiling.

"Nixon!" Ralph yelled at the top of his lungs. He yelled so loud that a few others in the cellhall answered him over the tier: *shut the fuck up, your momma, five-o, fucking noisy pig.* Sound travels in the concrete fortress.

Ralph drew out his walkie-talkie like a cop pulling a donut from a bag, "Industrial 35 to south cellhall desk officer."

"Go ahead," his radio crackled.

"Could you send someone up on 'G' tier to throw up the bar so I can enter 'G' 62 cell?'"

"10–4."

The bar was thrown at the beginning of the tier, locking and unlocking all the cells. Ralph rolled open the cell door and stepped in. Nixon lay on the bed, eyes open; Ralph could see both were tearing.

"Nixon, can you hear me?" At that moment Nixon mustered all the energy he could to raise his right elbow, wrist, and hand. He reached just enough to slide his hand off the bunk, hitting Ralph in the leg as he stood over him.

Ralph grabbed his hand and placed it back on the bunk. Nixon had had a stroke. Out came the walkie-talkie again, "Industrial 35 to south cell hall desk officer. I have a medical emergency, I repeat a medical emergency in 'G' 62 cell. Bring the gurney!" He looked down at Nixon, "Don't die on my shift, damn it! I don't want to do any paperwork today." The gurney arrived and Dorn Nixon was gone.

<hr>

When I arrived at medical, the rumors were flying around. Every prisoner was talking about Dorn. I had enough problems of my own. I was there to see the doctor again. I had already been shipped twice to the university hospital just outside of Long Lake to see the neurologist. "You've been to the hospital two times," the doctor said in broken English as he held up two fingers. "Two times I sent you." His accent was so thick he was hard to understand.

"I told them all my problems, but nothing they're doing is helping." The hospital doctor prescribed horse pills to stop the continuous migraines I had. Also I had neck, ear, and jaw pain.

At this hospital they had a ward built to house a few prisoners for medical surgery and appointments with specialists. After about three months of complaining to the medical staff at Gladiator School, they figured my problems were psychological. They attributed the problems to the fact that I had a life sentence.

The doctor at Industrial City gave up on me. "I am going to send you upstairs." With that I was escorted to clinical service to see the psychiatrist that day. They made me sit for two hours waiting for him to come in. A forced appointment.

"They tell me you're having pain and headaches."

"Yes. I am sick of this shit. I can't even think anymore."

"Do you want to tell me more?"

"Okay. I am not losing my mind like they say."

"Oh no, no one is saying that."

"Apparently you have not talked to the same medical staff I have." We talked for an hour. Believe me, all that time for one patient was unheard of. The psychiatrist came in from the outside. He had a regular practice out there. He would come in to see a few patients. Basically he was their pill doctor. But he wasn't corrupted by the state system yet; he was actually a nice guy.

Even he had trouble explaining things to me. No past history of prolonged mental illness. He showed me my file. We went through it together. They had me on 3000 mg anti-inflammatory painkillers a day! Even he was surprised they did not stop my headaches. At one point he asked me if I could still walk without being dizzy. Then he showed me the medical manager's letter sent to the **DOC** headquarters.

> Mr. Inmate has been seen on a number of occasions by the medical staff; twice he has been referred to the outside hospital, once to the emergency room where he claimed his limbs were numb. His mother has also called my office a number of times explaining that she knows her son, and she doubts he is suffering from any mental illness. It is the opinion of this department that he see the staff psychiatrist and be considered for heavy anti-depressants. He has been locked up for almost ten years and has a long sentence to do. It is our belief that he needs to come to terms with that.

This was signed by the manager, the doctor, and the head nurse. Their solution was the man I was in front of now, the pill doctor.

I agreed to take heavy doses of antihistamines to help counter my "mental problems." He also put me on light antidepressants—zine. With the antidepressants, the antihistamines, and the anti-inflammatory painkillers, I was so drunk it was a wonder I could walk. I had to stop my correspondence college classes for a while since I could not function.

I went right on complaining to medical for a year. The headaches were getting more intense. I had to climb a tough hill. The medical department didn't want to see me, the doctor said I was a nut, but the psychiatrist could not force me to take his pills. Believe me, on a few occasions, they were considering lockup!

✄━✄━✄━✄

Dorn Nixon came back from the hospital and stayed in medical for about a month. Then he came back to the cellhall. Old Nixon was not the same since he had the stroke. We were on our way to canteen when he called "Hey, Anon-Anon-ous."

"Hey, Dorn, how are you feeling?"

"Shit, better. My spe-ech is get-en bet-better."

"Good!"

"I just have to-to" he paused, "to keep going. They s-say the more I talk t-the bet-ter I'll g-get."

"You just keep on talking then!" I smiled at him.

"I just for-forgot many words I used to kn-know."

"I think I got my canteen list ready; you ready for the store?"

"That's what I wanted-ed to ask you, I need help."

"Sure."

"You just got to tell them guys-guys I got to think about shit-shit longer. I know what I want, just forgot the names."

When we went through the line I could see his frustration. A couple of times in line he let out a loud grunt and shook his body in anger. "Come on Dorn, we can work with this, don't get pissed." I remember he couldn't remember how to say "coffee" but he knew it was the red bag. He told me years later he forgot how much to put in the cup and he once poured half the bag in his cup! Cigarettes weren't cigarettes, they were the green ones. I helped him out for a while at the store. Once I knew what he wanted I could easily tell the guys working in the store what he needed. Each week I could see he was getting better.

Eventually, I convinced Dorn to come to my college test proctor's classroom for second hour reading. He was back in school again doing G.E.D. work. My proctor didn't have a problem with the idea, so Dorn was added to the class schedule.

Dorn had lost the motor skills in his right arm and hand so he learned to write with his left hand. I would arm-wrestle with his right arm to exercise it for him. Slowly he was able to use the right arm again.

Some days we got into heated discussions. "Man, I am sick of reading to you and looking words up in the dictionary," Dorn complained to me as he sat at the table.

"Come on, Dorn, I can see how it is helping you out. At first you couldn't do shit, now you can."

"I hated it then, but I couldn't tell you so I just did it. Now I can tell you!"

"Okay, fuck it, quit!" I told him.

"I will," Dorn fired back.

"Give up on yourself. I don't care. Stop." I grabbed the book and set it off to the side.

"I am," he pushed the dictionary away too.

"You want to quit. My proctor will take you out of this hour because, Lord knows, I got college work to do. Give up on yourself." I yelled at him, "Quit. You want to stay dumb all your life, it's up to you, Dorn. No one, no one is going to care. Yeah, you had a stroke but do you think medical cares about you? These people are not going to do nothing for you. You already told me you were having trouble getting tutors in your math class. It ain't fair. Lord knows, I know about medical, these damn headaches. But here we are. Remember you're quitting on Dorn."

"Fuck you, Anonymous! Fuck you!"

My college proctor would look over his book every now and then to make sure we were not going to fight.

The next day Dorn came back. He started reading, looking up words, and writing. After six months Dorn was doing great. He moved on to another regular G.E.D. classroom. He seemed to have about 90 percent of his motor skills back and verbally he was back to cussing like the rest of us. Being in prison, he had no choice but to come back. He got no physical therapy or other needed treatment.

Eventually a person I knew got Dorn to play handball with him. Dorn never played before so he was an easy target at first. Yet over a year, as Dorn improved, his skills did too. With time, Dorn was better. These things actually helped Dorn. As he experienced some human compassion, I felt rewarded and happy with what I could do for him.

About two years later, Dorn showed up at the door of my college proctor; he was being transferred. He came in, called me over, and gave me a big hug. I was caught off guard by this gesture. Again my proctor looked up over his book.

"Thank you for putting up with me for six months while I was reading. I hated doing it but you kept on me. I wanted to punch you!" He smiled. "I really hated you the day when you said I wanted to stay dumb and that these people weren't going to do anything for me. I did have to fight for myself. I'm leaving tomorrow so I snuck down here over class exchange from the cellhall. . . ."

"Okay, Dorn," I replied, "just don't hug me anymore!"

With that Dorn left on the transfer bus.

"Anonymous Inmate," the assistant at the hospital called, "you're next."

I went into the hospital's examination room with my two guard-shadows. There was a different neurologist this time. I explained that this was the fourth time I was here and I was glad to see someone new. She took about two hours with me. I told her she was my last stop. "I had to beg the prison to send me back." No one seemed to figure out my problem. After this they had told me if nothing was discovered I had to take antidepressants.

I explained I had ear, neck, and facial pain. Also that I had had a headache for a year now. No pills took it away. I swore up and down I was not a nut. "This isn't anything compared to my childhood; if anything that should have made me a nut."

She went through a battery of tests, then became focused on my jaw. This is when I learned about TMJ dysfunction, or Temporal Mandibular Joint Dysfunction. My bite plane inside my mouth was misaligned. After a year of struggling, someone had an answer that made sense.

"Mr. Inmate, I believe this is your problem. You said you haven't seen a dentist to have this examined. Your pain is greater in the mornings and after you eat. You told me you stopped chewing gum because that seemed to help."

"Yes."

"Well, all the symptoms you have point to TMJ dysfunction. I am going to set up an appointment with the specialist here and have him examine you. I am very surprised they did not check this."

⟩═⟨⟩═⟨⟩═⟨

"No," the medical manager spoke up as I sat in the doctor's office. "I will not approve another trip to the hospital."

"But these are the specialist's orders. You're not a doctor! The lady neurologist said, after much consideration I might add, that I need to have a TMJ alignment. I need to see a specialist, not just a dentist!"

"No, you have wasted a great deal of our time over here. This is probably another wild goose chase and nothing will change. You have refused to take the medication the psychiatrist prescribed. I am not the murderer in this room! Deal with that and maybe you will get better!"

"I want to follow the specialist's order." She had hit below the belt with that last comment. Everything was always a mental problem.

"No. I am overriding those orders. You can see the dentist here. Not another word or it is lockup!"

Needless to say I left the office. I set up an appointment with the dentist. *Man, these people pissed me off.*

⟩═⟨⟩═⟨⟩═⟨

"Mr. Inmate, you can come in now," the dental assistant held the door open. I entered and sat in the dentist's chair.

"TMJ dysfunction, why didn't they send you back to the hospital?"

"The medical manager says I complain too much and want attention." I briefly explained to him what had happened to this point.

"You should have seen the specialist for this. It is possible you have a TMJ dysfunction. We pulled the one upper tooth in the front that was behind your other teeth and a lower one that was in front of those teeth." He checked my bite for skid. "Yeah, you got a skid! I am going to try to see if I can remove your skid. This will stop your jaw from pulling to the left or right when you close. This should help the headaches."

He started grinding off my teeth. This went on for two or three months. He ground down the back more and more. It seemed the more he ground, the teeth would lift up more. Then I went off to the specialist to be fitted for a mouth brace. I have worn this brace since I got it.

Yet the migraines didn't stop. One day out of the blue the dentist decided to x-ray my lower back teeth. *Bingo!* Two years with a migraine before he decided to look at an x-ray. "Do you know your lower wisdom teeth are impacted?"

"No."

"This could be why the headaches will not go away. Look at this x-ray. See how the roots are pushing on the jaw nerve." The roots had literally grown into the nerve. "The tops are growing into the roots of your lower teeth. I think this is why your back teeth keep changing."

I believe what was happening was that as he ground down the back teeth and relieved the pressure, my wisdom teeth would push up on them. The more he took off, the more they would lift. Out to the specialist again.

✄═✄═✄═✄

"Mr. Inmate, we can do the procedure two ways. We can pull one now and do the other in a month, or we can pull them both today."

"Do them both now. It is going to hurt anyways, get it over with."

"I agree, but some patients prefer to do one at a time. It will be painful for awhile."

His assistant came in with the needle and stuck me once in both sides of my lower jaw. I turned white and my blood pressure felt like it had dropped to about zero. "Nurse, get his vital signs," the doctor ordered. "You there, come here and bag him."

I couldn't believe all the attention I was suddenly getting.

"Are you okay? Are you okay?"

"Hummm, yes."

"You're ghost white."

"It's that needle going into my mouth. I watched you get it, adjust it, and bring it to my mouth. I hate needles. When I was a kid I got a sewing machine needle stuck in my finger. I wasn't smart enough to know to turn the wheel on the machine to get it out. I had to wait awhile for my mom to do it. Ever since then I hated needles."

"Okay. I watched your blood pressure drop, then start to climb again. You're not allergic to seafood or anything like that?"

"No."

"I want to be sure you're not having an allergic reaction."

"No, just don't hold the needle in front of me like that."

He gave me a minute or two, then stuck me about ten times on each side. After that he stuck a piece of rubber in my mouth to hold my jaw open. "How are you doing?"

"Awh, huh, ho . . ." I mumbled. *Why do dentists want to talk to you when you can't talk?*

"Did you feel that?" He cut my gum with the scalpel.

"Woo, ho, awk, humm . . ."

"Good." He worked and worked. Two hours later both my teeth were gone and he pried the rubber piece out. "How do you feel?"

I looked around rubbing my numb jaw. "Okay," I said through all the cotton. Then my miracle happened. "Doctor, my headache is gone!"

"Good," was his only reply.

"No, no, you don't understand. I have had it for two long years. I have struggled to get those people in the prison to listen. All that pain. The zigzag in my vision is gone too." I started to sit up. I was so happy I wanted to hug him.

He pushed me back in the chair. "You better sit back, you're still very white."

White, I didn't care about being white, I thought. I wanted to move around, I wanted to catch up on two years of life!

✄━✄━✄━✄

"Here's a memo," the cellhall runner said as he handed me a piece of paper through my cell door bars.

I immediately thought that they were announcing a lockdown. Instead, it was a medical memo stating that all movement would be stopped tomorrow due to each inmate being tested and screened for hepatitis. If you refused the test, you would be placed in medical isolation for at least thirty days. "Why are they doing this?"

"You didn't hear? They had a guy working in the school hallway who had hepatitis. He's in medical now, but he was working down there for a month."

"Wow!"

"They want to test everyone so they don't end up with an outbreak."

The next day we went out to the rotunda that connected the cellhalls. They had a medical station set up to give skin tests.

On the fourth day we all went back out again to have the test checked. Everyone was scared. Some thought they wanted to inject us all for some type of government experiment. Others feared the test. "Man, they're trying to get us all!"

Me, I wanted it. I didn't want to catch hepatitis in this joint! "Yes, I'll take it. Where do I stand?"

✄━✄━✄━✄

REFLECTIONS

When I first entered prison everyone told me how lucky I was to get free medical. I was told I had it made. I even remember a news story I saw on television about a man who had cancer and couldn't afford the treatments. He entered a store, pointed a gun at the clerk, and demanded money. The clerk, fearing for his life, gave it to him. Immediately after, the robber put the gun away and told the clerk to dial 911 and say he was just robbed. He was arrested and went to jail. Then the TV commentator said, "and now he will go to prison to get his treatments for cancer." *Yeah, right!*

Medical in prison is not what everyone believes it to be. One is given the least costly, least care possible. If you have long-term treatment needs, you will get little and be told to deal with it. You will have to *beg* for any and all types of care.

I remember reading in the newspaper about some prisoners who died from lack of medical care. Some doctors and medical staff in prisons reportedly have restrictions on their medical licenses.

Medical care in prison is like it is in the third world. If you break a bone, they will set it. Yet if you fracture a bone, they will let it slowly heal while waiting for x-rays. If you need long-term medical or dental care, forget it. You might suffer for years, only to be told you will have to have the problem fixed when you get out if you don't die first.

11

Sex

303.13, Sexual assault. Any inmate who intentionally has sexual contact with another person without that person's consent and knowing is guilty.

DEPARTMENT OF CORRECTIONS MANUAL
APRIL 1990

303.15, Sexual conduct. Lack of consent is not an element of the offense of sexual misconduct.

DEPARTMENT OF CORRECTIONS MANUAL
APRIL 1990

Back at the receiving center when I was first incarcerated, a slender young dude named Zoom appeared at my cell door asking me if I had any of "those books." People are the most polite when they want something. But I was still green and didn't know what books he was talking about.

"I seen a officer every now and then give you a **jag mag.** You know, your books with the 'hos'."

I felt dumb that I hadn't known what the hell he was talking about. "I had a subscription but let it go. I got a couple left."

"Well, can I check 'em out?" Zoom asked, grabbing his groin through his pants, "I want to rape me a ho!" He chuckled.

I answered in the new language I was learning. "Yeah, you can check them out, but I want them back clean." Books like these seemed to always come back damaged.

"Oh, man, that means I can't rape me one?" he laughed again.

"Come on now, Zoom. I am trusting you with my shit." He was called Zoom since he always asked for some zoom-zooms and wam-wams to eat.

He grabbed two of my books and tucked them under his shirt, heading for the toilet stall in the bathroom. Well, he was getting started just as Skin and the other first-shift workers came into in the bathroom/shower area. "Hey, man," Zoom called, "can you guys keep it down out there?"

The guy next to him smiled. "Hey Zoom, you in there again? Damn, boy, you going to go blind pulling your meat and looking at them books."

"Man, I don't know about you, but I got to take care of my business," Zoom yelled out from the stall.

Skin laughed. "Four times a day! Your **swipe**'s going to get a rash."

"Hell," the guy next to him added, "rash my ass, he's gonna' pull it off!" Then he yelled more slowly, "You want us to call the nurse, just in case?"

"You call the nurse, and I'm gonna' stick her with this hard dick. Now get the fuck out of here. I can't think!"

A few days later I went down to get my books. "Hey, Zoom, where are they?" He looked through a pile of magazines on his desk before he told me that Ship had them.

Zoom must have had forty or fifty books in his cell. "Damn, Zoom, don't tell me those are all sex books?"

"Oh, man, they getting old. Yours are new!" He smiled again, showing the gap in his teeth. "I been locked up eight years, I got to do something."

"You say Ship's got them?"

"Yeah, he busted me in the bathroom and wanted to see them."

"Hey, Zoom, do me a favor, don't pass my shit around again," I said.

I walked to Ship's cell and asked about my books. He had given them to Skin, so I walked down to Skin's cell and knocked on his door.

"What's up?" he called out.

I swung his door open. "Hey, Skin, can I get my books back?" He was lying on his bed in his jockey shorts with my magazine resting on his chest. I quickly closed the door just enough so I could look in and still talk to him. "Skin, put some clothes on!" I was embarrassed.

"Why? Never see a man in his shorts?" He grabbed his bathrobe. "Why your face all red?"

I tried to sound casual but still tough. "I ain't accustomed to having a grown man holding conversation in jockey shorts."

"Man, it ain't like that. I grew up in a one-room house. A man's swipe gets hard, it gets hard," he said, drawing out the word *man*.

Prisoners like Skin, who grew up poor, were less bothered by lack of privacy than prisoners like me, who grew up in a middle-class home with more privacy.

Dudes were always moving on and off the unit. I was starting to fit in and getting to know other lifers. Kid had come out of the same city I did and we both were working in the kitchen so we had something to talk about. He was called Kid because he was only about five feet tall, with a twenty-six-inch waist.

Van arrived about the same time as Kid. Then they brought Tower, who had a twenty-year sentence for rape. Tower came from the Walls, the other prison across the railroad tracks. I had heard a lot about the Walls. Nothing good. Tower already had about ten years in.

"Hey," Tower was at my door, "check out my new magazine."

He handed me a motorcycle magazine. When I paged through it, I saw it was a sex magazine with a motorcycle on its cover. Like many sex offenders, Tower seemed preoccupied with sex like an alcoholic is preoccupied with getting drunk.

"Did you see the one with the girl on the beach?" Tower almost drooled. "She's got a starfish crawling on her breast."

He was not going to let that starfish go until I turned back to look at it. "Did you see it?" he repeated excitedly. "Hell of a picture collection." He laughed. "See how the starfish walks over her in each picture? Huh?"

"Yes, no big deal."

"No big deal! It's crawling right over her breast. It walked over her nipple."

"Eh-hum," I answered.

"She got off on it. Didn't ya see how hard her nipple got?" He looked at me grinning, raising his eyebrows up and down. "That starfish is making that woman come!"

"How do you see all that? It only shows her breast," I answered.

"Because I know women. She's coming, look at the other pictures! Damn."

"Tower, why don't you just take this book to your **house** real quick and handle your business? Hell, you sound like you're in heat."

"I already did." He reached for the book and paged through it. "Here, look at this one." Then he handed the book to me fast and told me to hide it. I tucked it under my pillow as Kid walked up in his kitchen whites. "Hey, what's going on?"

"Watching Anonymous's TV," Tower replied before I could say anything. It was like he had turned one switch off and another on.

"I got to go to work in a minute." Kid looked down the hallway toward the guard station, "How do you like that clerk's job?"

"It's okay," I said.

"Would you write me in for extra hours?" Kid asked. The whole unit wanted me to write them in for extra time. Man!

Then the guard called the kitchen workers, and Kid left. Tower was back to his magazine. I was glad when Van showed up. He was about my age, but he looked younger. He was in for robbery.

"Hey," Van walked up to the door. "You're the kitchen clerk, right?"

"Yeah." *Let me guess, extra hours.*

"What kind of job they going to put me in?"

"I don't know. They got some openings in the back and one in the front." The back was the kitchen area; the front was the dining room area.

"Can you help me get into the back? I just don't want to work the dining room and dish room with all those people."

"Tell the manager. He's cool. If he has the spot, he'll put you back there," I advised.

"Well, how will he know? If I get down there last, then I'll lose out."

"I'll tell him you asked about coming back there. Just don't fuck up since it'll fall back on me," I said.

"I won't. I used to work at Spring River kitchen."

"Well, I'll tell him."

"Thanks. I appreciate it."

Little did I know Van had just hustled me. He never worked in Spring River's kitchen. While he stood there, I handed Tower his magazine. "Dude be acting gay," Tower commented.

⬤⬤⬤⬤

I noticed that whenever Van was working, he'd hang out in the office with me when the manager wasn't around.

"Hey, what's up, Anonymous?" Van strolled into the office again. "I heard you and Gary talking."

Years later I learned Gary was gay. "Yeah, well, Gary is a trip," I said, as I watched Gary walk past the office window.

"I see you talking with a lot of dudes," Van smiled. Van was implying that I associated with African American men. This was not typical behavior of white men.

"Maybe, maybe not. I just give everybody his chance."

"You going to give me my chance?" He laughed a little.

I realized he was staring at me, so I spoke slowly so he'd understand. "As an associate. I only have associates and don't want anything more. You follow?"

"Yeah. As an associate," he replied. "I like that."

Just then, Kid came into the office. As the kitchen meat cutter, he pulled the meat out of the freezer every night so that it could thaw by the next day. He looked at Van, then asked me, "You got the 'pull list' out for tomorrow?"

I handed him the list.

Van laughed. "You gonna pull your meat. Gets cold back there, don't it?"

Kid went into the freezer. When he came out he handed the frozen packages to Van.

"I like you," Van told him.

"Thank you, I think you're okay too." Kid handed him a fifty-pound package. Van grabbed it. Each time Van grabbed another package, he'd put one hand between Kid's body and the package, and the other hand on the other side of the package. It didn't take Kid long to figure out what was going on, so he kept dropping the packages lower and lower.

⬤⬤⬤⬤

A few days later, when it was about time for evening lockdown on the unit, Van came to my cell. He wanted me to go with him to Skin's cell for some cigarettes. He didn't know Skin but I did, and so I agreed to accompany him just to get rid of him.

"Hey, Skin," I knocked and opened his door when he replied. Skin was standing in his jockeys with his bathrobe open.

"Come on, Skin," I started.

Van stuck his head in the cell. "Hey, Skin, I asked Anonymous to come down here. I need a pack of smokes until tomorrow."

Van was staring at Skin. When I saw Skin staring back at Van, I started to move backwards, out of the cell doorway.

Skin took off his robe and rubbed oil on his chest. "I got oil on my hands," Skin said. "Just have Anonymous watch for the guard and grab the cigarettes out of my cabinet."

Van seemed happy to step into his cell. "Where are they?" he looked at Skin as he knelt by his cabinet. "I don't want to mess up your stuff."

Skin moved right up on him and pointed with his hand. "Right there, top shelf in the back."

Van kept looking at Skin. Then Skin surprised me. "Hey, stop looking at me and look in the cabinet."

Van knew Skin had just caught him eyeing up his groin. He started to talk but Skin cut him off.

"Come on now, Van, you can't sit in here forever. I don't want the guard to know you're in here and Anonymous isn't going to watch all night. Get on!"

Van thanked him and we both left.

Skin showed up at my door minutes later. "Hey, what's up with your friend?"

"Hey, Skin, I only know him." But I knew what he meant.

"Yeah, he's gayer than a motherfucker," Skin remarked without hesitation. "Why'd he come by me?"

"Probably because you're always in your cell in your little shorts! I think he wants you." I couldn't help myself.

"You and him got something going?" Now he was upset.

I got very serious. "I just think he has jungle fever. Wants dark meat!"

"Not mine," Skin replied. "Not me!"

<hr />

Van's problems started after that. Skin told Greg, Greg told Zoom, Zoom told Ship, Ship told everybody. Hell, the only ones who didn't know about Van were the guards at the desk and before it was over, they knew too.

First I heard it from Kid. "Hey, Anonymous, you hear about Van? He's gay."

I could tell there was more to it than what he was saying. "Yeah, old news!"

"I hear him and Skin got something going?"

"I don't know."

"You know Skin?" he probed.

"Yeah, but I don't know him that well," I hesitated.

"I hope he ain't up to no shit."

"I didn't know you cared." It was unusual for Kid to care about anything unless he had an interest in it.

"Hey," he shot back, "I don't care like that. He just hangs around me and I don't want no heat from the guards. They ain't said anything to you about it while you're doing your job, have they?"

"No. I figure maybe they know but I don't know for sure." *So many questions. Something's on Kid's mind.*

Then Tower came along and Kid left. "Man, I heard Skin had Van in his cell."

"Ain't my business," I replied.

"Yeah, but we don't need no gay-ass dude on the unit. You know how much heat that can bring? That queer-ass Kid," Tower added, "he is up to something too."

"I didn't know Kid was a **fag.**"

"Yeah, over in the Walls, he was fucking around. Never got caught. But that was the rumor."

"I didn't know."

Tower gave me the details. "Well, I heard that Van was down in Skin's cell. I know you noticed, you talk with Van now and then. He has to be gay; then Skin wearing that small underwear." He paused. "I heard that Van saw him putting his baby oil on and started to help him out. Skin's meat got hard and Van sucked him off. Fucking gay-ass punk! That is what he is."

Although sex was often on Tower's mind, Tower was extremely homophobic.

⊱━⊰⊱━⊰⊱━⊰

The rumors got better. Skin had been sleeping with Van for a month already, the guard knew and was allowing it, Van was scared of Skin, Skin was punking Van out like a bitch.

About three days later I caught up to Skin in the dish room.

"Hey, Skin, you know the talk is out there about you and Van?"

"Yeah, these motherfuckers have to run their mouths."

"Well, I just thought I'd let you know. You were always cool with me."

"What you hear?" he asked.

"You know, what I said."

"No, you know more than that," he leaned against the dish machine.

"Yeah, well, you know," I looked at my shoes, then him, "I am sick of hearing it."

"I know Tower, your buddy, he is the one that won't let it die."

I nodded my head.

"He was like that at the Walls. He's a treejumper. Stays stuck on anything with sex." Skin had it pegged. Tower was running his mouth a lot.

I could see Skin was actually hurt and angry but could do nothing about it. I actually saw that Skin had a touch of humanity.

✖━✖━✖━✖

J–Bone and Rayfield, two of the kitchen workers, came over as Van and I were talking. "Hey, kitchen clerk," Rayfield said to me, "don't put us on the break list. We're staying to work."

"You got it squared away with the staff cook?"

"Yeah, he said okay," J–Bone answered.

Van headed to the cooler area. Rayfield followed him and J–Bone went over to help the staff cook.

"Van, I got to sweep your area." Rayfield looked at Van.

"Go ahead." Van thought Rayfield was a nice looking guy. Short. No more than 120 pounds soaking wet. But J–Bone was the asshole.

"I didn't wear any undershorts this morning, man," Rayfield grinned.

"Oh, is that your pick-up line?"

Rayfield grabbed Van's hand and shoved it in his pocket. He had cut out the pocket and was already excited.

"Damn, Rayfield, I don't fuck around." But Rayfield could see through that. Van had just let it go on too long.

Unnoticed by the staff cook, J–Bone made his way into the cooler area.

"Leave me the fuck alone," Van said.

J–Bone could not help but notice the front of Rayfield's pants were standing out. "I see you my brother!" he smiled. Rayfield smiled back.

They backed Van into a corner. J–Bone unzipped his pants and exposed everything. "Suck on it!"

"Fuck you," Van shouted. He saw no other choice: upside J–Bone's head he went. *Wam-bam.* J–Bone's head snapped back.

It was on. Rayfield jumped on Van while J–Bone quickly zipped up his pants. They hit Van from two directions. Van punched Rayfield in the eye, J–Bone hit Van in the side, Van punched J–Bone in the nuts, and Rayfield kicked Van in the knee.

It had gone on about five minutes when Steve, the prisoner cook, came in. J–Bone walked out of the cooler as fast as he could and Rayfield grabbed his broom and followed him out.

After a few minutes, Van came into the kitchen office. "What the hell happened to you?" I asked, looking at a cut above his eye.

"Those two jumped me in the meat cutting area."

"Why?"

"Come on, Anonymous, what do you think? They want me to suck their dicks!"

"You don't look too good. You all right?" I asked, handing him things out of the medicine kit.

"Yeah. Just make sure the staff cook doesn't write anything up. If he does, lose it, okay?"

Steve told Tower, Tower told Greg, Greg told Zoom, Zoom told Skin, Skin told me. Someone told Ship and Ship told everyone. *Van got beat up in the kitchen, Van got his ass beat, Van beat some ass in the kitchen. Van got knocked out. Those guys tried to rape him.* Boy, the stories were flying. Eventually Van got even. Van hid a homemade knife in J-Bone's cell and J-Bone eventually got caught. Sergeant Pot got himself another brother in segregation.

Van was not outwardly gay, but he was perceived to be gay because he flirted with other men. But when it came to being forced to have sex with another man, Van refused and fought back.

⋈⋈⋈

I had given up on the sex books. I was burning out. I looked at women like objects, since I was allowed zero social contact with them. A few times I thought about doing a few gay dudes but never did. I just couldn't.

When the buzzer sounded out for showers, we headed to the **bathhouse.** Everybody moved fast because showers were first come, first served. Many guys had their favorite shower.

In Gladiator School newcomers were always stunned by the shower arrangement. There were enough showerheads to do the whole forty-man tier. They stuck out of the wall in the open area. If you did not like to get butt-naked in front of forty men, you did not shower.

After my shower, I returned to my cell past the guard, a nice-looking female. The rumor was that she stalked prisoners in their cells. I never really believed it but was proved wrong. She would always stand in front of my next-door neighbor Mike's cell for awhile after she locked all the cells up to his. After about ten minutes, she'd move on.

She was already in front of Mike's cell. "Find someone else to help you with that," she said to him.

I had forgotten to take my mail with me so asked her if she could take it for me. She didn't answer. I repeated my question.

"Sure," she said to me, then turned back to Mike's cell. "Mike, you're something else." She really wasn't paying any attention to me and she didn't walk over to roll my door shut, so I figured it was okay to hand her the mail.

She was still talking to Mike about not doing something or not helping him with something when I grabbed my mail and walked over in front of his cell. As I handed her the mail, I couldn't help but see Mike and his muscle-bound naked body jagging right in front of her.

She didn't miss a beat. She grabbed my letters. I headed into my cell and closed the door.

Later Mike called to me. "Hey, Anonymous, she likes me." He laughed. He wasn't more than eighteen years old. Randy, my other neighbor, and I had branded him the Big Kid.

"I suppose she does," I answered, "you standing there doing your thing."

"Yeah, she thinks the taller we are, the bigger our you-know-what becomes," he laughed some more.

Since everyone on the tier can hear conversations between cells, Chuck joined in from a few cells down. "Who likes you, Mike?"

"Remember what I was telling you about that female?"

"You mean the guard?" Chuck asked.

I had heard rumors about Chuck, but not with females. It wasn't my business, though.

<hr>

REFLECTIONS

Many people in society seem to think all prisoners become gay or rapists **(booty bandits)** while in prison. A lawyer friend of mine wrote me a letter explaining that when he was in court, a victim's father shouted, *I hope you get raped in prison*, and the court audience started clapping. What a society we have!

Fortunately, this is not the norm. Sex in prison is just another part of life. Probably 90 percent of the people that pass through the prison doors masturbate. The other 10 percent have sex with other inmates or with staff members. Out of the 10 percent that have sex with another person in prison, about 99.5 percent of them have sex with other men.

A rapist does not stop raping just because he has come to prison. Although attempted rapes are more common than completed rapes, in my twenty years, I have heard about only five rapes that were reported. If a rape gets reported, everyone hears about it.

To curb prisoners' sex addictions the state eventually banned all pornographic material in prison. After this occurred, some prisoners swore up and down that it led to more homosexual activities. I do not know. I do know banning books does not help treat the mind-set of prisoners. Only the treatment phase can help stop rape, and even then the results are not highly successful.

No one really wants to talk about or change the policies on sexual harassment and rape, yet everyone knows those policies exist in prison.

12

The Barbershop Sex Scandal

"I am not sure if she was running a barbershop or a whorehouse."

OFFICER RALPH

SPRING 1987

"Mrs. Brown, we know it was impossible for some of these items to get into the prison without someone bringing them in. Mrs. Brown, you must talk to me."

ASSISTANT WARDEN ARIES

APRIL 1987

he years rolled on. Mike didn't live next to me any more, but Chuck was still there. Randy transferred down to medium security and a new fella by the name of Geneo moved into Mike's old cell.

Geneo was a convict barber, working toward a degree in hair styling. The barbershop was considered to be the gossip center of the institution. There was also a **staff barber** named Blue, who cut staff hair during the lunch hour. Some days no one came in for a haircut, so Blue and the barbershop teacher, Mrs. Brown, would be alone for that hour.

At that time Blue was a well-toned prisoner about ten years younger than Mrs. Brown. Blue started telling her how nice she was. When she said things like she was too fat, he'd tell her he liked his women full-figured. If word got out about him flirting with a staff member, he knew he could go to segregation. But he persisted anyhow.

Mrs. Brown told him to call her Amy, her first name. She had a husband at home but Blue was so polite. Once Amy asked Blue how a man pushing thirty years old could keep his waist so slender. "Playing basketball," he told her.

✄━✄━✄━✄

Blue didn't care much for Mrs. Brown. He just wanted some action and he could see he was slowly drawing her in. So he laid it on thick and he focused the talk on sex. He would go back to his cell each night and **jag** over their conversations.

Blue had his hair straightened with a perm. He would roll up his hair in the shop. This particular time he rolled it over lunch since there were no appointments that day.

"Oh, you're doing your hair," Amy smiled. He looked at her through the mirror. Then he dropped a few rollers on purpose.

"Let me help." Amy started rolling his hair. Each time she grabbed a roller out of the sink, she got closer and closer to him.

"You sure smell good today," Blue remarked. He felt his groin growing so he slid his hand down his lap like he was scratching himself and in the process realigned himself so it was sliding down his pants leg.

Amy watched what he did. "Thank you. You're excited today," she whispered.

"Man, Amy, I know you can see it. I am always ready for the right lady."

She pulled a pint of juice out of her pocket and gave it to him. "Remember, you told me you liked gin and juice?"

He picked up the bottle and drank some. She mixed it 50/50 like he said. *Gin and grapefruit juice. Damn, that tastes nasty.*

"What are you thinking?"

"Oh, why you're being so nice to me," he said slowly to her. He took a few more sips.

She grabbed another roller out of the sink and let her breast rub on his arm. "Gee, that sink is getting deeper. I can't reach the rollers."

Blue was excited. "I got nine and a half inches for you, Amy. I am a large man."

"Gee, I see it works but it doesn't look that long." She giggled just as the outer barbershop door slammed.

Amy moved away from Blue but kept rolling his hair.

"Just making my rounds," Landen, the guard, said, opening the door to the staff barber area.

Blue sat in the chair with his hands in his lap. The last thing he wanted was Landen to think anything was going on.

"Mrs. Brown, I need you to check in at the desk," Landen announced.

"Oh, shit," she looked surprised, "I forgot." She turned and walked out with him.

When she left, Blue pounded the rest of the juice. He knew he had about five minutes before the afternoon class would arrive. He stood up, rinsed the bottle out, unzipped his fly, and jagged right in the shop!

The flirting went on for the next two weeks. Amy continued to bring in gin and gave him earrings and other gifts. Blue started wearing the smallest pants he could get on, and pants where the fabric was worn and thin. His T-shirts got smaller, too, and he stopped wearing underwear.

It was ringout and Chuck and Blue were going to work. "Damn, Blue, you growing or are your clothes shrinking?"

"Got to be dressed for my barber girl," Blue smiled, not realizing that he had set himself up. He just broke a code norm: never tell others what you're doing.

"Yeah, I hear you," Chuck said.

Geneo was right behind them. He heard the conversation too and wanted to find out more. Geneo was a treejumper. Fifteen counts of first degree. He manipulated his way into the sports teams at college, then raped girls hanging out on the sidelines. He was cutthroat at getting what he wanted and selfishly worked to get it. Now he was going to work his way to the barbershop teacher. He started asking about becoming a staff barber.

✄━━━✄━━━✄━━━✄

"I don't know what I will do, Mrs. Brown," Geneo hinted. "I would like to stay here and keep practicing barbering. I want to be a staff barber or class tutor."

"We'll see. I only get one staff barber," she told him.

Geneo also worked hard to become best friends with Blue. He agreed with Blue's complaints and he laughed at his dumb jokes. One time he even helped Blue arrange a sexual encounter between Blue's friend Chuck and another convict named Hot Rod. Hot Rod was about the horniest guy I have ever heard of. He was always interested in sex and had many sexual partners.

"Okay, Geneo," Blue planned, "here is what we will do. I will give the clerk Chuck's name and number and get him an appointment at a specific time. You give him Hot Rod's stuff and get an appointment at the same time. I get cigarettes from him so I'll give you some out of the pack."

"No, that's okay," Geneo told Blue, "I don't need anything."

Turning down free cigarettes! Blue should have caught on.

When Chuck walked into the barbershop waiting area, Hot Rod was already sitting there. "How you doing, Chuck?" Hot Rod said in a high voice as Chuck sat next to him.

"I brought you some smokes if you need them, . . ." Chuck started.

Before he had finished, Hot Rod put his hand in Chuck's front pocket and pulled out the smokes. Then, looking directly at Chuck, he put his hand back into Chuck's pocket again.

"Lookit," Chuck continued, "they have an opening in wood tech where I work. Why don't you come over there?"

"I don't really want to be over there in all that dust. It will mess up my hair." Hot Rod was playing Chuck.

"Why don't you get over to the south cellhall with me?" Chuck asked.

"Well, I do want a different job. The paint crew isn't working for me," said Hot Rod.

The paint crew was painting cell door areas inside the prison. Hot Rod had a lot of traffic going with his job and was making a lot of money through prostitution, but he wasn't doing much painting and knew he was going to get fired. Other prisoners were talking and complaining about him.

"Then come over to the south with me. The north is burnt up." Chuck slid down in his chair. They were in the perfect spot. The barbershop waiting area had small hedges that screened one side of the chairs. It was late and they were the last ones there. If anyone came in, they'd stop doing what they were doing. But no one did. At least for the time being, Chuck and Hot Rod had become an item.

Just before the paint crew boss fired Hot Rod, Hot Rod applied for a tutor's job in education. The education office hired him and he moved to the south cellhall.

The education department had about thirty tutors, and at this time guess who was the second tutor in charge, very shortly to become the head tutor? Me. It was my job to assign tutors to the basic education lab area. We had some pull, even though staff signed all final assignments. It was a nice little empire and by moving up to head tutor, I was going to make the maximum allowed pay.

When I saw Hot Rod, I knew things were going to change.

✄✄✄✄

One day I went to hobby to enlarge a drawing I had made. The copy machine was housed in a small deep booth that was usually empty. The door was half shut, but as I looked inside, I saw Mac, the hobby clerk whom I'd known for years. So I walked in.

Mac had the machine pushed up close to the wall. I asked him to leave it on so I could use it when he was done. Then I saw Hot Rod sitting on the floor in front of him.

About fifteen minutes later, Mac came out grinning. Hot Rod followed him. Kim, the kitchen clerk, also saw them come out. Since both of us were cons, we just minded our own business.

I walked over to use the booth, and Kim started ribbing. "Ohh, you sure you want to go in there?" He laughed.

"I hope I don't slip on something," I whispered.

Then Mac came over for a minute. "I forgot my pen in there."

"Are you sure that's all you left?" Kim asked, poking him in the side.

"I ain't going to slip on anything?" I added to the ribbing.

Mac just laughed. "It's clean," he grinned so wide all his teeth showed.

"Why, Mac, are you glowing?" Kim kept on him.

"I don't know," I responded, "he looks drained to me!"

Shit like this was a natural part of life. Some dudes in prison would spout off at the mouth how they hated gay dudes. They were constantly downgrading them, so much on it that I wondered who was really gay. I never really cared if someone was gay or not.

You expected something like that around every corner. You could continue to hate or just move on with life.

It was easy to rib the shit out of Mac because he wasn't really ashamed of it. "I am a three-minute-brother," Mac returned our ribbing.

"You are?" Kim continued. "Why'd you take ten minutes? Hmm, inquiring minds want to know. I say we do a video for the cable news!"

"No, Kim, I don't think we really want to know!" When I said that, Mac's face turned purple.

This was Gladiator School.

✦━✦━✦━✦

I came back late from work one day. I was on pass for a college exam and no guard wanted to get out of his chair, climb the stairs to the third tier, and let me in my cell. So I stood on the tier outside my cell.

Eventually I got tired of standing, so I slid my books through the bars and went to look for a cigarette. The only person nearby that I kind of knew was Chuck. I heard a noise his way and thought I'd ask him for a smoke.

"Hey, Chuck," I called before coming up to his bars.

I heard a little scrambling, then he answered, "What's up?"

When I heard him answer, I walked in front of his cell. "Hey, can I get a cigarette? If you want one back I'll give it to you later."

He was in his undershorts. "Sure, you can have one." He held a pack up to the bars.

"What were you doing, getting ready to wash up?" I noticed that he had his curtain half up in the back of his cell. Just then it slid off the string.

Hot Rod jumped up from a chair behind it, butt-naked. Chuck looked at him, then at me. Hot Rod just stared at me. I didn't know what to say. I could see he was embarrassed, but yet he wasn't.

"I see you're busy," I said to break the ice.

"Yeah," he admitted, half grinning, "busy." Hot Rod grabbed the curtain off the floor and started putting it back.

Finally class exchange came and the guard let me into my cell. When they were ringing out, I saw Hot Rod walk by. Soon Chuck was standing in front of my door. He spoke through the bars. "Hey, Anonymous, let's keep that little incident between us."

I started grinning. "Chuck, your life is your life. I ain't gonna' tell a soul."

I didn't ask Chuck for too many cigarettes after that.

✦━✦━✦━✦

While all of this was going on with Hot Rod and his multiple sex partners, Geneo had to figure out a way to get rid of Blue without getting Amy in trouble. So he plotted. She continued to bring in gin and even some weed for Blue. Blue told Geneo it made the sex more fun. *Smoke some weed, then have the bitch suck my dick.*

So Geneo decided to set up Blue so he could get the staff barber position. Just another example of prison politics again. The security office got some notes that Blue was smoking marijuana. Geneo also started the rumor that Blue was selling weed in the barbershop.

One day Officer Landen called Geneo over to the desk. There was no one in the hallway.

"Is it okay if I smoke here?" Geneo asked.

Landen wanted information, so he pushed his ashtray toward Geneo. "I sure hope you're not involved. I like the way you cut my hair better than Blue."

Geneo had always volunteered to help on the days when a lot of staff wanted haircuts. Immediately he was on guard. "Involved in what?"

They were playing each other. Landen was trying the weak-ass guard game: suck up to a prisoner, then pump him for information. Geneo was relieved that he was the one Landen had called over.

"Come on, Geneo, the drugs being passed in the barbershop."

"No, I don't fuck around," Geneo replied, *knowing damn well he did.* Geneo even shared his weed with Blue.

"Well, I have to start searching everyone coming out of there when you guys go back for lunch."

"Yeah."

"Oh, you know it, so I hope you're not carrying any barbering supplies. I'll bust you for that." Landen knew the whole barbershop stole supplies.

Geneo looked concerned. "You'd do all that?"

"Yeah," Landen sat up, "unless I got to know who was doing it." He slid paper and pencil toward Geneo. All he needed was something in writing. "So what do you think, Geneo? I'll call it an anonymous letter."

"Well, I don't want no trouble," Geneo said. He looked up and down the hallway. Then he grabbed the paper and wrote a short line on it, folding it when he was finished.

Geneo knew this would do it for Blue. Officer Landen put his hand over the paper and Geneo went back to the shop. Landen unfolded the paper and read Blue's name on it. Later the officer came into the shop looking around and waited for the staff member to get out of Blue's chair. As soon the chair was empty, Landen moved in.

<hr>

"I'm going to do a couple of pat searches," Landen announced. He stood with his hands on his hips. One finger was flicking his keys on the ring attached to his belt. He looked around at everybody, then looked at Blue, "Start with you."

*Oh shit, the **package** in my waist is still there.*

"Step away from the chair," Landen ordered.

"Okay," Blue could feel the little package of weed he had hidden in the side of his pants.

"Take off your shoes and socks. Everything out of your pockets. Pull your pockets out and take off your barbering shirt." Landen spoke like a general. When he started digging through his stuff, Blue slid his hand into the waist of his pants and cupped the package.

Nothing in this stuff. Maybe it's still on him.

Geneo watched with anticipation. *The cigarette pack, you idiot, come on, the cigarette pack, the cigarette pack.* Geneo had made sure something was in Blue's open pack of cigarettes.

"Okay," Landen said, "do me a favor and turn around and put your hands on the counter." He kicked at his ankle, "Spread your legs more."

Just don't ask me to open my hand.

Landen ran his hands down each arm, over Blue's chest, back, then ran his finger in the waist of his pants, pulled on his front pockets, patted his back pockets, and ran a couple of fingers down his fly, placed one hand up into Blue's inseam hitting his groin, put the other on the outside of his leg, and kneeled down, running his hand down to his foot.

When he felt him jab his groin, Blue groaned. "Hey, come on, man."

"Sorry," Landen said. *Next time I will do it harder.*

He did the other leg and checked his pants cuffs. While Landen was kneeling, Blue looked around the counter for somewhere to hide the stuff in his hand.

The smokes, you dumb fuck, Geneo thought, *the smokes.* Landen still didn't see them on the counter. He stood up empty-handed, knowing it wasn't going as he hoped.

The smokes, Landen, the smokes, the words formed on Geneo's lips.

"Are you done?" asked Blue.

Just as Geneo thought Landen was giving up, he looked at the counter. "Are these your cigarettes?"

"Yeah, they're mine," Blue answered. He was still leaning on the counter, the package in his hand. *Just don't ask to see my hands.*

Landen grabbed the pack of cigarettes, bounced them around. As he looked in the pack once again, he finally found the one fat joint. *Gotcha.* "Okay, get your clothes on and sit in the chair." He set the pack on the desk by Mrs. Brown and told her to watch them.

She was a little surprised at how Landen had bolted into her shop without giving her any advance warning.

He ran another dude through the same routine, but patted him down faster. Then Landen grabbed the cigarettes and told Blue, "Come out by my desk and have a seat."

Blue knew something was up with those cigarettes, but he didn't know what. As Landen walked out, you could hear him on his radio calling for a captain and an escort.

Landen was first out of the shop, so Blue dropped the weed he had been holding in his hand as he followed him. No sooner was Blue gone that Geneo snatched the weed from the floor.

⟩═⟨═⟩⟨═⟩⟨═⟩

With Blue gone, Geneo became staff barber, just as he'd planned.

Amy missed Blue, and in her time of need, Geneo offered what she thought was a sympathetic ear. He used her, never thinking it would end, just as Blue had thought it would never end. But as always, things like this eventually end with innocent people getting hurt. And Geneo was worse than Blue in many ways.

"Oh, Amy, could you bring me a little more gin? I'd like to take some back to my cell," he begged.

Next time it was, "Oh, Amy, I like the watch you gave me but it doesn't go with my sweat suit. Bring me another?" When she did, he'd say, "Oh, Amy, I wrote you a love poem. Why don't you ever write me one?" Or "Amy, let's take some Polaroids together doing things."

⟩═⟨═⟩⟨═⟩⟨═⟩

When Geneo's cell was searched, evidence of Geneo and Amy's relationship came out in the open, and the next morning, the assistant warden grabbed her arm before she had a chance to check in.

He headed her into the security office. The institutional security director was there already. He was a big man, about 300 pounds, and had four chins. She put her purse on his desk and sat down.

"Mrs. Brown, can I look in your purse?" the assistant warden asked.

She stumbled over her words. "What's this about?"

"Mrs. Brown, may I look in your purse?" he repeated.

"Well, I guess, ah, maybe." She was scared. *There was a bottle of booze in her purse.*

He had it open while she was still stammering.

The security director just stared at her when he saw the bottle sitting in front of him on the desk. He didn't move, he didn't smile or frown, he didn't blink.

"Mrs. Brown, do you know it is illegal to bring alcohol into a maximum security prison?" the assistant warden's voice was cold.

She didn't answer.

"Mrs. Brown, we could easily call the authorities."

She stared at him. Her eyes started to water.

The assistant warden pulled some photos out of an envelope and threw them one at a time on the desk. "Can you explain how Gene Stewart came to have these pictures?"

She looked at the pictures she and Geneo had taken in the barbershop. Her breast showed in one, her hand was in his pants in another. Her skirt was around her waist, Geneo's pants were down, and on and on.

"Mrs. Brown, that is you in the pictures?" He didn't need an answer.

"I don't know what to say!" She was in tears.

"Mrs. Brown," he said again, "we found these things in Stewart's cell."

She watched the security director put the pictures back into the envelope.

"Mrs. Brown, do you know where some of this stuff came from?" he paused. "Mrs. Brown," he said louder.

"Hmm, ah, well," she stumbled, more tears running down her cheek.

"Mrs. Brown," the assistant added, "we know it was impossible for some of these items to get into the prison without someone bringing them in. Some are metal and would have set off the detector in the visiting room."

It was all over. Job, career as a teacher, over.

"Mrs. Brown, you must talk to me."

"I don't know where this stuff all came from." She **dragged** out the sentence. *She didn't know why she said that, she just did.*

"Lookit, Mrs. Brown, you have alcohol in your purse, sexually explicit photos of you and Stewart, and two buckets full of items that had to be carried into this prison."

She was very scared of the assistant warden.

"Yes, Mrs. Brown?" He paused, crossing his arms until she answered.

"Ah, don't you have something to say?" She looked at the security director. The security director didn't move. He didn't shift or flinch.

"Mrs. Brown, I am talking here," the assistant said. "We can handle this two ways, Mrs. Brown. Two ways. Either you give us your resignation now . . ."

As he spoke, the security director pushed a form across his desk. The form was already filled out with the incident and reasons for termination. Only the signature line was blank.

". . . or, Mrs. Brown, we can call the police."

The security director pulled a pen out from a desk drawer and dropped it on the desk in front of her.

"Well, what about the union?" She finally mustered something in her defense.

He looked at her as if she was a little kid. "Mrs. Brown, Mrs. Brown, I do not think your union can help you on this one! Alcohol, pictures, contraband coming in, possibly marijuana."

"I guess not," she managed to mumble.

"My advice to you is resign," he said as he held the pen out to her. "Or we call the police. The media will pick up on this for sure. Do you want that? You are married, right?"

"Yes, I guess you're right," she took the pen from his hand and signed. "May I clean out my desk in the shop?"

"Everything you had in and on your desk is in that box behind you. Everything allowable in a prison, that is. I don't think you'll care about the rest."

"No, I suppose not. No." She reached out for her purse. "What about Gen—I mean, Stewart?"

"Mrs. Brown, Mr. Stewart is going to be in segregation for a long time. Then he'll be transferred. Please just gather your stuff and leave the premises."

"Just go." She picked up her purse and reached to grab the box. "Leave the premises." She was better now. But it was over for her. She wanted to say something, anything to make this all go away, but couldn't.

"Good-bye, Mrs. Brown," the assistant said flatly as she opened the door.

She took one look and left.

After she was gone, the security director spoke up. "Good job," he said, "I was afraid that she wouldn't sign and wouldn't admit anything. If she pressed this with the union, it would take a year to tie up!" He was pleased.

The assistant warden sat down, relaxed. "She's married. She doesn't want the neighbors to know!"

"What about Stewart?"

The assistant warden looked at him as coldly as he had Mrs. Brown. "Give him the ticket, eight days in adjustment and 360-days **program.** And handle it yourself so no one fucks up the process."

"Maximum on everything?"

"Yes. Then call Grangeville Prison, tell them we have a segregation transfer. Talk to Roy and tell him to make Stewart do every bit of his seg time."

"You want to do a seg swap?"

"As fast as you can. I'll tell the Warden. He won't oppose it. Get rid of Mr. Stewart."

⟩━⟩━⟩━⟨

REFLECTIONS

I found out about this incident through some teachers while I was working as head tutor. One of the teachers was the union representative and had tried to convince Mrs. Brown to fight how the resignation was handled.

I saw Geneo again years later at Ridgewood medium prison. He verified what happened. In the meantime, Geneo's name had become supper conversation. I couldn't believe what I heard: attempted escape, busted in the visiting room in front of his family, Amy Brown was pregnant, Geneo was bisexual, he wanted a threesome, he tried to blackmail her, and on and on.

What most impressed me was how no one gave a second thought that Geneo's selfish plans led to all this. When I asked him about it years later at Ridgewood he said only that she shouldn't have wanted to fuck around. Like it was all her fault. He never gave it a second thought. That left me with a bad taste in my mouth. Yet this was prison and that is how this type of stuff occurred. People in prison do not care about what happens to another person, only to themselves.

In the state prison systems that I've been in, sexual relationships between prisoners and staff are a minor problem. Other than Mrs. Brown, I knew of only two other staff women having sexual relations with inmates over the last twenty years.

The prison seems overly concerned with nonsexual relationships between male prisoners and female staff. It seems that everyone assumes that sex is occurring or will be occurring. A female employee got the axe when she received letters from inmates. Contrast this to the following: I had three male teachers who helped me obtain my bachelor's degree. Over time, these three teachers dropped the "Mr." Label, and I got to know two of them on a personal level. I knew about their family, dislikes at work, and voting practices. They even came to me for security advice. It seems that the system treats same-sex staff/prisoner relationships as more acceptable than opposite-sex relations.

Sexual harassment of female staff is more common than staff-prisoner relationships. Most men in prison, especially sex offenders, have been brought up to treat women as sexual objects and will harass them behind their backs—rarely to their faces. Some women guards have complained that they suffer more open sexual harassment from other male guards than from the prisoners.

EDITORS' DISCUSSION OF PART II: PRISON LIFE

The life of the prisoner is perhaps one of the most commonly studied features of prisons. A great deal of attention has been paid to how people who are incarcerated organize and structure the stressful prison society in which they live. The chapters in this section examined the political nature of some prison relationships, the sexual nature of other prison relationships, and the economic exchanges and entrepreneurial endeavors that occur. These features illustrate that prison is in many ways a microcosm of outside society. With the lack of solitude and quiet, combined with strained family ties and friendships on the outside, the prison experience could be considered a source of "cataclysmic" environmental stress (Evans and Cohen, 1987).

Medical Care

One theme in this section was the quality of health care prisoners received by medical staff. To some inmates, prison clinics may seem substandard compared to the quality of care that they are accustomed to in the free world. For others, prison clinics represent the only medical care that they ever receive. One study by Gaes (1994) found that in the federal system, prisoners in the early stages of their sentence made more visits to the clinic. Furthermore, the longer an inmate was incarcerated, visits to the clinic declined (except for those who contracted a terminal illness). A higher number of clinic visits was linked to prisoners experiencing more stress during the earlier stages of confinement (Gaes). More stress and coping problems early in the sentence are also supported by the higher number of disciplinary infractions that inmates receive (Toch and Adams, 1989; Zamble and Porporino, 1988).

A small number of prisoners never required clinic services, while one third of prisoners utilized clinics as often as eleven or twelve times per year (Gaes). A number of reasons exist as to why prisoners made more visits to the clinic than on the streets. First, prisons regulate all prescribed and most over-the-counter medications (such as aspirin and ibuprofen). A second reason is that confinement in close quarters is more likely to spread colds and viruses to more people. Third, some prisoners (such as drug addicts and alcoholics, among others) did not take care of themselves on the streets and their immune systems are less able to fight off viruses and diseases. Finally, at the time they are admitted to prison, compared to that of the general population, prisoners represent a disproportionately higher number of the population who require extensive medical and/or psychiatric care. For example, there are a disproportionately higher number of HIV positive individuals in prison (Alarid and Marquart, 1999). Prisoners may require continuous long-term medical maintenance, such as dialysis for kidney failure, blood sugar for diabetes, and high blood pressure. Given these results, comprehensive guidelines have been established to deliver adequate medical care in large facilities (Anno, 2001). Prison administrators should develop and sustain a more effective orientation program for a prisoner's integration into prison, such as giving greater attention to a prisoner's psychological and medical needs (Gaes).

The Convict Code

To the casual observer, life behind the walls might not always make sense. This is because some elements of prison life are inconsistent with the world outside prison. One of these differences is the intense interpersonal and often confrontational relationships that exist for those who live and work in correctional institutions. Much of this behavior is defined in men's prisons by the unwritten codes of conduct for convicts and officers alike. Although differences occur between facilities and are somewhat dependent on both prisoner characteristics (such as age) and management philosophy, common features of prisoner conduct include:

- loyalty to convicts over staff;
- being a stand-up character, paying debts, honesty with other convicts;
- doing your own time, maintaining your reputation, not whining;
- no "snitching" or **"ratting"**;
- willingness to use force to protect your interests or reputation;
- lack of trust for the guards (Irwin, 1980; Silberman, 1995; Sykes, 1958).

Other pieces of advice for new prisoners include "do no favors and request none" and "volunteer as little information as possible about yourself and your personal life" (Ross and Richards, 2002, 70–71). Adherence to this code of conduct is more likely to be expected of prisoners in maximum security prisons where there is a greater incidence of inmate-on-inmate violence (Harer and Steffensmeier, 1996). It must be pointed out to readers that a book written from a prisoner perspective will reflect this code of conduct and likely portray correctional officers in a stereotypical and negative light (the same situation would apply to inmates in books authored by correctional officers). In either case, it is most instructive if the reader is aware of this dynamic and how it affects daily interactions and perceptions in prison.

The Correctional Officer Subculture

Over the past few decades, a small body of work has sought to define and describe the culture and actions of correctional officers and staff. The officer subculture does correspond in many ways to the convict code (Toch, 1998). For example, officers are taught to protect themselves from manipulation by remaining detached and somewhat aloof in all prisoner communication. In a very definite fashion, formal correctional academy trainees learn that there is a world of difference between "us," the staff, and "them," the convicts. Even when training is conducted in counseling, crisis diffusion, and suicide prevention, the instructor cautions officers not to get too personally involved and to maintain emotional distance from prisoners.

Kelsey Kauffman (1988) has described an "officer code" among line officers that stresses group solidarity by such norms as:

- "Always go to the aid of an officer in distress;
- Don't 'lug' drugs;
- Don't rat;
- Never make a fellow officer look bad in front of inmates;
- Always support an officer in a dispute with an inmate;
- Always support officer sanctions against inmates;
- Don't be a white hat (supervisor);
- Maintain officer solidarity versus all outside groups; and
- Show positive concern for fellow officers." (pp. 86–114)

These values are constructed in part because officers are severely outnumbered by inmates and must be unified to sustain control of a prisoner population. The similarities between the officer and the inmate codes are a value placed on group cohesion among themselves, while at the same time, viewing the "other" as an opponent or rival. Despite the existence of the code, many officers are instrumental in being positive role models and helping first-time offenders adjust to prison life.

Most violence in maximum security institutions tends to be inmate-on-inmate, but the officers are all aware that they too can become victims of assaults and stabbings. One study found that facilities that had unresolved conflict between prison administrators and line officers, coupled with a "visible gang presence" also had significantly higher rates of inmate-on-inmate homicides (Reisig, 2002, 99).

Officers, like the prisoners they monitor, have to work in a stressful environment. Authority and daily activities are regulated, but often the administrative and management presence is not seen on the unit floor, leading to broad discretion on the part of some officers. In many institutions, officers see themselves as alone or unsupported by management. Thus, officers may feel detachment from supervisory and administrative staff, as well as from the inmates.

Uniformed custodial staff, like many law enforcement positions, are often hired and promoted within the same institution. The "us against them" mentality, coupled with promotion from within, can be difficult for sergeants to discipline line officers for misconduct. For example, in a use of force situation, a sergeant may concur that the officer used the proper amount of force. Upon further review, if the captain were to take adverse action, he or she would not only be correcting the officer concerned, but would be ignoring or countering the subordinate command structure.

Society has an expectation that after a period of incarceration, most prisoners will learn their lesson. Ironically, one study found that the prisoners who made the best transition in adjusting to their prison stay were the same ones who had the most difficulty making the second transition back to freedom (Goodstein, 1980). In their ultimate focus on security concerns, prisons lack enough coping strategies that will improve a prisoner's chance for successful reintegration upon release. In sum, the elements of the convict code and the correctional officer subculture would seem only to increase mistrust, anger, and prejudice—none of which is healthy and none of which will reduce recidivism, or the return to criminal behavior. Lozoff (1995, 70), an exoffender, believed that convicts should adopt a new set of unwritten rules: "We need a code that allows people the maximum opportunity to become human beings, not one which keeps us and them stuck in the worst parts of ourselves and our past." Weakening the influence of the convict code and the correctional officer subculture is a complex task. While it may be feasible in a minimum-security institution, breaking down stereotypes becomes exceedingly difficult in a maximum-security prison where security concerns are heightened and there are increasingly more prisoners aligning themselves with gangs. It seems therefore, that to reduce the influences of unhealthy attributes learned in prison, incarceration should be reserved only for individuals who pose a genuine threat to public safety.

QUESTIONS FOR FURTHER STUDY

1. Why is prison considered a microcosm of society?
2. Why is the prison experience considered stressful?
3. What challenges may exist for doctors and nurses in the prison setting?
4. What commonalities exist between the convict code and the officer subculture?
5. Why is it so difficult for administrators to dismantle the influence of the convict code of conduct?

REFERENCES

Alarid, Leanne F., and James W. Marquart (1999). "HIV/AIDS Knowledge and Risk Perception of Adult Women in an Urban Area Jail." *Journal of Correctional Health Care* 6(1): 97–127.

Anno, B. Jaye (2001). *Correctional Health Care: Guidelines for the Management of an Adequate Delivery System–2001 Edition* (NIC #017521). Longmont, CO: National Institute of Corrections.

Evans, G. W., and S. Cohen (1987). "Environmental Stress." Pp. 571–610 in D. Stokols and I. Altman (Eds.), *Handbook of Environmental Psychology.* New York: Wiley.

Gaes, Gerald (1994). "Prison Crowding Research Reexamined." *The Prison Journal* 74: 329–63.

Goodstein, Lynn (1980). "Inmate Adjustment to Prison and the Transition to Community Life." *Journal of Research in Crime and Delinquency 10*: 246, 265.

Harer, Miles D., and Darryl J. Steffensmeier (1996). "Race and Prison Violence." *Criminology 34*: 323–55.

Irwin, John (1980). *Prisons in Turmoil.* Boston: Little, Brown.

Kauffman, Kelsey (1988). *Prison Officers and Their World.* Cambridge, MA: Harvard University Press.

Lozoff, Bo (1995). "Revising the Conduct Code—One Step Further." *Prison Life* (July/August): 32, 69–70.

Reisig, Michael D. (2002). "Administrative Control and Inmate Homicide." *Homicide Studies 6* (1): 84–103.

Ross, Jeffrey Ian, and Stephen C. Richards (2002). *Behind Bars: Surviving Prison.* Indianapolis, IN: Alpha Books.

Silberman, Matthew (1995). *A World of Violence: Corrections in America.* Belmont, CA: Wadsworth.

State of New York (1972). *Attica: The Official Report of the New York State Special Commission on Attica.* New York: Bantam.

Sykes, Gresham (1958). *The Society of Captives: A Study of a Maximum Security Prison.* Princeton, NJ: Princeton University Press.

Toch, Hans (1998). "Hypermasculinity and Prison Violence." Pp. 168–178 in L. H. Bowker (Ed.), *Masculinities and Violence.* Thousand Oaks, CA: Sage.

Toch, Hans, and Kenneth Adams (1989). *Coping: Maladaptation in Prisons.* New Brunswick: Transaction.

Zamble, Edward, and Frank J. Porporino (1988). *Coping, Behavior, and Adaptation in Prison Inmates.* New York: Springer-Verlag.

The Disease of Violence

EDITORS' INTRODUCTION TO PART III

"Prison is a place where the protective custody inmates, generally the
nonviolent intelligent ones, have to live with limited privileges, whereas the
regular inmates, who are generally the violent ones and losers, have all the
privileges permitted."

- JAMES W. HARKLEROAD
(IN JOHNSON AND TOCH, EDS., 2000, 164).

Recall from the previous section that prisonization is the process of prisoners
adapting to the prison through losing contact with their preprison identity and seeing their prison identity as their true identity. The prison
identity is grounded in hatred, learned racism, and a willingness to resort to
violence when necessary.

Part of the prisonization process involves the realization that the definitions of
character—"weak" and "strong"—are opposite in prison to that of outside society.
In outside society, a person earns respect through giving respect, and acting with
kindness and compassion. In prison society, a person earns respect through impos-
ing fear on others and a willingness to use violence. In outside society, a strong person is considered to be a person who thinks before acting. In prison society, a strong
person acts before thinking. In outside society, it is acceptable for a strong person
to express a range of emotions. In prison, rage and hatred are the two primary

emotions expressed openly, while self-pity and fear are the two primary emotions that are felt privately. In outside society, racial diversity and individual differences are embraced. In prison society, problems are avoided by blending in and staying with your own race. In outside society, eye contact is seen as a sign of confidence. In prison society, eye contact is seen as a challenge or threat. In outside society, the reputation of people is generally not harmed if they discount or overlook gossip and rumors about themselves. In prison society, the reputation of a person is at stake every time rumors and gossip surface, even if they were found later never to be said. In outside society, people receive attention through loving and healthy relationships with family, friends, coworkers and pets. In prison, people receive attention through associates, gangs, and negative behavior (e.g., insults, harassment, and violence). In outside society, people have a multitude of options at their disposal to solve problems. In prison, there are few options to settle a variety of situations like unpaid debts, personality clashes, and theft. In outside society, people are encouraged to ask for help from authority figures. In prison, the code of conduct hinders people from asking for help from correctional officers or other staff.

In both prison society and outside society, a strong person is a survivor of his or her world. However, the means by which the person becomes strong in each society differs greatly. According to Harkleroad (2000), many inmates lack control over their actions and react to events based on emotion rather than reason. When emotions override reason, it is considered to be a weakness in character from the standards of outside society. However, many prisoners who react with their emotions believe that through fear and violence, they are strong, because the structure of prison society rewards those behaviors (Harkleroad).

Despite this way of thinking about violence that proliferates the prison, most serious acts of violence are committed by a small number of prisoners targeting other prisoners (McShane, 1996). Fighting and assaultive behavior exists, in part, because significantly higher proportions of people who exhibit predatory behavior live in a stressful environment. The prison is noisy and space is confined without much privacy. Individual temperament, combined with scarce resources, economic instability, a perception of racial inequality, and the need to maintain one's reputation publicly can lead to episodes of unpredictable violence (Lombardo, 1994). Studies have found that while incarcerated, black inmates have significantly higher incidences of assault and fighting than white inmates (Harer and Steffensmeier, 1996). Another study found no racial differences in self-reported rates of fights and arguments (Wright, 1989), nor were there any racial differences as to how likely offenders would be to respond violently to a confrontation with another prisoner (Alarid, 2000).

Individual-level violence exists as a conflict between two prisoners, or between a prisoner and a correctional officer. The most common type of conflict occurs between two prisoners. Some of the causes of personal conflict are unpaid gambling debts, disagreements, and responding to rumors. As we read about previously, the rumor network, intimidation, gossip, and manipulation are inherent parts of the prison society as a way to fill idle time and to lessen deprivations. Individual-level prison violence occurs as a means to solve personal conflicts, or to establish or maintain a reputation.

COLLECTIVE VIOLENCE

On the other hand, collective violence involves two or more groups in conflict. The groups in conflict typically vary by race/ethnicity (for example, black and white prisoners having racial conflict), gang membership (for example, the **Gangster Disciples** and **Aryans** fighting about drug territory), or by prisoners protesting against prison administrators. Collective violence occurs primarily because of interpersonal conflict among "connected" inmates. Connected prisoners have many close friends or associates who are present to provide back-up support during the conflict.

Members of prison gangs are an example of groups that are intensely connected. Prison gangs are classified as a type of security threat group (STG) because the group jeopardizes the safety and security of the prison institution (Alarid and Cromwell, 2002). STGs desire to earn a profit through intimidation, violence, and illegitimate activities designed to give the group money, power, and a more comfortable prison existence while incarcerated. Many STGs also have an ideology built around racial hatred and self-protection. STGs have been known to compete in drug trafficking, prostitution, gambling, extortion, and theft. Larger gangs also establish "turf" in certain areas of the prison where only their members are allowed to use such things as weightlifting equipment, handball courts, or to eat at certain tables in the chow hall (Knox, 2000). Groups who compete for power and profit are at war with each other inside the prison. Because of this, gang members are more likely than nongang members to be involved in disciplinary infractions and prison misconduct (Cannon, 2001). With an ongoing concern about numbers, some gangs are engaged in active recruitment for members. For the last decade, gang membership inside prison has been on the rise. It was estimated that in 1999, one fourth of all male prisoners in state institutions were gang members, with a significantly higher level of gang involvement in maximum security level units (Knox, 2000, 5).

SOLITARY CONFINEMENT

Chapter 14 in this section discusses what happens when prisoners commit a major infraction while incarcerated that may jeopardize institutional security. Current managerial practices involve isolating violent and/or disruptive prisoners from the general population. Prisoners are socially deprived from contact for twenty-three hours per day with the goal of violence reduction. Temporary housing for management problem prisoners is known as administrative segregation. Many prisoners in administrative segregation suffer from the inability to trust anyone and thus feel the need to use violence as a self-protection device (Gilligan, 1996, 156). Long-term administrative segregation in maximum and supermax facilities seems to have psychological consequences that extend beyond the initial problems of institutional security (Haney, 1993). To date,

there are no empirical studies that examine the impact of administrative segregation on recidivism and future criminal behavior compared to the rest of
the prisoner population.

REFERENCES

Alarid, Leanne F. (2000). "Along Racial
and Gender Lines: Jail Subcultures in
the Midst of Racial
Disproportionality." *Corrections
Management Quarterly* 4(1), 8–19.

Alarid, Leanne F., and Paul F. Cromwell
(Eds.) (2002). *Correctional Perspectives:
Views from Academics, Practitioners, and
Prisoners.* Los Angeles: Roxbury.

Cannon, Devin D. (2001). *The Effect of
Gang Membership on Prison Rule
Violations.* Unpublished doctoral
dissertation.

Gilligan, James (1996). *Violence: Reflections
on a National Epidemic.* New York:
Vintage Books.

Haney, Craig (1993). "Infamous
Punishment: The Psychological
Consequences of Isolation." *The
National Prison Project,* (Spring),
3–7, 21.

Harkleroad, James W. (2000). "Prison Is a
Place." pp. 163–64 in R. Johnson and
H. Toch (Eds.), *Crime and Punishment:
Inside Views.* Los Angeles: Roxbury.

Harer, Miles D., and Darrell J.
Steffensmeier (1996). "Race and
Prison Violence." *Criminology, 34*(3),
323–55.

Knox, George W. (2000). "A National
Assessment of Gangs and Security
Threat Groups (STGs) in Adult
Correctional Institutions: Results of
the 1999 Adult Corrections Survey."
Journal of Gang Research, 7(3), 1–45.

Lombardo, Lucien X. (1994). "Stress,
Change, and Collective Violence in
Prison." Pp. 291–305 in M. C.
Braswell, R. H. Montgomery, and
L. X. Lombardo, (Eds.). *Prison Violence
in America,* 2ᵈ ed. Cincinnati, OH:
Anderson.

McShane, Marilyn D. (1996). "Violence."
Pp. 471–475 in Marilyn McShane and
Frank P. Williams (Eds.). *Encyclopedia of
American Prisons.* New York: Garland.

Wright, Kevin N. (1989). "Race and
Economic Marginality in Explaining
Prison Adjustment." *Journal of Research
in Crime and Delinquency, 26*(1), 67–89.

13

Racism and Hatred

"They call me a racist, I am only trying to survive in a jungle"
ARYAN BROTHER
NOVEMBER 1999

"All whites are blue-eyed devils."
MUSLIM BROTHER
DECEMBER 1985

"We all are brothers in the eyes of God."
K. C. CARCERAL
JULY 1994

"Cell search, Washington. Step out while I search your cell." With Sergeant Pot, everything was an order and everything was official. He never questioned authority and blindly followed the Department of Corrections line. He was a cold, calculating, power-hungry sergeant. Everything was *I'm the officer; you're the inmate.*

Pot would have made a good German soldier in World War II. He never questioned authority. He meticulously carried out every command given him. He had the rule book memorized and knew he could enter any cell at any time and find multiple violations of the pettiest rule.

He came from a small town and had never seen a black person in his life until prison. He never expressed racist attitudes but he acted in certain ways so that black inmates would talk back to him. Then he would write them up for the "3 Ds" of rule violations: disrespect, disobeying orders, and disruptive conduct.

"What did I do?" Washington was dark-skinned, short, and solidly built like a linebacker. He wasn't the smartest man, but he knew how to do his time. He left everyone alone. If he wasn't at **rec,** he was in his cell.

"I said step out of the cell!" Pot commanded.

"And I understand dat. I'm only asking ya why ya searchin' my cell?"

"Because it has not been searched in awhile. Now step out of the cell!" Sergeant Pot waited.

"You ain't searchin' no other cells. Why me?" Washington said, standing by his bed.

"I told you why!" What Pot did not tell him was that there was no particular reason to search his cell. They just didn't like him. Besides, Minks, the officer working with Pot, seemed scared and lacked experience with blacks. So Pot had decided to show the junior officer how it was done. "Are you refusing an order?"

"No, I ain't refusin' no damn order," Washington fired back.

"I'm giving you a direct order to leave your cell," Pot said, taking one step into the cell. He knew Minks was behind him.

"A-r-e y-o-u d-i-s-o-b-e-y-i-n-g?" Pot asked, slow and loud.

Well, by this time others were watching.

"Stay in your cells or in the **dayroom,**" Dave ordered.

Now Pot's authority was being challenged publicly. He was not going to let any inmate, especially a black one, make him look bad.

"No, I ain't disobeyin' and I ain't your motherfuckin' kid for you to talk to like dat. I ain't slow 'n dumb. I just ask you, why me? You ain't searching no other cells. You never search these honkies' cells. Why you want to fuck with me?" Washington still didn't leave his cell.

"I am not fucking with you, I am ordering you out of the cell now!"

"You are fuckin' with me," Washington replied in the same tone. "I don't fuck with no one on the motherfuckin' unit, and you can't be fuckin' with me." By this time Washington was shouting.

"Are you threatening me?" Pot shouted back.

"No, I ain't threat'nin' you. You threat'nin' me by coming in here like 'dis."

"You sure? Sounds like you're threatening me," Pot yelled.

"I don't fuck with no one until they fuck with me."

"There. See, you're threatening me." Pot said triumphantly.

By this time communications were at their worst: total breakdown.

"The only way I am threat'nin' you is if you're fuckin' with me. I **ain't no punk.**"

"Okay, Mr. Washington, okay." Pot moved out of the cell and back to the desk. "Officer Minks, watch him. He is not to leave his cell or close his door."

Mink stood there and watched every move Washington made. He backed against the wall so no one could get behind him, and now and then looked down the hall towards Pot. *What the hell you leaving me down here by myself?*

Pot was on the phone. "Captain, I have an inmate, Washington, down here who will not let me search his cell and has been threatening me." More conversation came over the receiver. "I gave him four direct orders, then he threatened me."

"Yes. Others are watching and he is trying to lead them in. Instigating a potential riot."

⫸⫷⫸⫷⫸⫷

In minutes the captain and two other officers showed up. They marched directly to Washington's cell.

"What's the problem, Washington?" the captain demanded. He really did not want an answer at this point.

"I asked Pot why he was fuckin' with me."

"Sergeant Pot did not tell it to me that way," the captain stated taking out his cuffs.

"He's a damn liar," Washington's voice was suddenly high-pitched.

The captain was there for only one reason. "We can do this two ways. You get cuffed now and walk, or we carry you. Choose now," he commanded.

By that time, the two officers that came with him had moved into the little cell. That made the cell a full house. Pot stood in the doorway smiling and Minks still leaned against the wall.

I guess Washington realized he couldn't win. Pot had set him up. So he walked to seg. Pot walked back to the desk with his shoulders out. He kept Mink down by the desk all night except for the one round they made. He was explaining proper procedure.

The dayroom was full of talk about Washington. "Dat motherfuckin' honkie got to ride another brother out," Zoom stated with disgust.

"Yeah, so far the past three months, he ride out eight brothers and one honkie," Big-Man complained.

After the fifth time I heard the word *honkie*, I left, once again reminded about how white I was.

Near the end of their shift, Pot and Minks made a round together. At least they tried to make it look like a round, but they headed directly for the dayroom. They had overheard the conversations. Everyone lowered their voices to whispers as the two officers neared.

"What's going on back here?" Pot broke in.

"Nothin'," Zoom retorted. Heads turned back toward the TV.

"Is this a gang meeting?" Pot demanded. Minks stood next to him, looking around but saying nothing.

"No," another black inmate answered.

"All I see is black men in here." Pot's statement was important since gang meetings never occurred when members of the opposite race were around.

Everyone stared at the TV.

"I suggest we return to our cells," Pot commanded, "before I have to lock up more people."

"We're just watching TV," Skin replied.

"Doesn't look that way to me. Now I suggest we break it up a little." What he was really saying was: *Clear the damn dayroom.*

A couple of brothers walked back to their cells. Others came out into the hallway. Someone said, "Motherfucking honkie wants to lock up all us niggas!"

"Who said that?" Pot spun around and saw four blacks entering their cells. No one bothered answering him; they just emptied the hallway. Pot and Minks stood by themselves.

⋙⋘⋙⋘

Very few people in prison ever associated with others outside their own race. However, I was one of the few white prisoners who associated with some of the black prisoners, although I sometimes got tired of their complaints about whites. One day I was at the picnic table in the rec yard when Shorty-D, K'billa, and Rosh came over. Rosh was a racist, but I was okay with Shorty-D and K'billa. I had met Shorty-D in the hobby shop. He had a mellow personality and got his nickname because he was barely five feet tall. K'billa was not much taller than Shorty-D, but he had more of a temper. Hence the nickname K'billa.

"Hey, Anonymous," K'billa adjusted his prayer cap. "What's up?"

"Oh nothing. Same stuff, just relaxing."

He sat down. "I'm getting tired of this place."

"You and me both," I replied, smoking my cigarette.

"How do you do it?" he asked.

"I have no choice," I wondered where the conversation was going.

"Man, I am so **tired** of these racist guards and these **boot licken'** niggas, damn."

I didn't realize I was in for the speech of my life.

"If it wasn't for the white man, Anonymous, his white courts, his white jury, and his white racist prison guards, I would not be in this mess."

As a white man, how was I supposed to reply to this?

"It's a conspiracy against us, my brother," Rosh added.

"Yeah, it is," Shorty-D agreed.

"What conspiracy, Rosh?" I asked.

"It's a conspiracy against the black man. From international bankers controlled by the whites, to the white president, through the Jews in America and overseas, down to the drugs on the corner. They want to kill us all." he paused.

"He's right, Anonymous," K'billa replied. "You all been killing us since slavery and still want to."

"You all," I smiled.

"Yes, y-o-u a-l-l," he fired back. His face was serious.

Rosh spoke to me, choosing his words carefully. "Come on, Anonymous. You know. The white man has been murdering and locking up brothers since he brought us here. You came over to our motherland, the land where life began. Where kings ruled. You took us from our homes. The white man enslaved us, and now he murders us and puts us in prison." His voice rang out and he banged his fist on the tabletop.

I shook my head. I didn't want war with three Muslims.

K'billa cut in. "And since the motherland was the beginning of all life according to the holy books, we as the founders should have our place. We should be worshipped as kings and queens."

"We are the dominant people who should control the earth, not be imprisoned on it." Shorty-D said proudly.

"You all ever study Hitler?" I asked, hoping they might pick up on my subtle suggestion.

"That racist whore. But at least he killed his own kind. Jews, too! Even Hitler was part of the conspiracy," Rosh answered.

"He was?"

"Man, right after Hitler got killed," Rosh stated, "what happened? America brought the Jews over here and gave them the media. Then they brought over those crazy scientists who experimented on people to experiment on us."

Again I could only shake my head.

"Tell 'em, Rosh," K'billa said.

"Who did they experiment on?"

"On us brothers!" K'billa returned.

"When?" I asked looking at Rosh.

"Man, I don't know the exact date," he said, "but they conspired. Then they put drugs in the ghetto to kill us. The CIA, FBI, international bankers, all of them."

"Well, if you know drugs are so bad, why not stop using them?" I knew this was a simple question to a complex problem.

"Man, the reason brothers don't is because they are not enlightened like us."

"Enlightened?"

"Tell 'em, brother Rosh," Shorty-D fired at him.

"Yeah, all part of the conspiracy. The brother ain't got no schools to teach him. If he had he wouldn't use no drugs."

"They don't teach nothin' but the white man's way."

K'billa spoke up. "That college stuff you're doing, it ain't teaching you the truth."

"How many courses you take about brothers?" Rosh added.

"Well, it's not all about brothers alone," I calmly replied. *This shit's gonna give you a heart attack some day.* I smiled politely.

"Yeah, but it's white man's thought," Rosh threw out.

"Well, it's Western education."

"Yeah, see," Rosh replied equating white man and Western together. "Now how many courses about brothers?"

"Let's see, I took two semesters of black history, two semesters of Indian culture, one semester on minority groups. Then criminology, and two courses of sociology," I listed.

"Yeah, well. Well, how many courses were taught by those people?" Rosh paused. "Did a brother teach you black history?"

"No," I replied.

"Exactly," Shorty-D said.

"It's part of the conspiracy," Rosh added again.

"I'm not saying it's perfect, Rosh, but nothing in the world is perfect," I replied.

"Allah, the creator is," K'billa interjected.

He had me stumped on that one. "What we have to do is get some guns and kill the government," Shorty-D added.

"Violence begets violence." I quoted a well-known saying.

"This country was founded on killing and revolt," Rosh interrupted. "Look at the Revolutionary War."

"By all means necessary. We have to do it by all means necessary," K'billa shouted.

"Yeah, being peaceful hasn't got us nowhere. Killing the conspirators, that's what we have to do." Rosh pounded the tabletop.

"You mean killing whites?"

"If they are a conspirator, yes."

"Well, are you going to kill me?" I asked. "I'm white, blond-haired, and blue-eyed."

"Are you a conspirator?" Rosh asked.

"Hell, I'm locked up like you."

"You do represent the blue-eyed devil we were warned of," professor Shorty-D calmly stated.

Oh boy, it's time to get out of this conversation.

"No, you have understanding . . ." Rosh said, ". . . Only we have to reeducate you."

I'm not touching that with a ten-foot pole.

"See, Anonymous," K'billa said, "you're all right."

"Yeah," I replied. *Damn, this was just like a white guy telling a black guy that he has black friends.*

"But if you were a racist white you would have to die," Rosh added coldly.

At this point I stood up.

"Yeah, Anonymous, we don't mind talking with a white boy who has knowledge like you," Shorty-D said.

I looked at each of them in turn. "You know something. I am tired of hearing that racist slur 'white boy.'"

They looked back at me, astonished. *What? Who is this honkie?*

"That ain't no racial term, Anonymous," K'billa said sarcastically.

"It don't mean that," Rosh said.

"To you maybe, but I find it very disrespectful. First you separate me as a white, then you call me boy," I replied.

"But it ain't racist," Shorty-D insisted. *"White boy, white boy, white boy"* was in his eyes.

"It is how you're taking it," Rosh argued. *Honkie, honkie, honkie. . . .*

I ignored him. "I'm getting my soda before they call us in."

━━◇━◇━◇━━

REFLECTIONS

In prison, the racial divide is always present. America entered the new millenium boasting about racial harmony, but its prisons still remain racial hate factories. We're stuck in the time warp of the '50s and '60s. Racism still determines where you go, how you go, who you go with, what you do when you arrive, who you arrive with, and what you say when finally there. It is a constant part of everyone's prison life. It took me fifteen years of living around blacks to be comfortable around them, as I'm sure the same was true for how most Black prisoners felt about whites. Both sides believe the other will sell them out.

There are two types of racism in prison: racism between prisoners and staff, and racism among prisoners. The relationship between prisoners and staff is different since staff has the power. Staff are treated generally with more respect. However, behind their backs staff are hated. The two-faced mentality thrives in prison. Also the racial mix of staff has a great influence on how prisoners are treated.

I have had the luxury of being in prisons that were controlled by mostly white staff and the hassles of being in a prison controlled by mostly black staff. Overall, if whites make up most of the staff who deal with prisoners on a daily basis, then blacks suffer more racism. For blacks in a white-staffed prison, racism is a daily complaint. That just seems to be how the system works and how America works.

One idea that transcends racism is hate. I realize they go hand in hand. Yet of the many factors that influence racism in a prisoner's daily life, such as upbringing, income, location, and education, learned hatred has the greatest influence. As hatred increases in the institutional setting, racism seems to increase also. To put it another way, when prisoners are happier at a particular prison because of its design, structure, and benefits, then racism recedes. In prisons where prisoners have more things to hate, racism becomes much more intense.

Hatred is an evil seed that grows in many forms. One can feel hatred toward staff, other prisoners, food served, clothing issued, even the temperature of the hot water in a cell. *It's hate!* Hatred of being poor, seeing others gaining more benefits, down to hatred of one's self. *Amazing, all this hate.* Hatred for all the rules, unequal enforcement, hatred of strip searches, hatred of showers where one gets naked in the presence of thirty others, hatred of a cellie. *And it still continues.* Hatred for being unemployed, hatred of the rec layout, weight equipment, old beat-up basketballs and baseballs, hatred of the lack of property. Hatred of lazy staff, hatred of not being answered, and hatred of the cheap soap handed out to wash with. Hatred of the schedules or lack of amount of time, hatred of the chow-hall seating policy. Hatred of the food items sold at canteen, the prices charged, and cleaning supplies given out. *Even hatred for the type of toilet paper.* These and many more make the list of what men hate about prison. Prisons are hate factories. Their product: *hatred!*

To understand prison is to understand hate. I did not know the true meaning of hate until I got to prison. I have learned to think of it like the disease of alcoholism. It transcends all lines in prison. Once the seed is planted it is passed on and on to new prisoners. This hatred drives racism.

But there are other factors besides hatred that drive racism. For a start, there is the self-imposed segregation. All prisons are legally desegregated. However, staff and prisoners help segregate the population. When I was first locked up, a black prisoner and a white prisoner were never housed in the same cell. It was frowned upon. If it did occur voluntarily (since that was the only way it would occur back then) no one expected that the two could be associates or friends. Either one prisoner was taking advantage of the other or they were having sex. Nowadays, it is indiscriminately done since almost all prisons are double-celled. This fuels the hatred and racial fire.

Next, in any prison that allows prisoners to sit where they want in the chow hall, there is an unwritten rule where whites and blacks sit. If forced seating occurs, fights will break out between men of different races at the tables. Or men will just simply refuse to sit at a particular table.

Then there is religion. The Muslim movement was limited when I was first incarcerated, yet with the influx of black prisoners, the religion has spread. Muslims have directly and indirectly affected the mainstream life of prison. For example, in the past, prisons regularly served pork, but nowadays it is unheard of. One outcome is the conflict between some Christians and some Muslims. At least some of the people in each group feel they have the proper, established route to God, and that anyone else is incorrect. This helps build more tension.

Then there is outright verbal disrespect expressed socially. Verbal disrespect has a long history in the white culture and from white hate groups. Now in the new millennium, there also is outright disrespect toward whites verbalized by black men within the prison walls. In my experience, people of any race can be prejudiced.

The game of racism also plays into prison funding. If racial hatred and racial violence is maintained in the prisons, then the central administration, the guard unions, and the support staff can cry to the media and to the legislature that they need more funding. This equates to more guards and more overtime for greater control.

Finally, many prisoners believe that punishments for rule infractions are unequally handed out. Some inmates believe that in prisons run by white staff, white prisoners actually get harsher punishments for the same infractions. They say this is because the white administration and the white staff assume that rehabilitation is possible only for white inmates. Blacks, they assume, will continue to commit crimes and cannot be rehabilitated. The result is that these inmates assume that whites are punished more harshly for rule infractions because they are expected to obey the rules. In contrast, blacks are considered hopeless, so they are expected to get into trouble.

I don't know for certain. But I have been in prisons where a large majority of staff were black, and it seemed to me that punishment was handed out somewhat more equally.

Of course, many blacks believe the opposite. They believe that whites are given a break because of their skin color. Whatever the truth is, the fact still remains that racism on both sides exists in how punishment is handed out. *This spurs more hatred.*

Finally, in an environment that has little distinction between its members, awareness of skin color is heightened. One of the first things other prisoners taught me was how white I was! During my first years of lockup, I could not escape the fact that, in other prisoners' eyes, I was white. The black prisoners reminded me daily, almost hourly, how white I was. The white prisoners reminded me how black the black prisoners were. The racial lines were continually drawn and handed to the new fish.

I learned that racism really had little to do with physical features and was more of a mind-set. My mind was not yet set to view my new living environment as white or black. I had to be converted by the other established prisoners. Once I put it all together, I decided that the theme song of the prison was a tune from a popular children's TV show:

I hate you,
You hate me,
We are all one racist family!

14

Segregation

"Isolation, deprivation, and restraining do not seem to harm a human being
and I see no reason to encourage different treatment."

STAFF PSYCHOLOGIST
NOVEMBER 1997

"Punishment is used to deter improper behavior."

WARDEN JOHNSON
JULY 1993

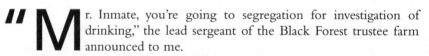

"**M**r. Inmate, you're going to segregation for investigation of
drinking," the lead sergeant of the Black Forest trustee farm
announced to me.

"I didn't do nothing!" *Famous last words of any prisoner going to lockup.*

"This is Ridgewood Control. We have two prisoners from the Black Forest
farm designated for segregation. They will arrive within the next ten minutes."

"Step into the empty shower, please," a Ridgewood guard said to me.
"Another officer will be here in a minute to process you."

Mad and depressed, I got into the shower. I hated this shit. I was mad at them
for hauling me off. I was mad at myself for falling into the trap of the prison game.

I heard a familiar voice. "Anonymous, what did you do?"

I looked at the officer. "Gaiter. You work here now?" Officer Gaiter and I talked a little until my clothes were taken away. In case I'd forgotten, that, and the search of my butt-naked body, reminded me I was in prison. Then I got segregation-issue orange linen. Seg prisoners wear a different color than GP prisoners to tell the two groups apart; the bright orange color stands out in the event of an attempted escape.

Eventually I was secured in **TLU** (temporary lock-up unit). The state places you in TLU while it determines if you broke any rules. But once you're in TLU, you can be pretty certain that you'll get some kind of ticket for a rule infraction. So no matter how hopeful I was, I knew that after I was found guilty of the charges, I would spend some time in **adjustment segregation (ADJ),** and then I would be transferred to **program segregation.**

⋙⋘⋙⋘⋙

TLU, day one. *Single room all by myself. It is quiet, so beautifully quiet. Ah, the heating vent, that's all I hear.*

I paced and thought this way for about an hour. Then the trap door on the cell door opened.

"Here's your bedding. Sheet, blanket, pillow case, pillow, washcloth, towel, and roll of toilet paper."

"Can I get a toothbrush and toothpaste?"

"The cart comes around with that stuff Tuesday and Thursday. We don't hand it out now," the voice mumbled.

Great. Today is Saturday. Another reminder that I don't even control simple things.

I couldn't see him then or any other time. All I ever saw were hands. Some hands were big, some were small, some voices deep, some high; but I knew that they all came from keepers who were depriving and restraining me.

TLU, day two. I awoke to more silence. I had gone from driving to work in a van every day, answering the phone, programming computers, doing account receivables, and writing out paychecks, to being locked in a cell. Prison is all or nothing; no gray. I was now enjoying the nothing. Everything gone. No one to talk to.

TLU, day three. I paced. Twelve, no thirteen steps to the door, turn around, thirteen steps to the smoked-glass window. I did ten laps turning to my right, then ten laps turning to my left. Just me and my cement surroundings. I had already gone over what happened ten thousand times: I am in segregation. They won't tell me why but I know. After three straight hours of pacing, lunch came. My ankles were sore and I felt dazed.

TLU, day four. Finally I could get my toothbrush and toothpaste. I brushed for about an hour. I paced until I could not take it anymore. I lay down and looked at the ceiling. Needs to be cleaned. Spiders were in the corners and I was missing my old life. I had been tired of doing what I once did, but now I was willing to take anything over this. I missed my shit. I enjoyed my property. Here in TLU, I had nothing. No TV, no radio, no books, no stamps, writing paper or envelopes, no comb, no deodorant or soap. No razor, no mirror, no shoes, no socks. I didn't even have a paper clip to bend into different shapes. My mind was now entering the mental trip.

TLU, day five. Breakfast, then lunch. My segregation slippers were wearing out. The heel on the right side was wearing down faster than the left. *I better turn to the left more often than the right.*

"Hey, cell fourteen, you want a shower?"

I must have been hearing things; he probably wants the other cell.

"Hey," the voice shouted again and someone pounded on my door. "You want a shower or not?"

Hey, he is talking to me! "Yeah," I yelled out. "You got soap?"

I went to the shower in handcuffs. Most guards would allow a man twenty or thirty minutes in the metal shower stall. That was the only break from the cell.

TLU, day six. "Man, I wish I had a cigarette," I said out loud. "Fuck this shit. Hell, I'm talking to myself." My beard was growing out because I had no razor. My hair was a mess because I couldn't be issued a comb. I was tired of pacing. *Time, too much time.* The days dragged now. I was constantly talking to myself and thinking about what was going to happen.

TLU, day seven. "Okay, 643 bricks make up this cell. No, no, 648. Now, each brick is one foot long, twelve going that way, eight that way. Come on, Mr. Inmate, in school you could figure out volume on paper. How come the numbers are getting too big to focus in your head? Okay, okay, twelve that way, eight that way, toilet's on its own wall. Figure the volume of the cube, then remove the area for the toilet. I can do this."

TLU, day eight. A voice from behind the door. "Hey, Inmate, you're going to court. Get ready."

"Now? I don't even have a ticket."

"At the desk they said you're going to court. Just get ready."

The voice was gone.

Despite all its glory, court was a simple process. They spoke, then I spoke. My goal was to make it sound like I was as innocent as Jesus; their job was to ignore me and find guilt. I got eight days in adjustment segregation and ninety days program segregation. Well, it had been a nice break from the cell.

ADJ, day one. I was back in my cell. Adjustment. Eight days of nothingness. "Okay, today is Monday, no wait, today is Saturday. No, I went to court today, it has to be Monday. They don't have court on Saturday. Damn! I did ten days in TLU and forgot two days." I spent a couple of hours pondering this. "How could I miss two days?" There was no answer. "Okay, today is Monday, eight days is Tuesday. I'll be out Tuesday. No, no, I will be out Wednesday because Monday is the starting date. Monday is day zero. It doesn't count. Wednesday will be my out-date."

ADJ, day two. "Damn, I wish I had a cigarette. No smoking today," I reminded myself. I paced.

ADJ, day three. This was actually the twelfth day in a cell with nothing. *No one to talk to, nothing to read, no nothing.* Even the guards made a point not to talk to me. The cells around me were empty. Everything was concrete. The bed was formed from the floor. No wall hooks, no shelves, no table to eat from. There was no mirror and no hot water in the sink.

The trapdoor on the cell door opened. "Inmate, here's your hygiene bag." A plastic bag fell through the door.

"Officer, wait," I yelled out.

"What?" he asked.

As I looked through the trapdoor, I just saw his knees, but then I spotted a pile of magazines and books on his cart. "Let me get something to read."

"You're in adjustment segregation. You can't have anything!" He said this so easily.

"Come on, dude. When I was in TLU I got nothing. I have been in here for twelve days. What's a magazine going to hurt?" I was in my very politest mode. I didn't want to piss him off.

"Sorry, can't do it!" The trap closed on my face.

I sat back on my bed. *These motherfuckers, one simple magazine. It isn't like I'm asking for the world.*

However, in their eyes I was. The point of adjustment was to teach me a lesson. It was to take everything from me. It didn't matter that I had previously done all those days in TLU. That was the past. I am now in adjustment so I get nothing.

ADJ, day four. Once again I paced, doing what every other human being in the cell had done before me. I examined the floor as I walked. I studied every inch. I could see from the dark path worn into the floor that I was following the footsteps of others.

By now I was fully into the mental trip of segregation. I was talking to myself all day long. It sounded better out loud. I actually talked to myself, answered back, then started another conversation in my mind. It was easy! "Two times two is four. Four times two is eight. Eight times two is sixteen. Who is on second." *No, Who is on first!* "Right. What is on second."

ADJ, day five. I examined that cell like an adolescent discovering his body. "Hmm, got a crack running up to the ceiling in the left corner facing the cell door. Starts two blocks from the floor and runs past the wannabe window."

Right then I discovered something exciting. The smoked glass in the window had a small edge that was clear so I could see out. "Oh boy, a kid in a candy shop!"

I got up and looked through the edge. "Man, this ain't easy," I told the wall. I had to turn my head about a quarter to the left, tip it forward. "Damn, corner would have to be right there." I ground my forehead into the corner as tight as I could. "A little more."

Bingo, I could see outside. There was the smoked glass, then the sill with bars, then clear glass. I could see the grass and part of the walkway leading to the segregation building. *Wow, this is exciting.* "Four dandelions, a piece of paper, and something that looks like dog poop!" *No. There aren't any dogs in prison. Ain't poop.* After a careful analysis, I decided it had to be a stick from a tree. *Some tree lost part of a branch. It must have floated around and made it to the grass in front of my window!* I stared and stared, but just as quickly as this got exciting, it got old. I went back to pacing.

ADJ, day six. By this time I had no set schedule for sleeping. A man's body goes through many changes in segregation. For one, you sleep whenever possible. So you end up sleeping lightly during the day and pacing at night. You feel tired all the time.

"Breakfast." This morning the guard left the trapdoor open, which meant I could see what was outside my cell. *Wow, a hallway!*

There was no one across the hallway, but they had moved someone in the cell next door. Suddenly I heard another voice.

"Hey, next door."

"Yeah," I was overjoyed to have another person to talk to. *Thank you, God, for this gift. I will never cuss again. Well, almost never.*

"What you doing down here?"

"Eight and ninety, you?"

"Eight days, that's it."

"What you do?"

"Fighting. You?"

"Drinking at camp." I replied.

"Man, you fucked up!" He was one of the many who told me that over and over again.

"Yeah, what can I say?"

Our conversation was interrupted by the guard. "Give me your tray." The trap closed.

Suddenly I heard banging on the wall and dude's voice again.

"I can't hear you!" I screamed at the cell door.

"Go . . . door crack."

"What?"

"Bottom . . . door . . . crack . . ."

I knelt down on the floor by the door and put my ear to the crack. Each door had about one inch between the concrete and the bottom of the door.

"Can you hear me now?" His voice rang out.

I turned my head and spoke into the crack. "Yeah, I can now."

We talked for a while. I would turn my head to hear, then turn it back to talk. Eventually, I just laid across the floor. Every now and then I saw footsteps going past my door.

There is nothing really to talk about in segregation, so men just talk about anything. Stuff that happened two days ago, stuff that happened two years ago, their future. They never talk about being in the cell with nothing. You do everything in your power to avoid the here and now!

ADJ, day seven. That morning I was actually somewhat hopeful. From the way my neighbor talked I knew he was a brother, but segregation is about the only place in the prison where racial boundaries are ignored. Each man is just happy to have someone else to talk with.

"Hey, next door," I yelled into the crack below my celldoor. I waited but heard nothing. I yelled again, then again. Finally, I pounded on the wall a couple of times and yelled again. There was nothing. *Must be asleep,* I thought.

I tried again later. Still nothing. My neighbor was gone. The officers apparently moved him out. *Nobody to talk to.* "Welcome back to prison, Anonymous. Never get comfortable with something they can take," I said to myself.

ADJ, day eight. To be on the safe side, I called to my neighbor a few more times. Still no one answered. I looked out the edge of my window at the grass. I talked to myself and I paced. "Tomorrow I start my first day of program, ninety more days. If I'm cool, maybe forty-five." *Man, this is a long day.*

ADJ, day nine. Finally. I knew I'd get moved today. My nineteenth straight day, TLU or ADJ, it was all the same. My beard had grown out. My hair was a mess. I couldn't sleep anymore. I was tired of watching mysterious hands give me my food. The only thing I thought about was that it would be over soon. "I ain't gonna lose my mind in here!"

The longest day in adjustment is the last day.

If you were a troublemaker while in ADJ or you were being transferred back to maximum GP, they'd keep you in the main segregation building. If you were cool and didn't snap by banging on your door or cussing at the officers whenever they came by, they'd move you to the program segregation building. "Inmate, get your stuff ready, you're moving." The voice came over the intercom system. *Like I had a lot of stuff to gather up!*

❖❖❖❖❖

I knew I would have to go through the three steps of program segregation. Usually if you were good, they'd cut time from your stay in program. *Usually.* You could end up doing two-thirds of your program time.

Your time also depended on where you were. Some institutions let a prisoner out of segregation early, but then they'd house him in another building commonly called **reconstructive learning.** That was program segregation all over again with a different name.

They could keep a guy forever in those buildings.

Over in program seg, I figured I'd get three showers and an hour of recreation three times a week. *It was the times out of the cell that counted.* Then after I had about a third of my time in, I'd get my reading material and mail. My property!

Program segregation was a mixed blessing. In program they mixed people together. They didn't care who you got put in with. If you got stuck with an idiot, you could get into trouble for his mistakes.

I was in with an older guy named Wilson. Wilson had mental problems. Wilson was paranoid and assumed everyone was out to get him. I discovered this about the third day we were cellies.

As the guard walked by, he started kicking the cell door. "Hey, where's my medication?"

"We're getting it. Takes time."

When you're in segregation, time is different. Every minute seems like an hour. Within ten minutes, Wilson was snapping. He wanted his bump. The state had strung him out on downers and every day his internal clock rang *bump time.* He purposely saved his breakfast food so his stomach was empty. Then he'd get his pills and wait about half an hour to eat. The medication would kick in and he would lay back.

He hit the door furiously. "I want my goddamn medication."

"Hey," the officer replied, "don't talk to me like that."

He ignored what the guard had just told him. "Every fucking morning you bring my medication late. I want my pills."

"You know I can write you a ticket for talking like that?"

"Write me a ticket. It'll get me out of here. At least in segregation they don't treat me like this!"

"Like what?"

"They bring my pills with every meal right there on the spot."

"We do it different here." The guard was calm.

"Yeah, you punks fuck with a motherfucker to piss him off."

"If you can't handle this, how do you expect to make it when you're out?"

"What the hell does that have to do with me being released? On the streets ain't no dumbass, cocksucking guard gonna' give me that shit! I'll take it myself, fool." Wilson was really wound up now.

"You need to calm down."

"You need to learn who you're dealing with. 'What am I going to do when I get released?' You dumbass guards always say stupid stuff. Of all the ignorant remarks. You just want to run something, you bitch. Now get my shit."

The guard looked so astonished that Wilson had spoken that way that I figured he was a rookie. He even gave me a look, like I might have had a string attached to my cellie to somehow make him speak like that.

Wilson was right. Guards like to say stuff like that, dumb stuff to let you know who is boss.

The guard walked away. That made Wilson even madder.

"Write me a ticket to get out of here! Send me back to max!" he screamed.

What could I say? Wilson was a grown man and knew what he was doing. I was tired of hearing him but I had no control. I had to put up with it.

"Why you all got me locked up anyways?" He started out again. "You cocksuckers, you're all dirty, that's why." He was swinging his arms and yelling at every guard that came by. About an hour later he got his pills. Once he popped them, he ate his breakfast and jumped back into bed.

⚊⚊⚊

The next day we went out to recreation. *Fresh air and sunshine!* I was happy. I paced in a large circle like everyone else. Other prisoners were getting cigarettes but I didn't want any. *Why smoke a couple of cigarettes outside, then have to do without inside?*

When we were back from rec, Wilson snapped again.

"Where's my shit?" he asked the guard as he walked past our cell.

"Hold on. I'm checking to make sure everyone's in their cells."

"Don't you walk away from me, you dirty cocksucker. I want my shit back." The guard walked away as Wilson carried on.

By this time I was getting sick of it. I stared him down. "Dude, give it a break!"

"Oh, so you're in on it too."

I cut him off quick. "No. But I don't want to hear a grown man screaming all day about nothing. I live in this cell too."

Well, that lasted about one minute until Wilson saw the guard.

"I want my shit back, punk," he screamed again.

"What shit?"

"The shit you dirty cocksuckers took out of this cell."

"We didn't search today. No one entered any rooms."

"Lookit, you're all dirty. My cellie is tired of hearing me and I want my shit. You cocksuckers steal people's shit, then don't want to give it back. You're all dirty."

"I'm tired of your mouth," the guard answered and looked at me. "What do you have to do with this?"

Surprised, I looked back at the guard. "I don't have anything to do with this. He's talking to you. I'm tired of hearing the noise."

"Oh," he said, his tone disbelieving. Then he looked at Wilson again. "And you. You keep talking to me like that and I'll write you a ticket."

Wilson wouldn't let that go. "Write me a ticket, you cocksucker! At least I'll be out of here. Send me back to max. I didn't do anything wrong to get over here, punk," he screamed at the guard.

"Okay," the guard smiled and left.

"Come back here, you dirty cocksucker, I want my shit back." He screamed and screamed. "Fucking punk bitches."

Then he saw the sergeant. "What's wrong now, Wilson?" the sergeant asked. I could tell he had dealt with Wilson before.

"You dirty cocksuckers took my shit and I want it back."

By this time I was thinking, *dude needs a beat-down.*

"No one searched this afternoon."

Suddenly Wilson looked at me, then back at the guard. *Did Anonymous take my shit?*

I knew nothing had been taken out of the cell, but Wilson wanted to bitch and I wasn't going to play that game with him.

"You're all dirty," he yelled. "You all are dirty cocksuckers. Steal my little shit, then lie about it."

"We didn't take any of your shit. The sergeant looked at me. "You got his shit?"

Like if I actually did, I would admit it! Now I was officially dragged into it. "I don't have anything of his," I said calmly. "And I don't appreciate you all putting me in with a nut. Give this dude his pills and his shit back, and maybe he will chill."

The sergeant gave me a long look "Oh, so you're saying we have his stuff? Is he taking his pills or saving them?"

Guards are sometimes so naive. Like an experienced con is going to tell on his cellmate while in lockdown. "I don't know nothing about all that. Don't play games with me, Sarge. I do what I do and he does what he does. Now move me out!"

"I don't know if we have any cells."

I was getting angry but I kept my cool. "What did I just tell you? Don't play games with me. Either you all deal with him so he chills out, or move me out."

"I am not playing games." He was going to say more but I interrupted him.

"Excuse me. I am the easiest-going dude in this place. I told you what I wanted. I am done." Once again, I spoke calmly, then just climbed back on my bed.

The sergeant tried to wrap up the conversation, but Wilson would have none of it. "Are you done, Wilson?"

"No, you stealing bastard, I want my shit back."

"All these tantrums you're going through . . ."

"You're all dirty. You took my stuff," Wilson repeated.

The sergeant walked off in midsentence. This pissed Wilson off even more. He raged for the next two hours. I watched him pace back and forth. His muscles were tensed, his fists were clenched, and his face had an evil, contorted look to it.

Now and then a guard would come by and look in. This just made Wilson more full of rage.

What bothered me was I was stuck in a cell with a nut. *They didn't seem to care too much about that.*

This went on for another week and then on the way out to recreation I told the guards to move me. "I don't give none of you any trouble, and you have me in with this nut case. I'm sick of it. I ain't raising no hell. Move me or I will get moved myself."

"Getting tired of him?"

"Dude, I got to go." I pleaded. A con's worst nightmare is being placed in a cell with a dude that is a **crank.** It is hard enough doing time without being in lockdown for twenty-three hours per day with a nut case. Fights break out—fast **caged** matches. I hadn't wanted that to happen.

The next day they told me to get ready and that I was moving to the second step of the program segregation phase. It was a lie but I didn't care. Wilson was pissed though, since he thought I was moving to the second phase before him. They shuffled me into a cell by myself for a day, then put me in with a new cellie right next door to Wilson. Wilson was still screaming and I knew his new cellie was sick of it.

My next cellie was a little better. He talked with the guards a little too much, but he shared his magazines with me. After I finished reading the first one, I tried to discuss some of the articles with him but I soon learned that he didn't—or couldn't—read very well. I believe it was the latter.

━━◇━◇━◇━━

Almost a month went by and I was trying to get some canteen. I wanted paper and pencils to help speed the boring days. After about a week with any cellie, you have little to talk about.

Eventually the unit manager came around, so I questioned her about my canteen and also about the book cart that was supposed to come through twice a week.

"Well, we're short of help. And you came from another institution."

State workers are so good about excuses. It's funny: they always tell a prisoner not to make excuses. But when they don't do their job, they always have the same excuses.

This used to confuse me, but then I learned this was called "*rehabilitation.*"

Program segregation was taking a toll on me, though. I was only human.

Next door, Wilson was screaming for a week that he couldn't shit. Literally. Segregation slows your bodily functions down. A human being's large intestine works off gravity and movement. The more a prisoner lies in a cell, the less his bowels want to move. Sometimes this can lead to cramps. And that is difficult to deal with under twenty-three-hour lockdown.

When my cellie was moved to the next step of program, he took all his magazines. The unit manager provided me with two books but they didn't last long.

I had no energy. None. I would wake up in the morning only to be half-awake and half-asleep all day long. After breakfast, I would lie down not able to fall totally asleep, yet I had no desire to get up. I would think about the life I had led. It wasn't much. I was coming up to the age where I'd spent half of it in prison.

Another day, another week. My aches and pains caught up with me. I had headaches every day, just as I had for the past ten years. What was new was that now I had nothing to distract me. My neck was tight and my back tense.

It wasn't happening fast enough. The dog days of summer were coming up and I knew I was going to suffer where I was. The daytime temperature ranged around 95 degrees outside with 80 percent humidity. In prison, this meant the water puddled under the toilet and ran down the walls. Plexiglas™ covered the window in my cell. An air vent blew the hot, humid air in from outside. When I got out of bed, the sheet was glued to my body from sweat. Clean linen came once a week, but by the third day of summer in prison, all your clothes, sheets, and your cell smelled. There was no deodorant in this phase of the program.

One day I got a new cellie. He was a young gangbanger who was out to impress everyone. His stay only lasted that day. I don't believe he wanted to be in the cell with a white man. He never said it directly but the words he yelled out at the bottom of the door meant it.

I could feel the stress getting to me. The noise and constant yelling cell to cell were getting to me. The heat was getting to me. And the guards were using their favorite saying, *it sucks to be you.* All in all, I was a time bomb just ticking away.

Finally I was to the point where I would be transferred to the last phase of program segregation. I would finally get all my property or what was left of it. *Some correctional employees like to steal prisoners' property.*

My fan, TV and radio, books to read, my drawing and writing supplies, and some junk food. And full canteen and more time out of the cell.

The guard opened my door and told me to go to the storage room for my stuff. They didn't use shackles on phase three. I was excited to say the least. I figured each day I could keep busy for weeks.

I was in for a big surprise.

The guard set a shoe-box sized container on the counter in front of me. Every electron in my brain went off. "This is only the shit I came in here with. Where is my property?"

He was calm, like he'd heard this before. "All we have. Come look around for yourself."

That was an invitation I could not refuse. I looked at the shelves, praying I'd see my name on about five other boxes. However, they were not there! I walked back around the counter and sat on the stool that was by the door.

"Are you okay?" the guard saw my face.

I didn't even think. I just said to him, "You got a cigarette?"

My question surprised him.

Then I took a deep breath. "I am just fine. My property isn't here. You don't know where it is. Now I have to wait some more. I sat half a month on TLU with nothing, then another half a month in ADJ. Now I've been here in program for two months. And you still don't have my property here!"

"I'll call around to see where it is."

I grabbed my little box and walked out without answering. *I didn't believe he was going to make any calls anywhere.*

When I got back to my cell in phase three, I had a cellie. His property arrived the same day as he moved to phase three. To say the least, I was pissed.

The next day I was called to the property room in the main building. There was my stuff. Half of my hobby supplies and all my baking books were gone, but I did recover the rest.

"This is all we got."

Stealing-ass guards. I left with what there was. On the way back I ran into a number of people I'd known from before. They all cussed me out for being back in medium.

I was also able to go outside for recreation. There were two separate segregation pens for everyone in phase three to breathe outside air. The blacktop we paced on felt like 105 degrees. Sweat started rolling off me the minute I went out.

Prisoners typically segregate themselves by race during all group activities, including recreation. There is a designated, but unspoken white pen and a pen for black prisoners. There was one older white man in the pen with the black prisoners.

"Why ain't ya on the other side with your honkies?" a young black kid asked him.

The older man said something but I didn't catch it.

"Fuck you, honkie," the kid said bitterly. "This side for the blacks!"

"I didn't pick the side. The officers just told me to go in there. You think I want to be with a loudmouth kid like you?"

They yelled at each other for a while but finally the kid backed down. Then everyone started up with complaints. I was left wondering whether it was good to be back or not.

⋇⋗⋇⋗⋇⋗⋇

REFLECTIONS

Segregation is the ultimate in deprivation. It is the final stop for every man in prison. It is prison at its worst, mankind's modern-day horror. A man is stripped of everything, including his dignity. First, he is isolated from human contact. Then, if he doesn't screw up, he is slowly blended through a three-phase program back into regular population again. He only hopes he can hold on long enough to make it through the mental trip.

The hardest time of all while I was in segregation was the day my mother came to visit. She hoped I'd be released some day. She knew that being sent back to medium security was not going forward. *She was right.*

"I'm getting too old for these changes. Don't you want to get out of prison?" she asked.

To be honest, I had no answer for her. I really didn't know how to answer. I thought I wanted to get out, but then I got myself back in seg.

I knew she didn't like seeing me back at medium custody. She didn't say it, but she was hurt. The guards at this prison disrespected the visitors: that hurt. She didn't like coming here: that hurt. I felt about two inches tall and figured I'd just better keep quiet and let her talk.

I never had the courage to tell her that I had lost hope of getting out. I might have been moving to a lower security level, but I did not see the state ever releasing me.

While I was in segregation, I looked back and saw how both my victim's family and my own family had suffered. The true price I've paid is loneliness and loss of control for over twenty years now. I know many people would quickly say I did this to myself. I agree. But those people also let lawlessness run wild in a prison. Meanwhile, I have given half my life to a past I cannot change. I live with only sorrow and hate.

15

Retaliation

"There are two choices in this world: got or be got."

DIRTY RED, GANGSTER DISCIPLE
DECEMBER 1989

303.26, Battery. Any inmate who intentionally causes bodily injury to another.

303.327, Fighting. . . . situation where two or more people are trying to injure each other by any physical means, to include hitting, biting, kicking, throwing or swinging objects, or using weapons.

DEPARTMENT OF CORRECTIONS MANUAL, OFFENSES AGAINST BODILY SECURITY
APRIL 1990

>✖✖✖✖✖✖<

The years rolled by. I wasn't as green anymore. I spent more time watching how other men behaved in these situations and was well into being a convict.

"Hey, Red," Baby-G said, stepping into the shower.

"What's up, **dog?**" Red replied.

Baby-G didn't answer and Red was puzzled. Usually he always had something to say. "That it?"

"Well, you know, I heard some stuff," Baby-G didn't look towards Red, even though in the showers men took special care to maintain eye contact lest they'd be accused of looking at something else!

"Heard stuff. What's that to mean?" Red asked.

"I heard Que talking about you and the shit you did. Said you ain't no good. Think he called you a punk," Baby-G said softly.

"First of all I ain't no one's punk. That Que, he ain't no good. Man's breath stinks so bad his teeth jump. Never showers."

Baby-G was an expert at kicking up shit. "Well, I don't know about you, but if a man called me a punk I'd do something about it!"

"You ain't me!"

"So you saying it's okay to call you a punk?"

"Watch your mouth!"

"Hey, don't get mad at me, I'm just asking. I just said if a man called me a punk, I would do somethin' about it."

Baby-G dried off and headed back into the sleeping area. He greeted C-Note and Que. Then he laughed. "Check this out. Red told me Que's breath stinks so bad his teeth jump out of the way."

"What'd you say?" Que asked.

"Man said your breath stinks so bad your teeth jump." Both Baby-G and C-Note were laughing.

"Fuck you. I don't know why you're talking, anyway!" Que turned away.

There was no love lost between C-Note and Que. They had a feud going for years. C-Note was arrogant, so I suppose they just did not like each other.

C-Note and Baby-G left the sleeping area as Red came in.

"Hey, Red. We can keep what I told you in the showers between us. I mean I don't want to get in no shit. I just thought you should know so you can keep your ears open to find out for yourself," Baby-G said.

"Yeah, yeah, man, I'll find out!" Red said, heading toward his bunk.

"What's this about?" C-Note inquired.

"I just spread the word that Que was talking about him." Baby-G told C-Note what he had said.

Red walked back to his bunk in the sleeping area and looked at Que. "Hey, Que, heard you were talking about me?" He flexed a little.

"What? I didn't say shit about your **lame** ass," Que fired back. *Once again, denial is the best approach.* Whether Que said anything or not, he wasn't going to tell.

"Motherfucker told me you was talkin' about me like a punk," Red stared at Que.

"Motherfucker told me you was talkin' 'bout me," Que fired back.

"Yeah, well, I ain't no punk, remember that!"

"I never said you were." Que grabbed his coffee cup and headed out of the sleeping area. He was mad at Red. Red was mad at Que.

⋘══⋗⋘══⋗⋘══⋗

After a couple of days C-Note came up to Que. "Shit, I never liked your big ass anyway, but motherfucker told me if he catches you running your mouth, he is going to **open up a can of whoop ass** on you," C-Note announced.

"Who? In their dreams. Ain't nobody gonna' whoop this ass!" Que answered.

"Ain't what Red said," C-Note let out.

Then Red came into the sleeping area and went to his bunk.

"Red, you gonna' whoop my ass?" Que asked.

"What you talking about, man?"

"C-Note here says you gonna' whoop my ass if you catch me disrespecting you."

"First of all C-Note should get it straight," Red shot C-Note a sharp look. "I said if anyone here is disrespecting me and I catch him, I am going to whoop his motherfucking ass, count on it!"

Now Que and Red had their eyes on each other. Both were built dudes. Que was naturally big while Red was a **bay-bay kid** from way back who played ball all the time.

Baby-G and C-Note kept stirring the pot for about two weeks. It all came to a collision one Saturday morning.

✂━✂━✂━✂

"Man, I just heard it, that's all," Baby-G was running his mouth, but he stopped when Red entered the sleeping area.

"Red, what's up with you?" Que shot out.

"What's up with what?" Red asked as he headed to his bunk.

"You know, all that disrespect going on," Que said slowly.

Red stayed standing, purposely not sitting on his bunk. He didn't know where Que was going with what he was saying. "What disrespect?"

Que walked towards him. "You running your mouth, that's what!"

"I ain't said shit about you, but if there's something you want to get off your chest, get to the point." Red stared at Que while he moved away from the hard metal bed frame. He had positioned his right leg behind his left in typical boxer stance.

Que wasn't giving him any space.

As I watched, I didn't know whether they were going to fight, or whether one was going to take flight. In prison sometimes even the experienced do not know what is going to happen.

"I am just saying if you want to talk about a motherfucker say it to his face," Que shouted.

Red began circling him. "And you want to call a motherfucker a punk, say it to his face!" He was spitting with anger. "You better keep your distance too."

"So what you gonna' do?" Que asked, pumping his chest.

The sleeping area got quiet.

"How many muthafuckas am I going to beat down today?" Red checked behind him.

Another man said "Fuck that mark, Que."

However, Red saw only one alternative. He wasn't sure if it was going to be just him and Que or others too. So he moved while Que was looking the other way. "No, fuck you!" he shouted, then swung at the side of Que's head.

"Punk," Que held and swung.

"Fuck you," Red hollered out.

"Your momma, punk," Que fired back.

After that the fight took off. Blows to the chest, blows to the head, Que tired out Red and threw him to the ground, Red jumped up and ran his head into Que's gut.

When Officer Harris heard the noise he looked into the sleeping area. "FIGHT! Derk, we got a fight!" he hollered as he opened the door.

The other officer, Derk, **bounced** out of his chair. "Green fifty-two, fight in the dorm." He yelled into his radio as he headed for the sleeping area.

The two guards broke through the onlookers. When Harris saw the blows Que and Red were throwing, he stopped so fast his arms swung out in front of him and the radio flew out of his hand. He wasn't about to go in alone and break it up.

Instead, Derk yelled at them to stop. Then he yelled again.

"Everybody back up. Get out of here." Harris motioned to the crowd.

"Officer down, officer down," Derk's radio cracked. "Fight, Dorm B, officer down. Attention all Green units. Officer down."

"Knock it off." Derk lifted his radio to his mouth. "There's no officer down," he shouted into the radio, then realized he hadn't pushed the button.

He was losing control of the situation. "I am giving you a direct order to stop," Derk hollered at Red and Que. "No officer down," he yelled into the radio again.

"Fuck your momma," Red screamed at Que.

"Punk," Que screamed back. No one was paying attention to either of the officers.

✕═✕═✕═✕

Two men can only fight full force for so long. Both Red and Que were sucking wind like wild vacuum cleaners. Que was blowing blood out of his mouth and Red's eye was black. Their punches got lighter and lighter.

When a guard sees that two gladiators are tiring, he knows it's safe to jump in. Any time after this, men will give up.

"I got Que," Derk ran behind Que and wrapped his arms around him, throwing his 250 pounds on Que's back. Que had a cut lip, a scraped arm, and red Kool-Aid™ pumping out his nose. Harris grabbed Red. Harris was lighter than Derk by about 150 pounds, so when Harris wrapped up Red, Red started to drag him around. Red swung a few more blows at Que. Harris slid his hands off Red's arms and put them around his neck. Que tried to swing back at Red but Derk's weight was full on his back. Que looked as if someone attached a great blue pumpkin on his back.

"One more swing out of you and I'll see you never get out of the hole for a year." Harris tightened his sleeper hold on Red.

Both he and Derk were sweating like pigs.

Then troops arrived. Thirty guards stormed the dorm, screaming at the top of their voices. "Back up," they yelled at the onlookers. "Back up or get locked up." They made it to the ring and saw Harris and Derk clinging on to Red and Que.

"Cuff 'em, damn it," Harris snapped at the other guards looking on. "Come on, cuff 'em."

He was still hanging on to Red's neck even though Red could barely stand. Two guards grabbed his arms while another spun the cuff onto one wrist.

"It's over now. Calm down, it's over." Harris let go of Red. He was breathing hard. "It's over."

Que gave up. With all those guards, he knew what was coming next and he knew when to stop.

Red and Que were taken to segregation and Derk and Harris headed to the staff room to recover.

Baby-G and C-Note had successfully **geeked-up** that fight. The rumors went out about how they had done it.

I had changed so much from my first days at Cold Springs that I saw this as just another incident in prison life. I was growing immune to the violence and I was tired of those who were geeking-up shit. I was also better at avoiding potential trouble.

✄✄✄✄

Soon after the incident between Red and Que, small items from our locker-boxes came up missing. One day two bottles of my shampoo disappeared. We knew we had a thief in the dorm.

"Hey, Chris, you see my shampoo?"

"That's funny, Al just said he couldn't find his sweat pants," Chris answered.

"Turner didn't kick them under the bed or do something with them?"

George came in and I told him that both Al and I had lost shit.

"Yesterday Dan from across the dorm asked me if I was missing anything since he said he saw Martinez in our area," George said.

"Why didn't you say something?" I demanded.

"I forgot!" George snapped.

"Good reason. I don't mean to be yelling at you. Just pissed that my shit is gone."

Martinez walked by then. Holding two bottles of shampoo. *My bottles.*

Chris looked at me, his eyes questioning. I nodded.

"Well, you have to do something. You just can't let him take your shit," George said to me.

"I will—not now, but I will," I answered.

Personally I didn't care about the soap, but he had stolen my stuff. It was the principle—it was what others would think about me. *It's not the cost, it's that he thinks I'm a punk!*

We weren't the only men to lose things since Martinez arrived. Shirts, canteen, shoes, and other stuff were turning up missing. Now he had invaded my area.

Al suggested we wait until after the holidays to get him. I had another idea. "We assault him, we all get locked down. Fuck the hole. I want to get even," I said. "Look. If we turn the game on him, he loses. Tomorrow when he goes to the can before rec, I'll switch my lock with his. He never locks it when he goes. Then when he goes out to rec, we stay back here and come out at the last minute. We'll have about two minutes to clear out his locker."

⚊✕⚊✕⚊✕⚊

It was 8 A.M. Everyone was going to rec because they wanted to start phoning home for the holidays. That was good because there would be no witnesses.

George saw Martinez head to the toilets. He was helping to make sure I wouldn't back out of what I said I'd do. It's the geek-up system.

I looked around. No one was paying any attention. "Chris, say 'fuck you' and throw your shirt over to Martinez's footlocker." I handed Chris the shirt he always wore for recreation.

"Fuck! I'm tired. I ain't going to rec." Chris shouted.

A few people looked at us. I walked over to pick up the shirt and swapped locks. Martinez's lock was hanging open, just like always.

Martinez came back, got on his rec gear, snapped the lock shut, and left. I walked back to his locker and looked around. No one was watching.

"Go out to the dayroom and make sure he doesn't come back here," I said to George. I opened my lock and unloaded everything that was worth taking. He didn't have much. He did have Al's sweat pants.

"If this don't work I am going to beat his motherfucking ass!" Al grabbed his pants and more.

Martinez's locker was almost empty. We replaced Martinez's lock on his lockerbox. I went over to my area and started packing everything we had taken in with my rec stuff. Luck was with me. I looked out the window and saw Mike pushing the laundry cart. "Hey," I yelled out the window, "Mike, hold up for dorm rec."

He looked up but didn't know who was yelling.

"It's me, Anonymous. Just hold up for about five minutes and meet us coming out for rec. I can't talk now, but wait." I closed the window and passed the word: drop the shit in Mike's laundry cart.

It worked great. I told Mike the stuff was hot and he should hide it, then sell it after the holidays. He had no problem since I told him to keep half of what he made.

⚊✕⚊✕⚊✕⚊

When we all came back after rec, Martinez opened his locker. "Where's my shit? Who the fuck took my shit?" he screamed.

Officer Harris was in the sleeping area in minutes. After Red and Que's fight, any noise brought the guards running.

We were playing cards.

"Someone took all my shit," Martinez snapped at Harris. "I gonna' beat the punk that did."

Harris tried to calm him down, but that didn't work. So he took him out to the desk.

Well, Officers Harris and Derk had no choice. Martinez threatened everyone, even called some dudes out to fight. That was a one-man riot. So off to the hole he went.

That afternoon, Officer Derk cussed out all of us. "We had a good crew up here. Now we got a thief. Someone took all that man's shit."

"He was the thief, Derk."

"Who said that?" Officer Harris asked.

Dangerous Dan walked over from the other side of the dorm. "I did. He was the thief."

It was quiet for a minute, then Chris agreed with Dan. Next Al spoke up.

"I see. And I suppose there's no point looking for his stuff?" No one answered Derk. "Why didn't somebody say something?"

"We're not snitches. We handle our own."

"Who said that?" Derk asked. No one said a word. We had just crossed the line. Derk could have had the whole dorm torn up, but he just turned around and walked out.

Of course, the rumors started. Everyone talked about Martinez but none of us admitted we took his stuff.

<hr />

As I got older, I just got more tired. I grew sick of seeing the fighting pattern that the guys went through, so I found myself trying to avoid fights by using the flight method, like with E.D. and his quest for my sugar packs.

"Hey, why ain't you giving me the sugars off your tray anymore?" E.D. asked me.

"Cause my cellie ran out of honey and asked me for a few until canteen," I answered.

"Well, I thought we had a deal worked out where you gave me your sugars."

"We did?" I asked. "Is this what this is all about? You don't sit at the table with me or Lee anymore and stay away from me for a week because of sugar packs?"

"Yeah, well, I thought we had a deal worked out!"

"I come over here to talk to you to see what's up because you're avoiding me, and it's sugars?"

"That and we had a deal."

"What deal? We didn't have any deal!" I said angrily.

"Well, you know, nothing written down but I thought we had stuff worked out."

"You mean you had stuff worked out, E.D. I never said anything."

"Well, you know, when someone does something for you and you do something back, that is like a deal," E.D. replied. *E.D. was a manipulator.*

"Well, if I have no plans for my sugars, you can have them."

E.D. started again. "I am just saying sometimes I just give burgers away to help a guy out."

"Never gave me no burger."

"No, but I would."

"Sure." I walked away. I was surprised that E.D. thought we had a deal worked out. He was a strange dude though. I was just trying to give him some respect since I knew he was another lifer with only a little time in.

⋙⋘⋙⋘⋙⋘

Things seemed to be going okay, but then they changed.

"You know, E.D., you say some bogus-ass shit," I said coming up the stairs behind him. He had just told Jim to watch his back since Lee wouldn't share any of his soda.

"Man, you say some crazy shit too," he remarked defensively.

I cut him off because I knew if I did not he would go into one of his famous speeches. E.D. would analyze a subject to death for hours. "You're threatening Lee over his own soda because he won't give you some?"

"I was joking."

Maybe E.D.'s still green.

"Man, you don't joke like that," I said.

"Oh, you're like the rest of these punk ass motherfuckers that want to run me!"

E.D. had me upset. *Punk.* You don't say that unless you want to fight. I have seen the worst come out in a man over that word. I couldn't believe he had called me that. Hell, I was just trying to be cool with him.

E.D. went into his cell, but it wasn't over. Later that morning I was helping my cellie clean our cell when E.D. stuck his nose out his door.

"What's up, punk motherfucker?" He laughed.

"Look, stop saying that shit to me. That shit ain't funny." I fired back with venom. Apparently E.D. just did not understand you don't call a man a punk. As I said, he didn't have much time in. It's like swearing in church, you just don't do it. In prison you do not call another man a punk, not even jokingly, unless you plan to beat the tar out of him.

I was done with him. *Done.* He said a few things to me that morning but I ignored them.

"Why you acting like you got an attitude?" he asked as I walked by him on the tier.

"Because of your mouth. You don't call a man a punk."

"I was joking." He tried to cover up.

"Lookit, E.D., clean that shit up, then talk to me." I was keeping my cool but inside I wanted to pop him in the nose.

"Well, you touched my apple." We had had apples for breakfast.

"Like a fool you were throwing balled up toilet paper at me before breakfast."

"You didn't give me your sugar."

"I used it this morning." Then I stopped. *E.D. was sucking me into his game.* Nothing was ever his fault.

"Lookit, E.D., I asked you politely to clean that shit up. You're just making excuses."

"You said I say a lot of bogus ass shit, you grabbed my apple like you were running something, and now I have to clean it up! Well."

"You're making excuses for saying the wrong stuff, plain and simple. I got nothing for you." I walked off.

By prisoner codes, I should have blasted E.D. He should have been in the medical ward recovering from mortal combat and I should have been exercising **bragging rights.** But I did not want that path, and I think E.D. knew that. So he was taking advantage of it.

I decided to avoid him. I had to live around him and would give him respect but no more.

After about a week of not getting his sugar fix from my tray, he apologized. I actually thought that he was going to clean up what he said. However, he spent twenty minutes telling me how it was not his fault because he was having problems: I touched his apple, and others were upsetting him. Then he said "Yeah, I can see how you would be upset over that."

E.D. thought we were now cool and life would go back to normal. But he never asked me if I was **cool** with him.

⟒⟑⟒⟑⟒⟑

About a week later E.D. came into my cell a few minutes after I got back from canteen. "Oh, I see you got peanut butter." He was casing my store items.

I wondered what was coming next.

"Why ain't you been giving me your sugar?" he demanded.

"Because someone else made me a deal and I'm going to make peach cobbler." I put my stuff away.

"So your cellie is getting it." He was being nosy.

"That's not what I said." I grabbed a cigarette and told him to come on out. I didn't smoke in my cell and didn't want him in there anyway. Obviously, he just wanted to see what I bought.

"Sure, you let another man tell you what to do," E.D. argued.

"I told you, E.D., someone else made me a better deal and I am going to make peach cobbler." I was stern with him like a man is with a child. However, he was not getting it.

"Well, damn, I just asked. You act like you got no time for me to even talk."

"Good! You're right. Motherfucker tries to give you some respect and you play games. I ain't your puppet," I fired back.

"Now I know why them dudes did something to you. You're letting your cellie control you. I would, too," he hissed angrily.

"Are you threatening me, E.D.? No one is going to do anything to me. You can kiss my butt. Leave me the fuck alone."

"I don't let others tell me what to do."

I was pissed. "This ain't got nothing to do with my cellie, you fool. Stay the fuck away from me! You run your mouth saying shit I would never say to a man unless I wanted to box." I wanted to educate his dumb ass on the finer points of prison the hard way, but worded my way around it.

He ran his mouth some more, but I just walked off. I wanted no part of his madness. I had enough problems of my own. I could care less about his little world. He didn't realize what he was doing. I never saw him talking to other dudes like that.

He had the nerve to try one of his fake apologies at lunch.

"Lookit, I was out of order for saying what I did."

"Fuck off, E.D." He could hear the anger in my voice.

"Oh, what . . ." he started, but I cut him off.

"You can beat it. I told you to stay away. I don't need your shit in my life. Wishy-washy ass motherfucker." I was red in the face by now.

"Okay, so you want it like that."

"What'd I just tell you? There is no room for discussion. You come near me again and we are going to **box,** dig?"

With that, he stormed off. I knew he was steaming, but it seemed I had to show E.D. the gorilla in me to shut him down. I was trying real hard to avoid the fight mode.

REFLECTIONS

Prisons in the United States have a reputation for being plagued with violence and retaliation. Raised middle class, I think that the amount of violence found in the system is extremely high. However, a gang member who has lived with this in the 'hood every day may see the amount of violence in prison as no different than the streets.

One myth is that a prisoner has to fight daily to survive. This is not true.

But prison violence has increased. There are many factors that may contribute to this increase. The entire world has become more violent. On the other hand, violent crime in society has decreased. Technology now affords individuals less human contact. People hide in their homes and care less about getting to know their neighbors. They have developed superficial friendships. I blame violence on the breakdown of the family. As families grow apart over the generations, they exhibit more hatred and violence.

Some prisoners blame prison violence on the inmate–staff relationship. It is true that the more the staff gets to know prisoners over a long period of time, the less likely prison violence will occur.

I also believe that idleness and boredom affect violence. The less a person has to do, the more minor irritations become a major part of his prison life.

Violence in prison may also stem from forced interaction, such as happens with double-celling. When you put two men into a room the size of a broom closet there are bound to be arguments. The stress can eventually lead to violence.

From my observations, violence in prison can be seasonal. The hole was filled over Christmas and just before the start of spring. The holidays generate a great deal of despair and social deprivation. Spring is a time when men know that they will soon go outside after being locked indoors all winter. As they anticipate outside recreation and greater movement, they become impatient, and the powder barrel ignites.

Violence in prison has grown over the years, along with sentence length. With the introduction of mandatory sentencing and the removal of early parole, incentives for good behavior are reduced. I came into prison thinking that hard work and good behavior would get me some type of rewards. Wrong! Fuckup or not, everyone ended up with the same privileges.

Following the deinstitutionalization of the mentally ill in the 1970s, jails and prisons became the new residences for homeless and/or persons with mental illnesses. Along with a population that was often older, these people provided victims for predatory prisoners.

Finally, the unwritten prison code of honor accepts violence. If someone steals, disrespects, or snitches on others, he will be assaulted. If he gets caught retaliating, prior actions are no defense.

For example, if someone steals from you or disrespects you in front of others, then other people will take the same actions against you. If you even the score by assaulting the other man and he covertly tells on you, then generally you are going to the hole. While he is moved to another area and never punished, you suffer the consequences of seg and a bad record.

Retaliation is a part of prison politics. I call this the fight or flight syndrome. To deal with disrespect or theft, a man can choose fight or flight. Flight also is avoiding fights by running, or trying to talk your way out of a situation. The problem is that if a person runs, he may be running his whole life.

Sometimes men were burglarized and didn't want to know who was the thief, even if their closest friends tried to tell them. They chose flight over fight. They only would threaten a whole unit of guys because they knew that the thief would never step forward. Their choice of flight worked and they saved face.

Regarding a stealing incident, it is not what happens if you *do* fight with the man you've caught stealing your stuff, but what happens if you *don't*. Your cell will be marked and more thieves will come.

When I was first locked up, most prisoners had rules for stealing. Most thieves would not steal from another inmate. They would only steal from the state. Now everyone seems to steal from everyone.

Another form of retaliation comes from disrespect. When you're in prison, the only thing you have left in life is your honor, and disrespect can result in an assault just as fast as theft can. When someone shows you disrespect, three times out of ten, he will say it to you directly. For example, if you are called a punk in front of fifty men, a fist to the jaw usually stops the conversation.

Other times, you will hear from a third person that a particular man is disrespecting you. There are so many lies and rumors in prison that no one knows for certain if the man actually said it. Also, some men feel that since they are not talking directly to you but just about you, they are not really disrespecting you.

Fights also start when one person talks about another person to a friend while that person is present. Others purposely set up another man by telling someone else that he said something about them. This is the geek-up system.

The geek-up system is the noise you hear from others on how you should or shouldn't have handled your problem. Those people are the true instigators in prison. At times the real sharks in the sea are not the gladiators, they are the instigators geeking-up the gladiators.

In the dorm in Gladiator School I learned how the fight or flight syndrome worked. I watched the gossips work their charm. The gossips instigated the violence. And the funniest thing about violence is that it is like a narcotic. Once it starts it spreads like a brushfire. While you're ducking and diving the predators, and throwing blows against victims, you're not focused on imprisonment.

At times I wonder who is the real perpetuator of violence—the brutality of prisoners or the structure of the system.

16

Gangs

"Wannabes come to prison, join a gang, and support what the administration wants: we fight each other, not them."

MINI-ME "D"

FEBRUARY 2000

"The reason blacks hate you whites so much is because of what you did during the slave years."

HAM GANGSTER DISCIPLES LEADER

AUGUST 1999

Big Ron ran the Disciples and their **contraband** store when I was in Gladiator School.

"Listen to me, Mad-Dog," Big Ron said as the group walked the recreation field's gravel path, "you keep the store in your **crib.** If it gets too full send some over to Money Mel's **crib**." Big Ron turned back and looked at Money Mel, "You take care of the overflow, okay?"

Money Mel had no choice. If he said no, Big Ron would have checked him by saying he was scared. On the other hand, Mad-Dog would have done anything Big Ron said. He wanted to be a member of the Disciples. He liked walking around with them, and developing a rep for **mean-mugging** people.

"Now listen. Anyone who borrows out of it, tell them two for one. If they got a problem, send them to me." When Big Ron wanted to emphasize something he said, he pounded the back of one hand into the other. "If any of you brothers take anything out, just put it back one for one. If you can stand it, then put back two for one to help all of us out. It's our store to help us out when we need something if we run short." He went on preaching about how brothers had to stick together.

"Should I keep the books?" Chicken Wing asked. Chicken Wing was Big Ron's right-hand man, and earned his nickname because his arms looked like chicken wings when he walked.

"Yeah, yeah," Ron agreed, "you men tell Chicken Wing when you get something so he can keep track. That way you have the store and he has the **list.** When the **police** come, no one will have everything and we can't get busted."

"Me and Rock will keep the pressure on these **peckerwoods** to get their shit. Keep them in debt and keep 'em paying."

One of the men knee-deep into owing Big Ron was Red. Part of Red's problem was he liked to gamble. During the weeks when he didn't have canteen, Red would get hungry and borrow from Mad-Dog. He thought they were looking out for him.

"Here's your shit, man, but they cut me two bags short of chips and a bottle of the spray shit you had down." Red said. He sat back on his bunk and looked away.

"Then you ain't got all my shit," Big Ron said as Mad-Dog looked at some tobacco on Red's desk.

"Where'd you get that tobacco?" he asked.

"I had a little money left over so I bought it," Red didn't want any trouble and thought that the guards were watching close enough to protect him. He fidgeted with a loose string from his blanket on his bunk.

Ron snorted in anger, "You got yourself tobacco and didn't get all my shit?"

"No, they didn't put the shit in my stuff when I asked for it." Red started rocking his right leg. He was lying but was hoping he'd get away with it.

"Fuck you, peckerwood," Ron snapped at him, "next time you have all my shit."

"And it is going to cost you," Mad-Dog interjected.

Big Ron told Mad-Dog to watch for the guards. They knew they were running out of time before someone came up from the front desk to make sure everyone was in their cells.

He stepped into Red's cell. Red's eyes shot wide open. He was only about five foot tall and Big Ron was well over six feet, worked out all day long, and had a serious attitude.

Big Ron grabbed his bag, then noticed four soda tokens on the desk. "Where did these come from?"

"Ah, a . . . someone owed me those from playing pool."

"You lie too much. They are mine too." Big Ron scooped them into the bag.

Red was in no position to argue. He had this big dude standing in his cell. *Where are the guards when you need them? I hope this gorilla doesn't want to fight.*

Big Ron pointed his finger at Red. "You have my shit next canteen and anything else too. Or I am through fuckin' with your punk ass." He stepped out of the cell and walked away.

All Red could say was *okay* to Big Ron. He couldn't move and he forgot Mad-Dog was still standing there.

"Hey, you all right?" Mad-Dog said to Red.

Red looked at Mad-Dog "I don't know why he was so mad."

"White boy, you owe him," Mad-Dog calmly replied. "Wouldn't you be pissed if someone won't have your shit?"

"I don't talk to him like that."

"Check it out. Make sure you get his shit. I'll talk to him. I'll cool him down." Mad-Dog knew what he was doing. It was all part of the game. *Good guy, bad guy.* He was making sure Red would not run out of his cell and go straight to the guards.

"Yeah, talk to him for me. I'll pay him."

"Just remember, he could have taken your tobacco, too."

"Yeah."

"I'll tell him you're cool. You didn't mean to piss him off. You'll make it good."

Mad-Dog went to Big Ron's cell and said "Red's okay. I kicked it with him. Told him telling would do no good. Told him to pay up. Said I'd calm you down."

Big Ron was happy, Red was scared, and they got most of their payment.

A few people I knew tried to talk to Red, but Red wasn't getting the message. Eventually I noticed he was gone and there was another man in his cell. There were rumors that Red was **beat down** or strong-armed for a gambling debt.

———————————

Oftentimes, when gang members see a **mark,** they will attempt to steal right from a prisoner's **house.** This happened to Ametch, a person with a bad temper and a drug habit that landed him in prison. Ametch was a big boy who was an avid sports fan. He lifted weights and worked out in his cell. His brother looked out for him so he was never starved for money.

When everyone came off the tier for chow one day, a young gang member about five cells down turned back. He went into Ametch's cell, grabbed the cigarettes on his desk, and stepped out.

When Ametch came back from chow he noticed his cigarettes were missing. He was upset to say the least. He left out a few more packs and the same thing happened.

The next day Ametch left out four more packs of smokes. He marked each pack. As he walked down the tier towards chow, he looked back toward the cell monitoring box at the end of the tier and noticed the celldoor light was lit. That meant his cell door was open. So he told the guard that he forgot to close his door. Since Officer Richy-Rich knew Ametch didn't play games with him, he nodded okay and then headed down to let the front-side tier out for chow.

Ametch hurried back to his cell and found the young gang member inside. He tried to get past Ametch to the door.

"Stealing my shit, huh, punk?" Ametch screamed, splitting his knuckle on the boy's temple.

The force put the boy on the bunk but he shot back to his feet. He swung and hit Ametch but the blows did not stop this raging bull. Actually, they might have made him more angry.

Ametch yelled "You don't ever steal my shit!" He hit his head three more times, then lifted him right off the floor by the waist and dropped him. The gang boy let out a piercing scream as the pain shot to his armpits and feet. More blows to the head. Nothing stopped Ametch.

The officer heard the noise in the now-empty cellhall. He headed down the tier and stopped in front of Ametch's cell. "Knock it off," he ordered. He grabbed Ametch from behind.

Ametch thought it was more gang boys coming up behind him, so he spun out of the grip. Then he saw it was Officer Richy, so he picked him off the floor and placed him outside the cell. Ametch jumped back in his cell and floored the thief again.

"Fight, fight! Ring the bell, fight!" Richy-Rich yelled to the officer on the catwalk. Sweat was rolling down his face. *I am not going in there to stop it.* "I'm giving you an order to knock it off!"

The bell went off and the troops arrived. By that time Ametch was tired.

Three guards dragged Ametch out and asked him why he was in the cell. He was breathing so hard he couldn't answer. But Richy-Rich could. "That's his cell!" He yelled to the guards, "Get the other one too."

Both Ametch and the young gang member went straight to seg.

⚯⚯⚯

REFLECTIONS

From my observations, interracial incidents and incidents involving gang members are more likely to involve retaliation.

"We should do something about Ametch, Big Ron," said Rock on the way back to his cell.

"Man, I don't have nothing to do with that. One of our boys ran into this dude's cell and stole from him, he got what he had coming!" Big Ron was firm. He knew a little about Ametch from the weight room and preferred to avoid that one. "Man disrespected him by stealing. Now how is that going to look if we jump Ametch?"

No one questioned Big Ron, but the talk after that was that Big Ron was getting soft. Rock wasn't too happy that his gang did not fight Ametch but he was a newer gang member. This was not the street. It was not his place to call Ron out on it.

Although there were some incidents like that, most fights came from gambling debts or two men disrespecting one another.

Turf gangs, regional gangs, East-Coast, West-Coast gangs, biker gangs—they've been in every prison I've lived in. I choose not to join one. I am writing under a pen name because I have criticized gangs.

When I first entered prison, gangs weren't as common, and every prisoner's enemy was the administration. Every man's goal was getting out. Some men tried to get their sentence overturned in state court. Others tried to get a reduction in time. Some challenged their condition of confinement. Others tried to escape.

Now it seems few men do any of this. They accept their prison life, their loss of self-respect and the prison degradation and violence. The choice is the illusionary lawlessness of incarceration. It is a part of escapism and leads to the time warp mentality.

While gangs are struggling with one another like little kids in the sandbox, the administration never gives them the tools needed to change and survive on the streets.

Gangs are like bullies—they prey on other prisoners. In a society where no one has any real power and control over their physical and, to a degree, mental surroundings, power in numbers is vital.

Even with gang intelligence, it seems like the administration cannot keep up with gang identification and gang-related incidents. Sometimes I think the administration looks the other way. When the administration tires of the gang activity, it does nothing to stop it but rather punishes all the prisoners by taking away privileges from everyone.

Gangs are like microeconomic systems thriving on money and power to gain status among peers. Gangs thrive on the contraband sales that go on in prisons: drugs, money, and services such as laundry, food, running mini-stores and cigarettes. A man selling drugs is guaranteed to have friends and protection. Even though a gang may have more power and status than money, it becomes a means of upward mobility.

Sometimes it seems as if every free-world citizen believes a man in prison has to join a gang to survive. This is a myth presented by the media and the guards union.

The main difference between gangs is where their ties are formed. Black gangs are usually an import from the streets. In prison they see friends they had on the streets so they band together.

Many Latino gangs also developed in the streets. In the system I'm in, the numbers of Hispanics and Asians are small, so there are more community ties rather than gangs running something. Also, few non-Hispanic people speak

Spanish in the prison system, so Latinos also come together because they can speak together. This is also the case with Asians. The number of Asian inmates has increased and the Asian prisoners do not relate much to the whites or blacks. The prison administration sometimes assumes that nonwhite groups are gangs when in fact they may be simply just a group of people who speak a different language, spending time with others of their culture.

Many white prisoners do not know others from the streets, so they usually join gangs in prison in order to survive the prison game. While squares generally avoid gangs and "the game," a weaker prisoner perceives he will gain status and strength through membership in a gang. I have watched a prisoner, who at one time wore the label of snitch, join a gang, only to physically challenge nongang members who **wear the snitch label.**

Gangs are a reality and nothing the state does will stop them.

EDITORS' DISCUSSION OF PART III

Individual and collective violence dominates most men's maximum-security prisons. While most men sentenced to prison are not sent there for violent crimes, the unwritten code of conduct dictates that "failure to take action justifies further victimization . . . [and] vulnerability attracts predation and fear invites exploitation" (Toch, 1998, 169). In other words, prisoners have to handle their own "problem" and be willing to use violence when necessary as a measure of self-worth. Correctional researchers believed that physical violence is overused in this "hypermasculine" environment as an uncomplicated way to measure achievement. This is because many men in prison might be considered by outside societal standards to be underachievers or failures in many aspects of their lives (Clemmer, 1940; Sykes, 1958). "In lieu of the respect and self-respect lost through imprisonment, status has to be attained among peers and imperviousness or autonomy from staff" (Toch, 172).

Awareness of the potential for violence by prisoners and minimizing risk exposure is a constant theme both at the academy and during in-service training of officers and other support staff (Conover, 2001; Fleisher, 1985). Officers and staff in contact positions minimize risk of violence through professional conduct that includes treating others with fairness and consistency, proper use of force training, accurate classification, and good communication skills.

Prisoners are also interested in minimizing their vulnerability to risk during their sentences. For prisoners, pathways to minimizing risk of violence may involve following the code of conduct, joining a gang for protection, curtailing time spent in heavily populated areas, exercising for physical strength, or intentionally obtaining a transfer to solitary confinement to escape victimization in the general population. We will discuss implications of some of these pathways.

Decreasing Gang Power for Risk Reduction

Gangs and other security-threat groups currently seem to have too much power within many maximum-security prisons. In a nationwide survey of 133 prison units, an average of one-third of all inmate–inmate violence was caused by gang members. In this same survey, 80 percent of wardens believed that the "gang problem" (collective violence) will likely increase over the next few years (Knox, 2000). Part of the reason why gang violence may increase is likely tied to active recruitment strategies based on a "blood-in, blood-out" approach. This means that the individual is loyal to the gang above all other groups. The loyalty is so intense that the individual is willing to shed blood for initial acceptance, either by enduring an initiation beating by fellow members or by stabbing or killing a rival member. Individual allegiance also means a willingness to assist other gang members and risk dying for the gang.

In his extensive research on prison violence, Silberman (2001) recommended to reduce prison violence in two ways: (1) empower individuals by allowing them more personal control over their fate, and (2) reduce the influence of prison gangs by removing resources that increase this power. Empowering individual prisoners can be accomplished through elected prisoner representatives who convey prisoner concerns directly to the administration and have voting power, and by creating alternative means to solve disputes, such as mediation.

Reducing the influence of prison gangs can be accomplished in a number of ways. One is through effective classification. Based on the chapters in Part III, we again see the critical need for an effective classification system that will serve two purposes: (1) separate rivals and enemies who may use violence against each other, and (2) identify potential victims and others who may be victims of violence. To reach this goal, it is necessary to consider the nature of gang membership. While the number has been growing, 68 percent of prisons surveyed (out of 133 units) reported that their institutional classification system considered gang membership as a factor when assigning housing and units (Knox, 32). Age should also be considered in the classification process, as it was found to be linked to prison behavior, whereby younger offenders were more likely to accumulate more disciplinary reports than older prisoners. One research study found that younger offenders also perceived prisons as more dangerous than older offenders (Hemmens and Marquart, 1999a).

A second method of reducing gang influence is through institutional transfer of identified members. Some state systems use solitary confinement in supermax prisons to control gangs. Knox (p. 4) found that about half of prison administrators in 133 units around the country believed that "no human contact" status (solitary) is ineffective for this purpose. Rather, 41 percent stated that gangs could be more effectively controlled if they were "transferred to a central-national federal unit." The conditions and effects of supermax are discussed later in this section.

Finally, a shortcoming of lifetime membership means that there are extreme consequences (e.g., death) for individuals who wish to leave the gang. Thus, few members ever leave. Based on a study of eighty-five former gang members in prison, one Texas study revealed less than 5 percent of gang members defected from their gangs after an average span of 3.4 years. Most of the defectors left the gang because they dishonored the gang concept of allegiance. In other words, they lost interest, refused to carry out a hit/crime, violated a gang rule, or matured in a different direction (Fong, Vogel, and Buentello, 1995). Although prisons offer some protection for defecting ex-gang members by way of solitary confinement, no security is provided once they leave. Thus, one way of further reducing gang influence both in prison and on the streets is creating a "gang defector relocation" program. Qualifying individuals who renounce their gang membership would be relocated to another part of the country, provided with a new identity, and assistance to begin a new life as a regular citizen. The German government is experimenting with this idea as a way to reduce gang violence.

Staff Role in Violence Reduction

Correctional officers are expected to observe inmate behavior with an eye toward averting incidents that may lead to violence. This includes observing and documenting inmate behavior and the "climate" of the unit. The quality with which this core task is performed, as well as the officer's ability to mediate inmate disputes is strongly related to whether a prison is peaceful or violent (Silberman, 1992). Many institutions also require crisis intervention training for staff, designed to give staff the tools to help diffuse problems and work on nonviolent resolutions to conflict. Reisig (2002, 99) found that the level of violence (particularly prisoner homicides) was higher in facilities that had tension or unresolved conflict between correctional officers and the prison administration. Thus the "exercise of official authority" can also significantly affect the quality of prison life.

K.C.'s experience in his assigned units suggests that the reduction of violence is in many ways the failure of human relations to work appropriately. Both staff and inmates should be encouraged to pay attention to how others will perceive their actions. When violence occurs, the custodial staff are trained in use of force techniques. The use of force in a prison is regulated by a legal standard that mandates that force must be proportionate and that it be used only to secure a legitimate correctional aim. While most uses of force are performed legally and appropriately, correctional officers who violate this standard can be prosecuted for assault or civil rights violations. Studies of violations of the use-of-force standard by officers suggest that the pressures of the work, combined with the animosity between the officers and inmates, contribute to the problem. Likewise, staff that are not well supervised are given a signal that this type of behavior is permissible (Baro, 1994).

A number of other factors outside of classification and good security procedures work towards a reduction in violence in correctional facilities. Reduction in stress among both staff and inmates can be alleviated most often by fairness, consistency, and avoiding too many rule changes with each new prison leader. One researcher found that effective access to grievance procedures for offenders, as well as third-party dispute resolution will reduce some of the stresses that contribute to violent behavior (Silberman, 1992, 2001).

Improving Race Relations

Another element tied to violence is the issue of race relations between inmates and staff, as well as among the prisoner population itself. Most correctional agencies have tried to improve race relations by providing staff training in cultural diversity. While overt racism between officers and prisoners has generally improved over the last three decades with the hiring of more women and minorities, significant problems remain. Hamm and his colleagues (1994) found that officers were more likely to write a misconduct report for jailhouse lawyers, prisoners who are African American, prisoners with mental handicaps, and political prisoners. These four groups were disciplined more often than gang members, gay prisoners, Caucasian inmates, or prisoners with AIDS.

In comparison to female prisons, male prison environments are separated by race. Male inmates generally agreed that racial conflict exists in correctional institutions and that prisoners chose their associations based first on race/ethnicity and secondly on compatibility (Alarid, 2000, 14). Two studies found that Caucasian and Hispanic prisoners were more likely than African American prisoners to favor racially segregated housing (Alarid; Hemmens and Marquart, 1999b). Despite these disturbing findings, nearly three-fourths of all correctional administrators felt optimistic that something could be done to improve racial conflict between prisoners. In addition, over half of all correctional administrators felt that improved race relations may reduce gang violence, although no administrator mentioned programs that were being implemented currently. At the current time, institutions seem more concerned with race relations between prisoners and staff, rather than investing resources to improve inmate–inmate relations. Alarid (p. 18) concluded that at the current time ". . . the institutional experience further corrodes race relations and encourages gang affiliation and violence to handle disputes. The institutional environment for men and women socializes and reinforces harmful perceptions and behaviors that are unlikely to aid offenders in adjusting to society after release."

Minimizing Risk through Supermax

Riveland (1999) reported that more than thirty states had at least one supermax facility that prison administrators used as a management tool for predatory inmates in solitary. The impetus to build these facilities originated from state legislators rather than corrections officials as a way to maximize control. Inmates housed in supermax facilities are individuals who are considered by prison managers to be disruptive to facility operations or dangerous to the physical well-being of other prisoners and correctional officers. The courts have so far upheld the constitutionality of supermax prisons provided their occupants are continuously reassessed on their level of dangerousness and transferred to a lower-level prison when they no longer pose a security threat. Prisoners who remain in solitary confinement for an extended period of time are faced with the ultimate form of sensory deprivation due to their long term separation from face-to-face human contact (Haney, 1997). Very little is known yet on the long-term emotional and mental effects of isolation, particularly for prisoners with preexisting mental illness and developmental disabilities (Riveland).

It is interesting to note that both prisoners and administrators view supermax facilities as one pathway to minimize risk during incarceration. While most prisoners in supermax would rather do their time with other inmates in general population, there are some prisoners who desire a transfer to supermax out of fear of living in general population. Fearful prisoners may be physically weak, unwilling to fight, have few associates, or owe too many debts. Whatever the reason, these victimized prisoners do not want a "snitch jacket" so instead of informing on their predators, the fearful prisoner intentionally creates a nonrelated disturbance or threatens a staff member with violence so that they will be automatically transferred to solitary confinement. The frequency of violence by fearful prisoners is unknown, but it is nevertheless ironic that victims must turn to staff threats or commit an act of violence as a call for help.

In conclusion, Toch believed that de-escalation of prison violence is possible, but highly unlikely in the current political climate. He believes that U.S. prisons are so violent because prisons are symbolic models of retributive punishment, which taxpayers currently want to be void of compassion. Thus, we must recognize that violence will be a fact of life in prisons, but there are many things that the management of corrections facilities can do to reduce it. These include effective supervision of officers, a working grievance procedure, adequate training for staff in crisis diffusion and use of force, and paying attention to inmate perceptions when making changes in operations.

QUESTIONS FOR FURTHER STUDY

1. Why is violence reduction inside prisons important?
2. What ways do prisoners use to minimize the risk of violence while incarcerated?
3. What do prison institutions do to minimize violence?
4. What are some other ways (perhaps not mentioned here) that you can think of to further reduce prison violence?
5. How much of the prison experience (e.g. learned violence) follows a prisoner once paroled into the community?

REFERENCES

Alarid, Leanne F. (2000). "Along Racial and Gender Lines: Jail Subcultures in the Midst of Racial Disproportionality." *Corrections Management Quarterly* 4(1), 8–19.

Baro, Agnes (1994). "Political Culture and Staff Violence: The Case of Hawaii's Prison System." In Michael Braswell, Reid Montgomery, and Lucien Lombardo (Eds.), *Prison Violence in America*, 2nd ed. Cincinnati, OH: Anderson.

Clemmer, Donald (1940). *The Prison Community*. Boston: Christopher.

Conover, Ted (2001). *Newjack: Guarding Sing Sing*. New York: Vintage Books.

Fleisher, Mark (1985). *Warehousing Violence*. Beverly Hills, CA: Sage.

Fong, Robert S., Ronald E. Vogel, and Salvador Buentello, (1995). "Blood-in, Blood-out: The Rationale behind Defecting from Prison Gangs." *Journal of Gang Research* 2(4), 45–51.

Hamm, Mark S., Therese Coupez, Frances E. Hoze, and Corey Weinstein, (1994). "The Myth of Humane Imprisonment: A Critical Analysis of Severe Discipline in U.S. Maximum Security Prisons, 1945–1990." In Michael C. Braswell, Reid H. Montgomery Jr., and Lucien X. Lombardo (Eds.). *Prison Violence in America*, 2nd ed. Cincinnati, OH: Anderson.

Haney, Craig (1997). "Psychology and the Limits to Prison Pain: Confronting the Coming Crisis in Eighth Amendment Law." *Psychology, Public Policy and Law* 3(4): 499–588.

Hemmens, Craig, and James W. Marquart (1999a). "Straight Time: Inmates' Perceptions of Violence and Victimization in the Prison Environment." *Journal of Offender Rehabilitation* 28 (3/4), 1–21.

Hemmens, Craig, and James W. Marquart, (1999b). "Race, Age, and Inmate Perceptions of Race Relations in Prison." *Corrections Compendium* 24(1), 1–5, 20–1.

Knox, George W. (2000). "A National Assessment of Gangs and Security Threat Groups (STGs) in Adult Correctional Institutions: Results of the 1999 Adult Corrections Survey." *Journal of Gang Research* 7(3), 1–45.

Reisig, Michael D. (2002). "Administrative Control and Inmate Homicide." *Homicide Studies*, 6(1), 84–103.

Riveland, Chase (1999). *Supermax Prisons: Overview and General Considerations*. Longmont, CO: National Institute of Corrections.

Silberman, Matthew (1992). "Violence as Social Control in Prison." *Virginia Review of Sociology* 1, 77–97.

Silberman, Matthew (2001). "Resource Mobilization and the Reduction of Prison Violence." *Research in Social Problems and Public Policy*, 8, 313–34.

Sykes, Gresham (1958). *The Society of Captives*. Princeton, NJ: Princeton University Press.

Toch, Hans (1998). "Hypermasculinities and Prison Violence." Pp. 168–78 in L. H. Bowker (Ed.), *Masculinities and Violence*. Thousand Oaks, CA: Sage.

PART IV

Conclusions

17

Correctional Policy and Prison Overcrowding

"Again I looked and saw all the oppression that was taking place under
the sun. I saw the tears of the oppressed and they have no comforter;
power was on the side of their oppressors."

ECCLESIASTES 4:1

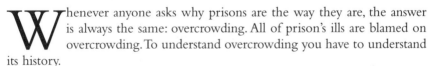

Whenever anyone asks why prisons are the way they are, the answer
is always the same: overcrowding. All of prison's ills are blamed on
overcrowding. To understand overcrowding you have to understand
its history.

In the early 1980s, when prison overcrowding first became a problem,
politicians more or less asked: How can we eliminate prison overcrowding
without actually spending any money? The solution to this problem largely was
found by changing the definition of the term "overcrowding." After all, a problem is only a problem if you define it as a problem. Thus, the meaning of that
term went through continual change over the years as politicians continued to
look at prisons through rose-colored glasses.

When I first entered prison in 1982, a prison's capacity was defined as the number of prisoners the prison was originally built to house. In the corrections business, this is known as "design capacity." For example, Gladiator School was originally built in 1935 to house 500 men. In 1984, when I arrived there, it housed between 675 and 700 men. Thus, it was overcrowded. Rather than build new prisons to handle the influx of prisoners, politicians simply redefined the meaning of the term. The next definition of overcrowding referred to the number of beds that could be put into a prison. In the corrections business, this is known as "bed capacity."

In the case of Gladiator School, the prison grounds remained the same size. For the most part, bed space was created by converting cells designed for one man into two-man cells and by converting large rooms into dormitories.

When I arrived there, Gladiator School officially had a "bed capacity" of 700. But staff considered the beds in the open dormitories to be unsafe. So as a practical matter, staff considered Gladiator School to be overcrowded whenever its population went above 650, since that's when the problems started. Thus, overcrowding was in the eye of the beholder.

The influx of inmates continued, so soon another definition of "over-crowding" was created. The new definition was based on "operating capacity," which refers to the number of prisoners that can be supported by the food, laundry, and social service facilities. From the politicians' point of view, this new definition eased the problem of overcrowding quite a bit. Why? Because no prison will ever hold more inmates than it can shower, launder, and feed. Increased operating capacity was achieved primarily by opening more dormitories, which usually are one of the most violent places in a prison.

At Gladiator School, for example, very little physically changed about the place. The prison was originally designed to house 500 men, was modified to hold 700 men, and now had an operating capacity of 1,000 men. If one looks at the problem of overcrowding this way, it is not so bad.

The goal of these changing definitions was to allow the politicians to reduce or eliminate prison overcrowding in the view of the public. The politicians could now tell the public that Gladiator School was operating at normal or a little over normal capacity. At least for a time, politicians wearing rose-colored glasses could argue that the problem of prison overcrowding had been solved.

✕═✕═✕═✕

But the fact is that only so many sardines can be squeezed into a can. Thus, most states ended up making the choice between letting people out and building new prisons.

In my own state, Governor "Robert (Bobby) Bullhorn" had a get-tough-on-crime strategy that would not consider releasing prisoners. So he started an unprecedented building strategy. In my state, expansion of the prison system became the buzzword.

In the late 1980s and early 1990s, my state just could not build enough new prisons or modify current prisons fast enough to keep pace with the influx of prisoners. To help get around this problem, new prisons were modified even before they were opened. Some prisons were constructed with a design capacity of 500 men, but before any prisoners moved in they were modified to hold 700 men. This basically was accomplished by putting bunk beds into single cells. This way the new prisons technically were not overcrowded when they finally accepted prisoners. It fell within the definition of operating capacity.

Despite these problems, Governor Bullhorn prided his reelection campaigns on his record of opening new prisons. The state could afford it since the budget was running a surplus. While President Reagan spoke of how defense bases subsidize local economies, Governor Bullhorn preached of how prisons subsidize the state's local economies. The campaign to build new prisons and add new beds to old prisons rolled on.

<hr>

Somewhere along the line, the politicians wearing those rose-colored glasses realized that building new prisons and modifying old ones cost money. When I was at Ridgewood, I was told that it cost $1.5 million to construct one 250-man housing unit. From the politician's point of view, as I said before, the problem was how to reduce or eliminate prison overcrowding without actually spending any money. So costs had to be reduced inside the current prisons. Prisons needed to reduce their expenses. This resulted in the elimination of rehabilitation programs for inmates.

All cost cutting in prisons affects prisoners one way or another. But the wave of cost cutting that came with the expansion in prison construction was primarily aimed at the rehabilitation programs that directly touched prisoners' lives—education, vocational training, drug treatment, and so on.

After Governor Bullhorn had eliminated most of the rehabilitation programs in prisons, the next part of his get-tough-on-crime strategy was to eliminate most of the incentives for inmates to participate in the few rehabilitation programs that were left. This further increased the population explosion in the state's prisons.

Throughout the 1990s, the number of crimes being committed was decreasing, so you would think that the number of prisoners would also be decreasing. Well, not in my state. Sentences were increased on most crimes, some even doubled. Sentencing guidelines for judges stressed longer time. Parole was tightened. The "three strikes and you're out" law was passed, giving sixty years for third felony convictions. A law was passed to keep sex offenders in prison even longer than the time to which they were sentenced.

Then came "truth in sentencing," which required that prisoners serve at least 85 percent of their sentences. This made parole almost nonexistent. It was not enough that a judge could give a person sixty years for three burglaries, but the person could expect to serve almost the entire sentence.

The problem with having long sentences and not having parole is that prisoners then have no incentive to reform themselves. Why bother to change if you're not going to get out anyway?

Finally, the politicians eliminated "good time" credits. "Good time" is time off a prisoner's sentence in return for good behavior while in the prison—that is, prisoners can earn "good time" by not getting any "misconduct" reports for bad behavior. But with "good time" eliminated, prisoners have no incentive to behave themselves while in prison.

So inmates had no incentive to participate in rehabilitation programs, and no incentive even to behave themselves while in prison. Nothing mattered. No matter what you did, you wouldn't get out any earlier. Once the system eliminates its incentives, many men will not change!

Politicians like Governor Bullhorn argued that overcrowded prisons were the result of the failure of prisoners to reform themselves. These same politicians eliminated most of the rehabilitation programs that were designed to reform prisoners, and watered down the remaining programs so much that they had little meaning. They then eliminated all the incentives that prisoners had to participate in the minimal programs that were left. So the absence of reform in prisoners became a self-fulfilling prophecy for these politicians.

✕▷✕▷✕▷✕▷✕

All these cost-cutting measures did not slow the influx of more prisoners. In my state, operating capacity never dropped below 100 percent and often it was much higher. The state prisons were so stuffed that no more inmates could be squeezed into them. Thousands of men were backed up in the local county jails—they were supposed to be in the state prisons but there was no place to put them. The state's prison system was reaching a crisis point. A drastic solution was needed.

Governor Bullhorn's solution was to ship prisoners out-of-state to be housed in private prisons. Some prisoners referred to this as his "final solution."

In his reelection campaign in the late 1990s Governor Bullhorn boasted, "If you do a crime in our state, you'll do your time down South." He already had contracts to house prisoners in county jails in a state over a thousand miles away. Beyond this, he was working on a plan to solve my state's problem of prison overcrowding. His plan would make his state the number one exporter of prisoners in America.

Governor Bullhorn's "final solution" to the problem of prison overcrowding came in the form of private prisons, which suddenly rolled through Wall Street. The private prison industry hit America like a bull tiptoeing through the tulips. Private prisons promised that they could do it better and cheaper, and everyone started jumping on the bandwagon. Governor Bullhorn jumped on, too.

The deal that private prisons offered looked great. The euphoria of the private prisons was so high the state employees' pension fund decided to purchase stock in this company. Everyone wanted to make a buck on the convict. No one considered that this might raise an ethical concern because these state employees would have an economic incentive to keep people locked up longer in order to keep that stock price up!

Governor Bullhorn was so enticed by this savior that he rented out entire prisons. By the year 2000 the state had approximately 5,000 prisoners housed in four different southern states. They were paying about $40.00 a day per prisoner for a total of about $80 million a year.

Governor Bullhorn is a big supporter of family values, but not for prisoners. Instead, the prison buses roll to out-of-state facilities, the closest of which are hundreds of miles away from home. Prisoners no longer receive visits from their family and friends who had stayed in contact with them. Even the long-distance telephone calls are prohibitively expensive for many prisoners' families.

But Governor Bullhorn did not care about family values for prisoners. Nor did he care about the human rights violations that were coming out of these private prisons. Nor did he care about the riot teams the private prisons used to electrically shock or beat prisoners into compliance. He ignored the reports of the higher rate of violence and mayhem of prisoner-on-prisoner assault.

The politicians, looking through their rose-colored glasses, wondered why out-of-state private facilities had double the violence rates of in-state public facilities. The reason for this surge in violence is clear. Private prisons do not do it better—they only do it only cheaper. When money runs short, they simply don't provide for the prisoner.

Governor Bullhorn's get-tough-on-crime strategy is to house prisoners all across America. Millions and millions of state tax dollars subsidized other states' local economies. Eventually the private prisons' stock, as all overpriced stocks do, dropped like a rock that was hot. Luckily, I am not a state employee drawing a pension. But Governor Bullhorn wanted prison expansion, and prison expansion is what he got.

With inmates receiving longer sentences and with the parole commission not granting paroles, prisons can be expected to continue expanding. A compounding problem, however, is that the "truth in sentencing" law was only passed recently, and the full impact of the law, in terms of prison overcrowding, will not be felt until the people who were sentenced under it become eligible for parole. Thus, the full impact of this law, in terms of prison overcrowding, will not be felt until about 2010. At that point, its effects will be stacked on top of the current problems.

Without rehabilitation programs, inmates won't have the opportunity to change. Without parole, they won't have an incentive to change. Without "good time," they won't have an incentive to behave while in prison. And yet these inmates are not going to disappear off the face of the earth. They have to go somewhere and the taxpayer burden can only continue to grow.

A system has been created that gives little or no treatment, keeps those who want change around the same lawless element that doesn't want change, and demands perfection while in prison and out on the streets after prison. This is a system designed for failure, and it has failed both the inmates who end up within it and the taxpayers who pay for it all.

My state has chosen to destroy lives, instead of supporting family values and inmate rehabilitation. It has spent more on prisons than on the state's public universities. But taxpayer money put into the prison system, a system based on failure, and taxpayer money put into the college system, has two opposite and dramatic outcomes. One helps build the economy by creating a smarter employee. The other wastes millions of dollars and destroys lives, instead of supporting family values and inmate rehabilitation.

By the year 2001, my state was no longer running a budget surplus. It had dug itself into a budgetary hole with its failing prison system. But no one wants to look at any alternatives.

✂━✂━✂━✂

One alternative is community corrections. At the present time, each prisoner in an out-of-state private prison costs the state about $15,000 per year. At the same time, parole officers in my state often handle 100 or 200 parolees. Why not stop spending money on private prisons and use that money to hire parole officers?

For example, ten prisoners in an out-of-state private prison cost the state $150,000 per year. Suppose these ten men were paroled and put on the caseload of one parole agent. With that $150,000, my state could pay this parole agent a very good salary and have plenty of money left over to pay for rehabilitation services, such as vocational and educational programs and drug treatment, and for tracking programs, such as electronic monitoring, that would closely supervise the parolees' behavior.

With that kind of money, the tracking would be phenomenal. The FBI couldn't do any better. And the parolees would have access to a wide range of rehabilitation services at the same time.

Further, these parolees would be paying taxes because they would be working in jobs. Besides that, the state collects monthly fees from parolees for the privilege of being on parole. Thus, this program would actually save the taxpayer a great deal of money. It would be a win–win situation because it would help both the taxpayer and the inmate.

The governor could brag to America how a tightly monitored community corrections program is successful and boast about its cost effectiveness. But instead, the politicians would prefer to waste economic and human capital.

The millions of dollars that flowed out of state to rent beds in private prisons down south could have created the greatest system of community corrections that America had ever seen. But the politicians had no tolerance for this. They continued to tell the public the same old story: overcrowding causes all the problems in prisons, and the lack of reform in prisoners causes overcrowding in the prisons.

Put all these problems together, including the prisoners' daily life, and you have a ship sailing endlessly in the wrong direction. I may not have all the answers, but one thing I know for certain: this ship is bound for failure, continuously failing the prisoners held within it. Removing all reform incentives is not good for the prisoner or society. This is the greatest shame of all. The prisoner population has become too great to manage, and reform is not being considered for those who live outside the norms of society.

EDITORS' DISCUSSION OF PART IV

Herbert Packer (1968) characterized correctional policy and legal sanctions in civilized societies as a continuous compromise between society's need for social order and the value of social justice. Packer called these two competing philosophies "crime control" and "due process." Crime control functions to ensure that social order is maintained by preventing future criminal actions, while due process is necessary to ensure humane treatment within the confines of our Constitution. In order for our system of justice to function properly, Packer believed both philosophies must be present to a certain degree. This is the idea behind our scales of justice. The scales not only represent a balance between the punishment and the social harm of the crime, but the punishment itself must consider the future effect on the offender as well as on the entire society. Haney (1997, 500) maintains that the get-tough movement and our evolving standards of punishment over the last three decades has "virtually suspended the debate" on alternatives to incarceration. "The public not only has been kept ignorant of the harm that prisons can do, but they have been convinced that cruel treatment is a carefully considered, effective, and perhaps even the only viable strategy to be followed in achieving meaningful crime control" (Haney, 1997, 505).

Prison expansion is directly tied with political ideology and public opinion more so than an actual increase in crime. Political movements that have influenced this "march of folly" (Irwin, 1996) in the growth of our prison population include the decline of rehabilitation programs inside prisons, the emergence of determinate and presumptive sentencing to fill its place, and the use of punishment severity manipulated by fear of crime as a method to win public office. One result of the media frenzy with the marriage of crime and politics was an increased fear of crime (Haney, 1999). The continuing "get tough" political movement that has existed since the 1970s has evolved into ever more-draconian standards. If politicians want to be reelected beyond the first term, they are left with few choices. Haney (1999, 788) describes the reality of the situation: "When the crime rate is stable, we need more prisons to make it go lower; when it decreases, we need more prisons to make sure it does not go back up; when the crime rate goes up, we really need more prisons to regain control." In other words, to suggest alternatives to imprisonment or decriminalization is, in many jurisdictions, political suicide. As a majority of the voting population, Caucasian constituents are less informed and their families less affected by the war on drugs and other punitive prison policies than are Mexican Americans, Hispanics, and African Americans, many of whom have been devastated by these policies (Haney, 1997; Haney and Zimbardo, 1998).

THE NATURE OF
CORRECTIONAL CROWDING

To deal with the phenomenal growth in the numbers of men and women who are incarcerated from these mandatory crime control policies, correctional systems have typically taken one of three courses of action: live with the overcrowding; build new facilities; or use contracted or private prisons or jails to alleviate crowding. At various times some states have engaged all three population management schemes to deal with the prison population. Privatization seems to have contributed to the growth of the "punishment industry" more so than alleviated it. Due to the strong economic opportunities that private prisons have generated, private companies have a strong interest in maintaining prisons for punishment (Lilly and Deflem, 1996). Very few states have attempted to deal with prison crowding with policies designed to reduce incarceration rates and sentence lengths.

In explaining prison crowding, it is necessary to understand the three types of capacities: design, operational, and emergency. Design capacity is the number of beds the prison was designed to accommodate. The design capacity is often related to accepted national standards of space, ventilation, lighting, sanitary fixtures, program space, and food-service capacity. A 500-bed design capacity prison would be expected to house 500 prisoners.

Operational capacity is the number of prisoners that can be accommodated at the prison. This may exceed the design capacity. The most common form of this is "double celling" portions of the prison that were designed for single occupancy. In this example a unit might be able to accommodate 700 or more prisoners in the 500-bed design capacity prison without serious impacts on the ability to feed, program, and care for prisoners and maintain security and order.

Emergency capacity is the numbers of prisoners that can be held for a short time in an emergency. In an emergency, a prison with a 500-bed design capacity may be able to accommodate over a thousand prisoners for a short period if certain adjustments were made to staffing, hours of operation, and alteration of the programs and activities.

Regarding the legal ramifications of crowding, an overcrowded institution is not by itself unconstitutional. The courts are interested primarily in the quality of basic services like food, medical care, safety, and sanitation. The Supreme Court said that, in order to show illegality, prisoners must demonstrate a prison condition that deprives them of life's basic necessities (*Rhodes v. Chapman* 1982) or that prison administrators showed "deliberate indifference" (*Wilson v. Seiter* 1991) to a prisoner's condition or situation. Bleich (1989) said that overcrowding has previously been used as a justification for court intervention and as an excuse by prison administrators to obtain more money or resources.

The social science research on the impact of crowding is mixed. Gerald Gaes (1994) emphasized that other than anecdotal evidence, there lacks enough empirical studies that can scientifically show how crowding affects stress, prisoner health, violence and, recidivism. In one study, Walters (1998) measured all the units in the entire federal prison system for a period of nine years and found an inverse relationship between crowding and violence. He discovered that as federal prison units became more crowded, prisoner violence actually *decreased*. Walters also found that as more new staff members were hired, prison violence decreased, leading him to conclude that staff inexperience did not necessarily increase violence. Gaes provides evidence that crowding may be *linked to* but is *not the sole cause of* of many unconstitutional prison conditions. At times, poor prison management may be the actual cause, but administrators can easily mask it by claiming overcrowding.

On the other hand, research has also shown that crowded institutions create uncertainty, and increase idle time and stress (Haney, 1997), which in turn may contribute to weakened prisoner–staff attachments and higher rates of inmate misconduct (Ekland-Olson, 1986) and more violence (Ekland-Olson, Barrick, and Cohen 1983). In addition, crowding could conceivably create difficulty for staff to operate and deliver all the necessary daily services. For example, correct classification of inmates to maximize their safety and security requires a certain percentage of empty bed space in which to move the new or transferred prisoner. In crowded situations, classification breaks down when inmates are assigned to the first open bed.

Crowded institutions make it difficult for many of the programs and services to operate effectively, such as kitchens, medical, and treatment programs. For example, kitchens need to be able to produce nutritious meals at proper temperatures three times per day. Special meals often need to be prepared for medical or religious reasons. A kitchen designed to produce 500 meals cannot expect to maintain the same quality and schedule if they must prepare meals for 700 to 800 prisoners three times per day.

All of the factors that have thus far been discussed—the demise of rehabilitation programs, the war on drugs, favoring prison over community-based sanctions, longer mandatory sentences, and crowded institutions—seem to indicate that most prisoners will be worse off when released than when they entered prison. The remainder of this section focuses on prison conditions and the standards for sensible prison management, including a reduction in the use of imprisonment as a criminal sanction.

Logan's Performance Criteria

Logan (1993) proposed performance measures for prisons that narrowed the focus on prison management responsibilities to the internal workings of the prison. Logan argued that "The purpose of a prison is to keep prisoners—to keep them in, keep them safe, keep them in line, keep them healthy, and keep them busy—and to do it with fairness, without undue suffering, and as efficiently as possible" (Logan, p.25). Thus, being sent to prison *is* the punishment, and that the conditions in prison are *not designed to be* the punishment. In today's more ideologically punitive environment, many people believe that conditions in prison are not harsh enough. Like Packer's balance between crime control and due process, many corrections workers attempt to balance the needs of the inmates and the needs of security and order in the institution. Unfortunately, this mix is often skewed so far toward order and security at any cost, that treatment and rehabilitative needs are virtually forgotten. Much of what the author discussed in the preceding chapters illustrates this point from the perspective of the incarcerated person.

The performance criteria discussed here are based on eight dimensions of activity that are designed to work together in the prison to provide the *minimum* levels of operations of these facilities. These performance criteria do not reflect a mission that includes the rehabilitation of prisoners, nor according to Logan should prisons be held accountable if inmates return to criminal behavior when they are released. The performance criteria are:

Security: Security involves keeping the inmates from escaping, controlling movement, and regulating contraband items in the facility.

Safety: Safety implies that inmates will be protected from environmental and social hazards such as those arising from other prisoners (e.g., assault) or injury from unsafe equipment.

Order: Order is seen as minimizing prisoner disturbances and misconduct.

Care: Care is keeping the inmates healthy, by providing adequate medical and mental health care, nutritious food, and recreation.

Activity: Activity is keeping the inmates busy in some form of activity, ideally in constructive activities that might enhance success.

Justice: Justice implies that the facility operates according to constitutional laws and rules that are applied with fairness and consistency.

Conditions: Conditions implies that inmates should be able to serve their terms without undue suffering. They should be provided with basic necessities of adequate space, food, legal visits, and ability to practice their religion of choice.

Management: Management is running the prison as efficiently as possible. This includes adequate staff, proper training, and continuous in-service training.

Legality of Prison Conditions

Two recent changes have occurred in the courts over the last decade. First is the Supreme Court's retreat toward a revised "hands-off" attitude toward prison conditions (see Haney and Zimbardo, 1998). Second, researchers observed that in determining the legality of prison conditions, the Supreme Court has looked at the amount of harm inflicted rather than the quality of positive change by prisoners (Haney, 1997). It is noteworthy that we have lost the ability to define the effects of prison as to whether a person has been reformed. Now the effects of prison are measured by level of harm done. In addition, institutional crowding creates an uncertain situation that in turn makes the delivery of services harder or impossible to meet. If we cannot meet the objectives of Logan's confinement model, how can we expect that the individuals exiting prison will be reformed or rehabilitated?

WHERE DO WE GO FROM HERE?

The American prison system is facing a number of serious problems in the next two decades. While the population growth seems to be leveling off, many states and the federal prison system have not fully realized the impact of their sentencing policies implemented in the 1990s. New prison construction is costly, and every dollar spent on corrections is money not being spent on other programs, like health care and education. Even during the latest budget recessions, crime control agencies such as law enforcement and corrections seem to be gaining a larger share of the taxpayer pie, while other programs are cut.

One primary theme to be learned from this book is that increased public safety cannot be achieved solely by incarcerating more people. We are fooling ourselves if we think that the crime rate has decreased only because we are incarcerating more people. Some researchers believe, in fact, that the opposite effect may occur. "[P]risons themselves may act as criminogenic agents—in both their primary effects on prisoners and secondary effects on the lives of persons connected to them—serving to increase the amount of crime that occurs within a society" (Haney, 1997, 504).

Public safety can be more effectively achieved as a prevention mechanism at the front end, early in life, by focusing resources on healthy families, adequate schools, and economic opportunities that give rise to an overall better quality of life. Prisons are an expensive response that should be used sparingly as a punishment for violent people who are a real threat to community safety. It is estimated that between 35 and 40 percent of state prisoners and 50 percent of federal prisoners who are currently incarcerated could have been sanctioned for their behavior using community alternatives and/or restorative justice methods (see Karp, 1998; Van Ness and Strong, 1997; and Wright, 1996, for more information on restorative justice). For prisoners who must be separated from society, over 90 percent of them will eventually rejoin our community. The question we must ask ourselves is, what kind of a person do we want leaving the prison?

Revival of Rehabilitation

Decreasing treatment programs in prisons in the 1970s was a grave mistake. Research studies have found that the general public continues to believe that treatment programs should remain a part of sound correctional policy (Applegate, Cullen, and Fisher, 1997). Rehabilitation must be available and expanded as a choice for prisoners who are ready to seize the opportunity for personal growth. Treatment programs must also be targeted at the people who are most likely to benefit from the intervention. Psychologists note that ". . . prisoner change cannot ignore situations and social conditions that prevail after release if they have any hope of sustaining whatever positive gains are achieved during periods of imprisonment . . ." (Haney, 1997, 504). We wholeheartedly agree with John Irwin (1996, 494), in that "[b]efore we can take up the rehabilitative task again with any seriousness, we will have to greatly reduce the size of our prison populations."

QUESTIONS FOR FURTHER STUDY

1. What factors contributed to the demise of rehabilitation programs in the 1970s?
2. How did correctional policy become such a political hot potato?
3. Do severe punishments work to deter crime?
4. What is the benefit of reintroducing rehabilitation back into the prison environment? Can treatment work in a punitive controlled setting?
5. What alternatives to prison exist to sanction criminal behavior?

REFERENCES

Applegate, Brandon K., Francis T. Cullen, and Bonnie S. Fisher (1997). "Public Support for Correctional Treatment: The Continuing Appeal of the Rehabilitative Ideal." *Prison Journal* 77(3), 237–58.

Bleich, J. (1989). "The Politics of Prison Crowding." *California Law Review* 77(5), 1125–80.

Ekland-Olson, Sheldon (1986). "Crowding, Social Control and Prison Violence: Evidence from the Post-Ruiz Years in Texas." *Law and Society Review* 20(3), 389–421.

Ekland-Olson, S., D. Barrick, and L. E. Cohen (1983). "Prison Overcrowding and Disciplinary Problems: An Analysis of the Texas

Prison System." *Journal of Applied Behavioral Science* 19, 163–76.

Gaes, Gerald (1994). "Prison Crowding Research Reexamined." *Prison Journal* 74, 329–63.

Haney, Craig (1997). "Psychology and the Limits to Prison Pain: Confronting the Coming Crisis in Eighth Amendment Law." *Psychology, Public Policy and Law* 3(4), 499–588.

Haney, Craig (1999). "Ideology and Crime Control." *American Psychologist* 54(9), 786–8.

Haney, Craig, and Philip Zimbardo (1998). "The Past and Future of U.S. Prison Policy Twenty-Five Years after the Stanford Prison Experiment." *American Psychologist* 53(7), 709–27.

Irwin, John (1996). "The March of Folly." *Prison Journal*, 76(4), 489–94.

Karp, David R. (1998). *Community Justice: An Emerging Field*. Lanham, MD: Rowman and Littlefield.

Lilly, J. Robert, and Mathieu Deflem (1996). "Profit and Penality: An Analysis of the Corrections–Commercial Complex." *Crime and Delinquency* 42(1), 3–20.

Logan, Charles (1993). "Criminal Justice Performance Measures for Prisons" in *Performance Measures for the Criminal Justice System*. Washington, DC: U.S. Department of Justice.

Packer, Herbert L. (1968). *The Limits of the Criminal Sanction*. Stanford, CA: Stanford University Press.

Van Ness, Daniel, and Karen Strong (1997). *Restoring Justice*. Cincinnati, OH: Anderson.

Walters, Glenn D. (1998). "Time Series and Correlational Analyses of Inmate-Initiated Assaultive Incidents in a Large Correctional System." *International Journal of Offender Therapy and Comparative Criminology* 42(2), 123–31.

Wright, Martin (1996). *Justice for Victims and Offenders: A Restorative Response to Crime*, 2nd ed. Winchester, England: Waterside Press.

COURT CASES

Rhodes v. Chapman, 452 S.Ct 337 (1982).

Wilson v. Seiter, 111 S.Ct 2321 (1991).

Appendix A

A THEORY OF THE TOXIC-SHAMED CRIMINAL

By K. C. Carceral

Through my years of study and growth I have read a great deal of material on why people become criminals. I have always had a keen interest in human development, including criminology, but ultimately I also have been trying to understand myself and the people with whom I have lived for over twenty years.

And now, though I am far from perfect, I believe that the root problem in people who become criminals is that they have a toxic-shamed identity. Shame itself is a healthy emotion that allows me to know I am worthwhile even though I am human, even though I am imperfect, even though I make mistakes. When properly nurtured, shame is associated with normal embarrassment, shyness, community, creativity, learning, humility, and spirituality.

However, a person who is chronically shamed can come to believe that he or she is flawed and defective as a human being, and therefore worthless. At that point, shame becomes "toxic" rather than healthy. It becomes a "state of being" rather than an emotion. Toxic shaming results from improper socialization, first in the family and later in subcultures and cultures. I believe toxic shame is the key to understanding crime and therefore the key to understanding all that I have written about prisons and prisoners in this book. In developing this view, I have relied on the work of John Bradshaw, particularly as expressed in his book *Healing the Shame that Binds You* (1988). I have relied on Bradshaw's work because of its convergence with my own thoughts and observations about criminals, and also because I lacked access to other material. Though I believe most of his material was directed at helping the middle class overcome personality dysfunctions, I also believe that criminals could benefit in this type of experiential and relationship-oriented treatment in a more confrontive form.

⟩⟨⟩⟨⟩⟨⟩

Healthy shame is an emotion directly connected to our worth as human beings. When shame is properly nurtured, we become whole in our sense of self. We have appropriate self-esteem, realizing that we are not God and that we are not perfect. We have a sense of our own limitations, but we also have a sense of our own ultimate worth and value as human beings. We are grounded in our own reality, of who and what we actually are.

From birth, a child develops a healthy shame by building a bridge of trust and security to his or her primary caregivers. "When security and trust are present, we begin to develop an interpersonal bond, which forms a bridge of mutuality. Such a bridge is crucial for the development of self-worth. . . . If a child can be protected by firm but compassionate limits; if he can explore, test, and have tantrums without the caregiver's withdrawal of love, i.e., withdrawal of the interpersonal bridge, then the child can develop a healthy sense of shame" (Bradshaw, pp. 5–6). This secure bridge to the caregiver is necessary in order to set limits to build a healthy sense of self. This allows the child to develop his or her ego within appropriate boundaries. Once safe boundaries are developed, the intense ego needs of the child are reduced and the child can develop healthy shame along with other healthy emotions.

⟩⟨⟩⟨⟩⟨⟩

Toxic shame no longer is an emotion that signals our limits. Instead of helping to build a balanced identity with an appropriate sense of worthiness and limitations, toxic shame fuses with our identity and upsets the natural state of our core. Needs, emotions, and feelings natural to any human being are at that core. Once that core is fused with toxic shame, the toxic shame becomes a state of being. We develop a toxic-shamed identity.

Bradshaw (p. 10) explains this further: "Toxic shame gives you a sense of worthlessness, a sense of failing and falling short as a human being. . . . A shame-based person will guard against exposing his inner self to others, but more significantly, he will guard against exposing himself to himself . . ." Instead of giving the person a healthy sense of limits, it becomes the person's deepest darkest secret, a demon within.

A child develops toxic shame when his or her core wants, emotions, and needs are repeatedly and unexpectedly exposed. This exposure starts before the child has the ability to choose and before the child has a boundary structure to protect him or herself. As the shaming repeatedly occurs, the child comes to feel that his or her core feelings, emotions, and needs are incorrect, wrong, bad, and defective. The child comes to dislike, distrust, and disown those vulnerable parts of the self. Eventually, the child rejects those parts and objectifies them.

Thus, with toxic shame, ". . . we disown ourselves. And this disowning demands a cover up" (Bradshaw, p. 1).

✄━✄━✄━✄

The "cover-up" consists in constructing a false self. Where the true self is *human*, the false self is either *more than human* or *less than human*. This is one of the paradoxes of a shamed identity: ". . . it is the core motivator of the superachieved and the underachieved, the star and the scapegoat . . ." (Bradshaw, p. 14).

For example, embarrassment is a part of healthy shame that lets us know our boundaries and limitations. With toxic shame, we either are embarrassed about everything down to our deepest core, or we are embarrassed about nothing whatsoever. Neither of these states is normal; both are unhealthy. Healthy shame reminds us to be cautious when dealing with others, but toxic shame makes us either paranoid or fearless in our relationships. Paranoia leaves us alienated and isolated, while fearlessness leaves us vulnerable and exposed—either way, we are wounded. Healthy shame reminds us we do not know everything and opens us up to creativity and learning. Toxic shame leads us to believe either that we know everything already or that we can never learn anything. Either way, learning and creativity stop. Healthy shame reminds us we need community, we need love, we need relationships. Toxic shame leads us to believe either that we don't need relationships because we are superior to everyone else, or that we can't ever have relationships because we are too defective for others to love us. Healthy shame helps us see life's higher meaning as both beyond ourselves and also within ourselves. Toxic shame, in contrast, leads us to see meaning only within ourselves or only outside of ourselves, with the result that we never find life's higher meaning. Ultimately, healthy shame puts us in touch with our deepest human needs, while toxic shame cuts us off from those same needs.

✄━✄━✄━✄

Freud said that children have primary and secondary ego defenses and that these defense mechanisms work in stages: when the primary fail, the secondary take over. Bradshaw added characterological styles as a third stage of ego defense, with which an adult passes shame onto others by acting shamelessly.

I think about this a little differently, based on two relatively simple facts. First, individuals construct their views of the environment over their own life span, from their earliest beginnings as small children to their present situation as adults. Thus, their mature adult views of the environment have been built on the foundation of their very early, very simplistic, views as children. Second, individuals are egocentric and look outward at the environment from their own position in life and from their own point of view. As children grow, this outward-looking view of the environment changes over time and takes on a larger area. As this happens, individuals change their views; their "selves" make adjustments.

At the beginning, when we are children, the environment is very large and our caregivers seem all-powerful. As we age, our environment seems to reduce in size and our caregivers do not seem as powerful. When a child is shamed, he or she has to rely on his or her ego defenses, simple ways with which we defend ourselves against attacks from our caregivers. We have little experience in the world and our all-powerful caregivers are our survival. Hence, primary and secondary ego defenses are simple, inexperienced ways to defend off attacks. As we gain more experiences of life, our ego defenses become more complex, so we build on our simple ways to defend attack, to more complex ways. Hence, characterological styles develop as complex personality traits to defend against shaming. We developed characterological styles, or character patterns, to prevent exposure from shame.

Eventually, our response to toxic shame becomes automatic. It separates from our conscious thinking and becomes autonomous. Our brains can retain only a certain number of memories. Generally the more intense (or terrifying) the memory, the more we cling to it, but over time the memory weakens. Even though the memory itself fades, the emotional reactions to these events can remain and can begin to function autonomously. That is, we do the same things but without thinking about them or being aware of them. We now function automatically in ways that we previously thought about consciously.

Bradshaw discusses a rather long list of ego defenses. Freud conceptualized ego-defense mechanisms, or weaknesses that stem from anxiety. Toxic shame creates a heightened state of anxiety. These weaknesses are not mutually exclusive—a toxic-shamed person generally develops many such weaknesses. I mention a few of these ego defenses and have added a few of my own that seem to me to be especially relevant to prisoners and criminals, although I am not expert on this subject.

Denial, in my view, is the ego weakness that is the most common among prisoners, particularly with respect to their own offenses. Most people think that denial means denying that something ever happened. Instead, mostly it involves admitting that something happened but interpreting it in such a way as to lessen its impact or its meaning. For example, a person who killed may say that the victim deserved it, a person who raped may say that the victim really wanted it, a person who stole may say they were only borrowing it, and so on. These are examples of how denial works by lessening the impact to self. In reality, the toxic-shamed person is covering up, denying the full truth of the crime, so that the true impact of the action has been reduced to something more acceptable.

Repression is a way for the child to "numb out" his or her emotion. Bradshaw writes, "Whenever a child is shamed through some form of abandonment, the feelings of anger, hurt, sadness arise. . . . Since shamed parents are shame-bound in all their emotions, they cannot tolerate their children's emotions. Therefore they shame their children's emotions. . . . Once an emotion is repressed, one feels numb" (Bradshaw, p. 74). I believe that many offenders are numb to their own feelings, including the feelings they have about having committed crimes against other people. Offenders may express no remorse whatsoever, even for truly terrible crimes. In addition, I believe that repression in offenders manifests itself in insensitivity to the feelings of others. In particular, offenders may "numb out" any sensitivity to the feelings of their victims. If I cannot feel my own emotions in the proper sense, then I cannot understand another person's feelings and emotions.

A third ego weakness is *projection*, in which we attribute our own feelings to others. Toxic-shamed people deny and disown their own feelings, needs, and wants. But they often then project those same feelings, needs, and wants onto other people. They cannot see their own feelings in themselves and so they tend to see their own feelings in others. With inmates, for example, projection often manifests itself in judgments about other inmates: "Dude thinks he knows everything; he talks too much; he always wants to argue," etc. The person expressing these judgments usually has the same characteristics himself, but will never admit it. Projection also manifests itself in hatred and prejudice. Toxic-shamed people are intensely critical of themselves and are filled with self-hatred. These people cannot feel or acknowledge these intense feelings, so they tend to project the hated parts of themselves onto others, particularly others who are different in some way. That is, projection of self-hatred ends up taking the form of prejudice and racism. The problem is that hatred of others makes the toxic-shamed person feel better for a while, but it cannot heal the core of self-hatred that lies within. Ultimately, racism and prejudice are ways to hide our true selves behind the false self of racial and ethnic superiority. But the core of emptiness and self-hatred remains within, so that hating and hurting others can only be a temporary fix.

Similar to this is *paranoia*, a fourth ego weakness to cope with toxic shaming. When they think of paranoia, many people think of the old TV shows where the doctor drops his pen and the patient jumps, trembling in fear. But I think of how many men within prison I have seen exhibit paranoia over simple events in their lives. They believe the guards and the administration are out to get them in everything they do. The toxic-shamed person projects his perceived deficiencies onto others and therefore must always remain hypervigilant and constantly on guard.

A fifth ego weakness against toxic shame is *addiction*. Toxic shame is associated with moods that are very uncomfortable and distressing. Illegal drugs or alcohol are mood-altering substances, and the whole point of using them is to alter moods that can seem intolerable at the time. But food, sex, money, sports, work, shopping, TV, and exercise also can have mood altering effects and can be used in an addictive way to try to escape the intolerable moods brought on by an internal state of toxic shame. Crime can be addictive in this same way: burglars have told me about the rush of breaking and entering, and armed robbers have told me about the skill and the thrill of sticking up a person. But addictive behavior is another way to hide the true self behind a false self. Even worse, addictive behavior creates life-damaging consequences that manifest themselves in even more toxic shame. Finally, like hatred and racism, addictive behavior can only be a temporary fix. The real problem is in the core of the person, which is filled with self-hatred generated by toxic shame. This core cannot be healed by additive behavior, any more than it can be healed by hatred.

A sixth ego weakness is the endless desire to seek perfection, described by Bradshaw (p. 19) as *narcissism:* "The *narcissist* is endlessly motivated to seek perfection in everything he does." The endless drive for perfection causes extreme involvement with the self and a complete lack of interest in others. Yet the perfectionist has a very strong need for others because only others can approve and validate the perfectionist efforts. This is the paradox of the narcissist who is filled with toxic shame.

Finally, Bradshaw spoke about *grandiosity* as a seventh ego weakness against toxic shame. "Grandiosity results from the human will becoming disabled. . . . The will is disabled primarily through the shaming of the emotions. . . . When an emotional event happens, emotions must be discharged in order for the intellect, reason, and judgment to make sense out of it. As emotions get bound by shame, their energy is frozen, which blocks the full interaction between the mind and the will" (Bradshaw, pp. 21–2). As this occurs, the person loses the ability to reason and judge. In particular, the person loses the ability to curb the desires of the will. As Bradshaw states, "The will is an appetite. It is dependent on the mind (reasoning and judgment) for its eyes. Without the mind, the will is blind and has no control" (Bradshaw, p. 22). The result is that the person wants things that can't be, tries to control everything, becomes impulsive, and sees things as all or nothing. When he succeeds in getting what he wants, he becomes godlike, but when he fails he feels depressed and defective. This is the main theme of toxic shame: it is either more than humans can ever be, or less than humans actually are. It is all or nothing without anything in between.

<hr/>

The "ego weaknesses" described above essentially are *automatic, habitual and largely unconscious ways of thinking* that protect the person from toxic shame—i.e., they are internal to the individual. In contrast, the "characterological styles" or "character patterns" that are described below essentially are *habitual and largely conscious ways of acting*. In particular, character patterns are habitual ways in which people act shamelessly and pass their toxic shame onto others. "Acting shameless embodies several behaviors which serve to alter the feeling of shame and to interpersonally transfer one's toxic shame to another person. . . . These behaviors are all strategies of defense against the pain of toxic shame. . . . They are mood altering and become addictive" (Bradshaw, p. 88).

As with the ego weaknesses, these character patterns are not mutually exclusive of one another—in fact, I believe they are connected to each other and tend to come in multiples. On the other hand, as these behavior patterns become habitual, people tend to exhibit one particular pattern of behavior over and over again in many different types of situations. That is, these patterns of behavior become "characteristic" of the person; they become identified with the "character" of the person.

These character patterns are largely what I have written about in this book, since they characterize the people who fill the prisons in which I have lived for over twenty years. The theory I present here is how I understand these people, how I explain them to myself, how I think they came to be the people they are today.

This, then, is the heart of my theory of the toxic-shamed criminal. *In my view, many people suffer from toxic shame. However, when the toxic shame is intense, the person can develop habitual patterns of behavior (character patterns) in response to the intense shame that eventually leads the person to incarceration.*

<hr>

I have built on Bradshaw's list of character patterns since he did not tailor his writing to the criminal offender. The character patterns that I have developed are perfection seeking, failure seeking, power and control seeking, anger and rage, arrogance, criticizing and blaming, judging and moralizing, contempt, patronizing, people pleasing, care taking, manipulating, envying, rationalizing, minimizing, explaining, intellectualizing, extremism, sympathy seeking, and reenacting.

The first character pattern is *perfection seeking.* For the toxic shamed individual, ". . . parental acceptance and love is dependent upon performance. . . . Judgment and comparison-making lead to a destructive kind of competitiveness (Bradshaw, pp. 88–9). In response to toxic shame, then, some people endlessly seek perfection. They care little about others, but care greatly about their attention and praise. Yet the perfect measure of praise is never obtained, since to fail is human.

Failure seeking is the opposite of perfection seeking, but they are mirror images of each other. The failure-ist seeks failure the same way the perfectionist seeks perfection. Neither knows they are exhibiting this behavior. Both flow from the boundarylessness of toxic shame. Both seek attention through performance; one seeks positive attention while the other seeks negative attention. However, they only care for attention, not for the person giving it. They battle internalized toxic shame, yet they seek to resolve it through external means.

Next is the person who strives for *power and control*—this is a major behavior pattern exhibited by criminals in general. As children, while being shamed, these people felt powerless; as adults they strive to cover up that vulnerability. Control-ists perform well in highly structured environments such as prisons, where the hierarchy of power and authority is well defined. They use this clarity of power to climb in the hierarchy. As they climb, they relentlessly follow those above them but relentlessly subdue those below them. Loss of control would bring vulnerability and toxic shame. When this type of person lacks control, he suffers anxiety, depression, and frustration. People striving for power and control try unsuccessfully to get others to treat them the way they want to be treated. They want to be in control. Toxic shame develops a warped sense of being "greater than" human, leading to an addiction for control; yet all these efforts fail since we are only human.

Many offenders resort to *anger and rage* to cope with vulnerability. Bradshaw (p. 90) states, "Rage protects in two ways: either by keeping others away or by transferring the shame to others. . . . Rage often intensifies hatred. . . . If the person with internalized rage also acquires power, then it can result in violence, revenge, vindictiveness and criminality." Criminality often is revenge, vindictiveness, and violence—i.e., anger projected onto others. Those who internalize their anger and/or rage tend to be bitter and sarcastic. Rage-ists are related to control-ists. When control-ists cannot achieve their need for power and control, they turn to rage. Rage may be intensified by the person's environment, which can be frustrating and stressful and lack opportunity. But rage is rooted in the core of the toxic-shamed individual.

The next character pattern is *arrogance*, which involves ". . . offensively exaggerating one's own importance . . . . After years of arrogance, the arrogant person is so out of touch he truly doesn't know who he is" (Bradshaw, p. 91). Arrogance is an exaggerated form of the false self, developed because of the toxic-shamed self that lies within. It combines the effects of a disabled will combined with grandiosity, even though all these behavior patterns are, in one way or another, related to a disabled will. When people exaggerate their importance, they try to become more than human. This also is related to power and control. The person's false sense of importance leads him to believe he is "born to lead", i.e. have power over and control others, who are "less than" he is.

Another way to deal with toxic shame is by *criticizing and blaming* others. This character pattern is related to most of the other character patterns described here. Criticism and blame allows a toxic-shamed individual to justify his or her actions. It supports the false self and keeps the true self in hiding. "If I feel put down and humiliated, I can reduce this feeling by criticizing and blaming someone else" (Bradshaw, p. 91). Blame also plays an important role in responsibility. Blame is an outgrowth of denial: If I blame others for my own actions, it lessens or removes my responsibility for my actions. Once again, power and control is a counter-partner in blaming and criticizing. Toxic shame allows us to remove our own feelings of being flawed and interpersonally transfer them to someone else (projection).

Judging and moralizing are related to the perfection-seeking—they are a way to be "one up" on other people. "When one is using perfectionism, moralizing and judgment to mood alter one's own shame, one is acting 'shameless.' The children who are the victims of perfectionism, judgment and moralizing have to bear their shameless caretaker's shame" (Bradshaw, p. 91). It also can be used in connection with spirituality and religion: People can play a role of being "better than" others because of their spirituality or their relation to God.

Contempt is similar to judging and moralizing and to perfection-seeking since the self of another is rejected. Bradshaw states (p. 91): "In contempt one is intensely conscious of another person who is experienced as disgusting." The person to whom the contempt is being directed feels himself as rejected and disgusting. In the case of a child, he lacks ways to protect his self. Later in life he condemns others as he was condemned. The perfectionist uses judging, moralizing, and contempt to remove his or her toxic shame and place it on another.

Patronizing others is still another defense against toxic shame. Bradshaw (p. 92) says that you "patronize" another when you ". . . support, protect or champion someone who is unequal in benefits, knowledge or power; but who has not asked for your support, protection or championing." Patronizing can be an offshoot of contempt: it can be used to cover up contempt, but the contempt actually shows through.

Caretaking is related to patronizing: people help others but do it because of their own needs generated by a core of toxic shame. "Such a person can alter her feeling of defectiveness by helping and taking care of others. When she is care-taking others, she feels good about herself" (Bradshaw, p. 92). Both patronizing and caretaking help to cover up the person's toxic shame, and both also can transfer that toxic shame onto the other: "It robs the other person of a sense of achievement and power, thereby increasing toxic shame" (Bradshaw, p. 92).

People pleasing is related to both patronizing and the caretaking. People pleasing "is primarily a way of manipulating people and situations . . . [and] avoids any real emotional contact and intimacy. . . . By avoiding intimacy, he can insure that no one will see him as he truly is, shamed, flawed, and defective." (Bradshaw, pp. 92–3).

Manipulating is a way to avoid true relationships and to use people and situations to fulfill your own needs and desires. The difference between people pleasing and the manipulating is that people pleasers think of themselves as nice guys in order to cover up their toxic-shamed self. In contrast, manipulators are self-consciously selfish; they want to get their needs met but dislike confrontation. By manipulating they can get what they want without directly confronting others. Both avoid intimacy to hide the feeling of toxic shame.

Envying is everywhere in prison since prisons nurture envy. Bradshaw (pp. 93–4) describes envy as ". . . discomfort at the excellence or good fortune of another. . . . Such discomfort is frequently accompanied by some verbal expression of belittlement. . . . Ultimately self-assertion, admiration and greed are the disguises envy uses to cover up the core issue which is toxic shame." I believe prisoners' politics run on envy. Most prisoners see the world with envy, instilled from our social and cultural success myths. Jealousy and envy cover the toxic shame that leads the person to self-destructive behavior and creating more victims. Envy is the cover-up for toxic shame.

Rationalizing is a way that some people use logic to worm their way out of anything they are confronted with. All actions are rationalized so that there never are any mistakes. Mistakes would mean that you are flawed, but to recognize that you are flawed is to be filled with toxic shame.

Minimizing is a way to follow the same pattern: The person will minimize his actions to remove himself from them. For example, I knew a rapist who told me his story many times over the years, and each time his role got smaller and smaller.

Explaining is similar to both rationalizing and minimizing. The explain-ist has a unique way of explaining everything. When he talks, he talks and talks. He does all the talking and others do all the listening. The explain-ist controls the conversation so that the others cannot talk.

Some of these constant talkers really are *sympathy seeking*. In their conversations and actions, these people always pull for sympathy from the other person. They try, in every way possible, to make others feel sorry for them. Getting others to feel sorry for them helps them justify their actions (denial).

Intellectualizing is like explaining, but instead of talking all the time, the intellectual-ist thinks. This person will mentally go over and over thoughts in his own mind. He is the guy that never cries, or gets angry, happy, etc, because he is always thinking.

Extremism is like perfectionism—the extreme-ist has a disabled will and sees everything as all or nothing without anything in between.

Finally, some people engage in *reenacting* as a defense against toxic shame. Bradshaw (p. 103) describes reenactment as "repeatedly entering into destructive and shaming relationships which repeat early abusive trauma." In reenactment, a past victim can become a victim again, or can become the offender who victimizes someone else in a similar way. Bradshaw goes further, "What this means is that a criminal offender was once victimized in much the same way as he criminalizes. Children from violently abusing families, children from families where high voltage abandonment takes place, suffer terrible victimization" (Bradshaw, pp. 119–120). Finally, this is a person dealing with his toxic-shamed identity.

These are the character patterns that people who were toxically shamed as children express when they become adults. These character patterns (behavior patterns) stem from the ego defenses (thinking patterns) described above. They are not mutually exclusive and they come in varying degrees. These character patterns allow the false, shamed self to pass its shame onto others by acting shamelessly. There are many other character patterns that I see every day in prison. Each is, I believe, an outgrowth of denial and repression generated by toxic shame.

⋊⊏⊐⋉⊏⊐⋉

The major way that a person acquires a toxic-shamed identity is through the family. Every family has categories of rules, which are the family unit's social laws of reality. Bradshaw (p. 39) notes, "There are rules for celebrating and socializing; rules about touching and sexuality; rules about sickness and proper health care; rules about vacations and vocations; rules about household maintenance and spending of money. Perhaps the most important rules are about feelings, interpersonal communication and parenting."

With regard to these rules about feelings and communication, toxic-shamed parents create rigid and dysfunctional rules due to the family's need for balance. The rigid rules in a dysfunctional family are the way they pass the shame from the parent to the child. "In the shamed families, the rules consciously shame all the members. Generally however, the children receive the major brunt of the shame" (Bradshaw, p. 39). This is because the rules are hierarchical so that blame flows downhill: Dad yells at and blames everyone, mom yells at the kids, the older children yell at the younger children, and the youngest child kicks the cat. This is one of the rules of a dysfunctional family.

Bradshaw describes a variety of dysfunctional family rules. I have modified those here to make them applicable to my theory of crime.

1. "Control . . . the major defense strategy for shame" (Bradshaw, p. 39). If the parent shows vulnerability, he or she opens up to powerlessness and toxic shame.

2. "Perfectionism—Always be right in everything you do. [It] always involves a measurement that is being imposed . . . [yet] no one ever measures up" (Bradshaw, p. 40). The child learns that love is based on an exterior condition of an action and begins to love the actions to measure up, instead of the parent.

3. "Blame—maintains the balance . . . when control is broken down" (Bradshaw, p. 40). Criticism and blame are used to ease the feelings of toxic shame through vulnerability. Yet, criticizing and blaming also remove one's responsibility for his or her actions, allowing shameful behavior. This feeds perfectionism and teaches manipulation. It is my belief that none of the dysfunctional family rules are mutually exclusive; however, these three become enmeshed in spinning a web, which feed off one another. They are truly the three-headed demon of toxic shame.

4. "Denial of the Five Freedoms— . . . the basic human power of . . . the power to perceive, to think and interpret, to feel, to want and choose, and the power to imagine . . . " (Bradshaw, p. 40). These basic human powers stem from each individual's core. In a toxic-shamed family unit, other rules of power and control, perfectionism, criticizing, and blaming, etc. mask these natural freedoms by shaming them. Each freedom is affected to a degree by teaching a child to ignore them and accept the perfectionist's measuring tools.

5. "The No-Talk Rule— . . . prohibits the full expression of any feeling, need or want" (Bradshaw, p. 40). Toxic shame demands rigorous cover-up. Thus true feelings, needs or emotions are hidden and the loneliness and self-rupture are not spoken about. It is a very common rule of many sex addicts and alcoholics. The most amazing thing about toxic shame is that no one in the family wants to talk about the family's true problems.

6. "Don't Make Mistakes— . . . mistakes reveal the flawed vulnerable self. Cover up your own mistakes and if someone else makes a mistake, shame him" (Bradshaw, p. 40). I believe this rule should read, "hide your mistakes." To avoid revealing the flawed self, cover-up is demanded. Any mistake made has to be covered, hidden, concealed, and pushed out of sight. This is the heart of the toxic-shaming rule system. First, you don't talk about mistakes, but if they are discovered, you have to seek power and control through denial in criticizing and blaming to rid yourself of such shameful mistakes.

7. "Unreliability—Don't expect reliability in relationships. . . . Don't trust anyone . . . " (Bradshaw, p. 40). Since the parents did not have their needs met, they cannot be there for the child. Reliability has to do with keeping promises with a child. We start making so many promises which are broken that we are constantly lying to ourselves. Our lies allow us to act shamelessly toward them.

8. Don't Trust Rule—First, the child learns to not trust his own needs, emotions and feelings, then he or she projects this nontrusting onto others. If the child cannot trust, as an adult-child he or she will never learn intimacy. If a relationship is started, closeness opens the door for vulnerability. By not trusting anyone, there is never a letdown. As an adult, power and control strive to force a person to treat us the way we want to be treated ourselves, yet it usually drives people away.

9. No-Confrontation Rule—When the needs of children are not being met, they learn subtle ways of manipulation to get them met. This teaches a toxic "strategic interaction" to obtain needs, wants, and feelings through indirect means. If we lack the ability to confront others, either when they are harming us or we desire something, we manipulate the relationship to indirectly feed our needs. However, another outcome of this is gossip: we will tell a third party about our problems with another; unfortunately, it just isn't quite the same as confronting the source directly. When a person doesn't confront the source, the problem never really gets solved. Further, the gossiper spends time on everyone else's problem but never his or her own. It becomes a great way to act shamelessly before others.

10. "We're Fine Rule"—As toxic-shamed individuals present a false self, the toxic-shamed family does also. When asked about family relationships, the answer, however presented, is always equated to, "we are just fine." The dysfunctional family system demands cover up just as the individual seeks it. To present the truth to others would create painful social shame.

These are the rules that govern toxically-shamed, dysfunctional family systems. They are how toxic shame is passed from the parent to child and from generation to generation. I believe that criminal behavior originates with toxic shame learned in the family. I believe that when a child is chronically shamed by his caretakers, he develops defenses instead of boundaries that would have allowed the development of a structured life. The results are character patterns that lead to constantly trying to pass his shame onto another by acting shamelessly. The criminal usually incurs intense toxic shame and is acting out.

No theory is absolute, and neither is mine. Yet to spend your life seeking external rewards that can never replace internal joy is, I think, the saddest form of life. To change or curb the crime problem in this country, one has to treat toxic shame.

The ten unwritten but rigid rules listed previously for a dysfunctional family system are also ever-present in prison. In fact, they are the foundation of prison reality.

1. Control—Everyone wants to run something, anything. Some prisoners work their way into certain prison jobs just so they can treat other prisoners like shit.
2. Perfectionism—The system uses perfect compliance to the rules as a means to maintain rigid order. The control freak complains about the daily rules, yet in some perverse way he clings to them and the hierarchy.
3. Blame—Everyone's first defense is to blame. Your crime is never your crime if you can blame it away.
4. Denial of the Five Freedoms—Being able to think, interpret, feel, want, choose, and imagine are shunned for survival.
5. The No-Talk Rule—Is maintained by the population and the prison administration so the true problems never surface.
6. Don't Make Mistakes—Forces the prisoners to exhibit perfect records and innocence to the administration, so they learn not to admit to mistakes and manipulation. It becomes "don't get caught—and when you do, blame someone else!"
7. Unreliability—Don't bother being reliable to others because the system is not. Most offenders come into the system unreliable; the system only reinforces it.
8. Don't Trust Rule—Don't talk about personal matters and trust no one. Trust may let you down and lead to serving more time!
9. No-Confrontation Rule—Offenders have no power so they never approach staff about mistreatment. Prisoners never approach one another, preferring indirect means of communication. If one checks the weak, he feels proud and powerful.
10. "We're Fine" Rule—Individuals will never desire any help or want prevention programs. The assigned programs are a game to impress the system. To add to this, the system tells you if you come honest and admit to any more crime, they will tell you it is added to your history and can be used to hold you longer.

⟨▭⟩⟨▭⟩⟨▭⟩

The unwritten rules of dysfunctional family systems are also the unwritten rules of prison life because the prison system places a large number of toxic-shamed individuals into a small area where they interact only with other toxic-shamed individuals. Just as the dysfunctional family system has rigid rules, the penitentiary also has rigid rules. Like the dysfunctional family, the prison system works on power and control and hierarchy. The rules of the dysfunctional family are the foundation of the pecking order of prison society.

As children, most prisoners suffered abandonment and withdrawal of the emotional bridge to a primary caretaker, and so they lack attachment and the ability to socially bond. Many men in prison also lacked a male role model when they were growing up.

Men who suffer such abandonment tend to be selfish, controlling, insensitive, and lack the ability to enter relationships since they believe others are not treating them as they should be treated. The once-neglected child, now a prisoner, seeks attention through peer pressure and breaking rules. It becomes a paradoxical love–hate relationship with the people around and the prison's segregation system.

Each shamed offender also has plenty of other shamed offenders to mirror and to learn new ways of acting shamelessly. In addition, as individuals project their shame onto one another, each reinforces the others' false selves. Offenders constantly hide their true self. Men are surrounded by others from broken homes, which helps the "lack of attachment" and "indirect means" to drive relationships.

Associations among prisoners therefore utilize control, power seeking, poor communications, withdrawal, fighting, assaulting, manipulation, blaming, criticizing, and game playing. There are no productive, healthy relationships that an offender can bond to and mirror in order to help curb these character patterns. In such an environment, each offender continues to act shamelessly while passing his shame onto others by committing new crimes against each other. Physical and sexual abuse is reenacted over and over again within the prison. Physical violence becomes the norm.

><><><><><

CONCLUDING THOUGHTS

In this theory, I have argued that toxic shame is passed from generation to generation within family units, and that it is the root problem in people who become criminals and end up in prison. Having said that, I want to make sure that the reader does not interpret my writing as blaming my own parents for the fact that I am in prison. I am not now, nor would I support or try to promote, blaming my parents.

I do believe that toxic shame is passed from generation to generation within the family unit. I believe that my parents were enmeshed into their own toxic shame, and that they passed that shame on to me just as their parents had passed it on to them, and so on back in time. Toxic shame is a multigenerational disease. We reinstill toxic shame, with all its beliefs and character patterns through auto suggestion and repetition, keeping it alive within ourselves. When I keep toxic shame alive inside me, I am the course of my own downfall. Blaming my parents would only be another form of denial. If I did this, I would not only be lying to myself, but I would be lying to my victim's family. I would be discounting his death, the death that I caused. Further, I would be discounting the pain I caused his family and my own. Blaming Mom and Dad is not the route of recovery for me; it would be only a way to cloud the facts.

The facts are the facts. Someone is dead at my hands and sadly, humbly, I will never be able to change that fact or make up for it. I can wish that it did not happen but this, once again, would be denial, because the facts are the facts. It did happen. I can feel the pain of knowing that I ruptured another's family system in the most evil way by murdering one of their members. But I will never understand the pain of his parents. I will never be able to explain to them or to their children about his death, nor will they ever be able understand why it had to be their son.

The pain I see and hear in my mother and in my other family members is a pain I can understand. I can feel the pain I caused, the emptiness in my mother's heart that I am locked away in prison, the pain of seeing her and all my family growing old. This keeps me humble.

I have never been with a truly confessed murderer who could find any goodness in the heinous, hideous act of destroying another human life. I cannot and never will be able to. Over the years, I have discovered in myself that there is no reason I can give for murder. I can give the story of the events that occurred, but there is no reason for the death except me.

We are all part of a spiritual journey, and it is my belief that until we recognize this, we cannot accept our mistakes and start healing. If I am angry all the time, I invite anger into my life and seek out people who will be angry along with me. If I hate, I seek out those who hate, to be around me. But if I allow compassion into my soul, then I will allow compassion into my own life and into others' lives around me.

My prayer is not for myself but for those I have hurt. I pray that the acts I caused to change and affect their lives will not bind them into a life of anger, hatred, and bitterness, which can eat a person's soul. I pray this because I have destroyed one life; there is no need to destroy more.

REFERENCE

Bradshaw, John (1988). *Healing the Shame That Binds You.* Deerfield Beach, FL: Health Communications.

DISCUSSION OF APPENDIX A

By the Editors

Bradshaw (1988) argues that healthy people internalize views of themselves as valuable and worthwhile and lovable despite the fact that they have faults and failings and shortcomings. In contrast, people filled with toxic shame internalize a sense of themselves as defective and worthless and unlovable because of similar faults and failings and shortcomings. Highly talented people can be filled with toxic shame while people with few talents may nevertheless have a sense that they are worthwhile and valuable and lovable human beings.

Relying on Bradshaw's work, Carceral argues that the literature on toxic shame describes a wide variety of behaviors that emerge from a toxic-shamed sense of self, most of which are similar to the behavior of the inmates with whom he has lived for the last twenty years. He also argues that the environment of the prison is very similar to the environment of dysfunctional families, whose relations are based on the transmission of toxic shame.

Based on these observations, he therefore proposes a theory that the behavior of serious offenders, which at times can seem almost incomprehensible to ordinary people, ultimately arises from a toxic-shamed sense of self. While "many people suffer from toxic shame" who do not end up in prison, Carceral argues "when the toxic shame is intense, the person can develop habitual patterns of behavior (character patterns) in response to the intense shame that eventually lead the person to incarceration."

〓✕〓✕〓✕〓

Carceral's theory seems underdeveloped, as compared to other theories in contemporary criminology (for a review, see Vold et al., 2001). That seems an inevitable consequence of the fact that its author is a life-sentenced inmate largely without formal education in criminology and largely without access to the current academic literature of the field. However, this does not mean that the theory is without merit.

Compare Carceral's theory, for example, to Gottfredson and Hirschi's (1990) theory, which probably is the most influential theory in criminology today. Gottfredson and Hirschi argue that the failure of parents to consistently monitor and punish a young child's offensive behavior results in "low self-control" when the child grows up. This develops by age eight or so, is very difficult to change after that point, and is associated with higher rates of offending throughout the rest of the person's life. Carceral's theory resembles Gottfredson and Hirschi's in several ways.

Both theories place the causes of crime in early childhood experiences (the failure of parents to consistently monitor and punish vs. the failure of parents to love and nurture and approve while recognizing faults and failures).

Both theories argue that those early childhood experiences result in personality traits (low self-control vs. toxic-shamed sense of self) that remain fairly stable through the rest of the person's life and that are associated with the increased risk of offending.

Both theories describe the traits in similar ways. Gottfredson and Hirschi describe people with low self-control as being impulsive, insensitive, physical (as opposed to mental), risk-taking, short-sighted, and nonverbal (e.g., pp. 15–44, 89–90). Carceral describes people with a toxic-shamed sense of self as being selfish, controlling, insensitive, lacking the ability to enter into relationships, attention-seeking, and violent.

Beyond these similarities, however, there is a significant difference.

In Gottfredson and Hirschi's theory, the crucial early childhood event is the failure of the primary caregiver (usually the parent) to consistently monitor and punish the child for offensive behavior. As a result, the child grows up with a sense of freedom that, after age eight or so, is very difficult to restrain.

In Carceral's theory, the crucial early childhood event is the failure of the primary caregiver to provide love and nurturance and approval to the child while recognizing the child's faults and failures and shortcomings. As a consequence, the child grows up with a sense of self as either "more than human" (i.e., having no faults and failings) or "less than human" (i.e., having *only* faults and failings and therefore worthless and unlovable).

Gottfredson and Hirschi's theory is part of a "control" tradition that goes back at least to the ancient Greeks (see Bernard, 1983). This tradition assumes people have a natural freedom that, if unrestrained, would result in a wide range of criminal and deviant behaviors. Individuals therefore must be shaped and formed and molded (i.e., "controlled") in order to live in societies.

Carceral's theory, in contrast, is associated with a very different tradition, at least as old as the "control" tradition. It assumes that children naturally grow into healthy and productive and ultimately law-abiding adults if they receive appropriate love and care and nurturing.

This difference between the two theories might be illustrated by the old saying: "As the twig is bent, so grows the tree." Both theories reflect this saying because both describe how early childhood events (bending the twig) result in long-term stable consequences in adulthood (the shape of the grown tree).

In the context of this old saying, Gottfredson and Hirschi's theory might be said to focus on pruning unwanted and unattractive branches that naturally would grow on the tree unless something were done. This is the consistent monitoring and punishment of the child's naturally occurring offensive behaviors.

In contrast, Carceral's theory might be said to assume that the twig, if planted in good soil and properly fertilized, naturally will become a beautiful tree all by itself, even if some of its branches grow in odd directions. This is the love and acceptance and recognition of the child despite faults and failings and shortcomings.

❈━❈━❈━❈

There are several ways we find out which, if either, of these two theories is correct. We could, for example, interview offenders and ask them about their memories of childhood. Do they remember receiving consistent monitoring and punishment of their offensive behavior? Do they remember receiving love and acceptance and approval in the context of a realistic view of their own faults and failures? This type of research is *retrospective* because it looks backwards from the present to the past. It also is a *self-report* study because it relies on people to describe their own experiences.

Alternately, we could observe parents as they actually raise their children. We could see which parents consistently monitor and punish their child's offending behavior, and which parents provide love and acceptance and approval in the context of a realistic view of their child's faults and failings. Then we could wait twenty years to see which children turn out to be serious offenders.

This would be a *prospective* (as opposed to retrospective) study because it would go forward in time from the present to the future. It would also be *observational* (as opposed to self-report) because it would rely on independent observations rather than the person's own statements. As such, it would be a stronger research design—i.e., more likely to produce accurate information—but more difficult to perform.

❈━❈━❈━❈

Perhaps such studies eventually will be done. In the meantime, we will give our own "educated guess" on what such studies might find. But first, we need to explain our views about the "causes" of crime.

In our view, the causes of crime are like the causes of cancer. Everyone knows that "smoking causes cancer." But what exactly does that statement mean?

First, it does not mean that smoking causes all kinds of cancer. For example, smoking may cause lung cancer but not cause leukemia.

Second, to say "smoking causes lung cancer" does not mean that smoking is the only cause of lung cancer. For example, exposure to asbestos may also cause lung cancer.

Third, to say "smoking causes lung cancer" does not mean that everyone who smokes will get lung cancer. It's just that people who smoke have a much greater chance of getting lung cancer than other people.

In our view, a similar situation exists with the causes of crime (e.g., Bernard, 2000).

First, we believe that crime is a multifaceted phenomenon, much like cancer is, and that it therefore has many different causes. No one thing causes all the different types of crime, just as smoking does not cause all the different types of cancer.

Second, to assert that one specific thing does cause crime does not mean that nothing else causes crime.

Third, nothing causes crime every single time, just as smoking does not cause cancer every single time. But some things can substantially increase the risk of becoming a criminal, just as smoking substantially increases the risks of getting cancer.

In the context of this view about the causes of crime, we would guess that both the failure to consistently monitor and punish offensive behavior in early childhood, and the transmission of "toxic shame" in early childhood, significantly increase the risk of criminality over the rest of the life span.

We would further guess that the failure to monitor and punish early-childhood behaviors will be more important in the explanation of *less frequent* and *less serious* offending, and that the transmission of toxic shame in early childhood will be more important in the explanation of *more frequent* and *more serious* offending. That is, our guess is that Carceral's theory better explains the behavior of the prisoners with whom he has lived with for the last twenty years than Gottfredson and Hirschi's theory.

⟩⟩⟩⟩⟩

Carceral's theory is consistent with a fairly wide range of current theory and research in criminology. In fact, the theory presented in Appendix A is condensed from an unpublished book-length manuscript in which Carceral interprets much of the theory and research in contemporary criminology from the point of view of his theory. Space considerations in the present book required that all of that criminology material be eliminated.

In particular, we would suggest that Carceral's theory is consistent with a substantial body of research on the early predictors of later delinquency and crime, especially among males (e.g., Farrington, 1998; Garbarino, 1999). It is also consistent with other research suggesting that the most effective long-term crime prevention is achieved with "nurturant strategies" rather than punishment strategies (e.g., Vila, 1997). These nurturant strategies focus on improving the life experiences of young children and are said to take several generations to achieve their full effect. This is similar to Carceral's argument that "toxic shame is a multigenerational disease" that is passed from generation to generation and therefore would take several generations to eliminate.

〓✕〓✕〓✕〓

The specific evidence Carceral presents to support his theory are the stories contained in this book about the behavior of prisoners and about the organization of prisons. The stories themselves have a ring of truth to them, in that the author appears to have captured essential elements in his portrayal of these complex realities.

These stories are evidence in support of Carceral's theory because they are exactly what we would expect to find if his theory were correct. That in itself, however, does not mean that the theory is correct. It does suggest that we might profitably look further into this matter.

This type of evidence is called *anecdotal* evidence. In general, anecdotal evidence is the weakest type of evidence to support a theory. But it also usually is the first type of evidence, so that it usually is where the research process begins. If anecdotal evidence appears to be consistent with a theory, then researchers will take the theory seriously and set up more complex and rigorous tests, such as those described above. If researchers were to take Carceral's theory seriously, that would be the next step.

REFERENCES

Bernard, Thomas J. (1983) *The Consensus-Conflict Debate*. New York: Columbia University Press.

Bernard, Thomas J. (2000) "Integrating Theories in Criminology," pp. 335–46 in Raymond Paternoster and Ronet Bachman, Eds., *Explaining Criminals and Crime*. Los Angeles: Roxbury.

Bradshaw, John (1988), *Healing the Shame That Binds You*. Deerfield Beach, FL: Health Communications.

Farrington, David (1998). "Predictors, Causes, and Correlates of Male Youth Violence," pp. 421–75 in Michael Tonry and Mark H. Moore, Eds., *Youth Violence*. Vol. 24 of *Crime and Justice: A Review of Research*. Chicago: University of Chicago Press.

Garbarino, James (1999). *Lost Boys: Why Our Sons Turn Violent and How We Can Save Them*. New York: Free Press.

Gottfredson, Michael, and Travis Hirschi (1990). *A General Theory of Crime*. Stanford, CA: Stanford University Press.

Vila, Bryan (1997). "Roundtable: Human Nature and Crime Control." *Politics and the Life Sciences*, 16, 3–55.

Vold, George B., Thomas J. Bernard, and Jeffrey B. Snipes (2001). *Theoretical Criminology*, 5th ed. New York: Oxford.

Appendix B

GLOSSARY OF PRISON-PROPER TERMS

The following is a list of common words and phrases that are a part of everyday prison language. In the text, they appear in boldface type.

A.D.J.   see adjustment segregation

adjustment segregation—a classification designation of solitary confinement for punishment of a disciplinary infraction while in prison. Also known as A.D.J., segregation, or the hole.

A&E   assessment and evaluation. In other regions of the country, this process is also known as known as reception and diagnostics.

ain't no punk   a tough person; a situation or event that is described as hard or painful

A.K.A.   also known as; most prisoners are known by a different name than their legal name that they've established through reputation.

artillery   fists or fist-fighting

Aryan   when a person of another race/ethnicity refers to a white person; especially a white gang member

back-to-back   someone who is serving time consecutively for multiple crimes; he must finish the time on one before he starts time on the other.

baked   under the influence of prescription medication distributed by medical staff

bathhouse   shower and/or laundry area

bay-bay kid   a youth that is a troublemaker and does not respect parental control and authority

beat down   assault

beat-down crew   a group of assaultive inmates

Beirut mode   see "max mentality"

biker   a term that people of other race/ethnic groups use for whites; a cracker, redneck, honkie, or peckerwood

bird bath   wash up in the sink in one's cell

biscuit   female

bit   sentence

bitch   female, acting feminine

blue-shirt   line officers; a correctional officer at the rank of sergeant or lower (Note: Color of officer uniforms vary by state.)

bone   male sex organ, having sex

bones   game of dice or dominoes

bootlicker   a prisoner who is acting friendly or "sucking up" to a guard or staff member

booty bandit   male-on-male rapist

boss   correctional officer; turn-key

bounce   to leave or exit

box   radio, fight, segregation, female sex area

bragging rights   winner of a fight

break camp   run; get away

bring the drama   fight

bro/brother   black man, good friend, homey

bud   friend, associate, marijuana

bump it, bump that shit   radio playing loud

bush bandit   child molester

bust your hole   an attempted or completed act of perpetrated rape

cage   cell, home; crib

canteen   a prison store where prisoners can buy hygiene products and snacks

catwalk   a walkway patrolled only by correctional officers that is elevated above the ground (about 1–2 stories high) across a hallway or living area so that staff have a wider or longer range of vision

cave dweller   a prisoner who spends every moment inside his cell by choice, coming out only for the bare necessities (food, shower, medical); also refers to someone who stays in his cell and chooses not to shower (sometimes out of fear of victimization); also known as "viking"

cellhall   older prison housing unit with many cells in it

cellie   cellmate; a roommate who shares a cell

check   a warning for someone else to correct their disrespectful behavior (e.g., "check yourself, punk")

chester   child molester

chill or chillin'   to relax

chronic   marijuana

chow hall   place where prisoners eat

C-note   a $100 bill

Cobras   a prison gang of Latino origin

coke   crack or powdered cocaine

con   someone who has spent many years in prison

contraband   items that can be confiscated because they are illegal (e.g., cash, drugs) or legal items that a person has in large quantities (e.g., too many pairs of underwear)

cool   o.k.

corner   visiting room

cracker   derogatory term for whites

crank   a person that complains all the time, hard to get along with; methamphetamine

crash gate   electronically barred gate in a hallway that controls movement and minimizes disturbances

crib   current living place: cell, home

cuffs   handcuffs

cunt   female guard, female

dayroom   common area within a living unit that is connected with cells or dorms for the purpose of watching television or playing board games

death house   prison medical services

desert boots   state-issued boots; boots typically worn by members of the Aryan Nation

dig   understand; "do you dig?"

dipping   being nosy

dis   disrespecting someone

Disciple   an organized black prison gang

disciplinary report   a report for misconduct while in prison; also known as D.R., a case, or a conduct report

DOC   Department of Corrections

dog   road dog, associate, friend

doing time   serving one's sentence

don't get tore off   avoiding victimization (robbed, assaulted)

doors secured   all cell doors locked

dotted eye   receiving a black eye

drag   lie, story, excuses

drama   fight, bringing out truth someone wants to keep secret

dub   hand-rolled cigarette

dude   a general name for an associate; a way to get someone's attention

ear hustling   being nosy; listening to others' conversations; dipping

entertain me   talk

Esé   an inmate of Hispanic origin (can be a derogatory term if used by non-Hispanic inmates)

fag   fag ass shit, a gay man

feel-ya/smell-ya   degrees of understanding when in a conversation

fire in the hole   See five-0

five-0   a warning to other prisoners that a correctional officer is approaching; see man walking (Note: Other regions of the country use the term "fire in the hole.")

fish   new prisoner; naïve to the prisoner subculture; green to the system

flatten out   mandatory release date

fort   the prison

free world   society outside of the prison walls, "in the free"

freeze me   stop talking to, never talk to me again; freeze the bullshit

fresh meat   new prisoner; a fish

froggy   one who feels like fighting; jumpy

funk   cool; smelly

game   game of life, playing games on others, conning

gangbanger   a gang member

G.D.'s   Gangster Disciples; see Disciples

geek-up system   instigating or encouraging another to fight through peer pressure

general population   see GP

get some business   go away, stop bothering me

get your money   winning at a table game; conning a female; masturbation

Gladiator School   a large unit that houses young and violent inmates where violence is prevalent

GP-general population   being housed with the mainstream of the prison population (as opposed to being in segregation or other special housing)

green   naïve; see fish

green leaf   marijuana

greens   state-issued prisoner uniforms for general population inmates (there are tans, brown, oranges, greens)

gump   a gay man; see crank

gurney   a bed on wheels used to transport inmates to medical

guy   that's my guy; my friend

hanging tough   hanging out; being cool; maintaining oneself during hard times

hear-ya   degrees of understanding when in a conversation

high-tech shit   drugs or drug related; when someone has a good plan

hip   confirming a level of understanding; also known as cool

hit it   leave, masturbation

ho   a female; a male inmate who performs submissive homosexual favors; a prostitute; short for whore

ho smasher   rapist, see "treejumper"

hole   segregation; the box; see A.D.J.

hook   someone who purposefully starts trouble among other inmates

hook-up   create something; mixing soups; got me a hook-up; also a bad situation

honkie   the name that someone of another race/ethnicity will use when referring to person of European descent; a white boy, cracker, peckerwood, wood, snows, etc.

home team group of friends; "he's on my home team"

homey bro, associate, friend

hootch homemade alcohol; vegetables and fruits fermented in a container with yeast or sugar that prisoners use to get drunk; the pressure caused by the fermentation will pop the top of the container as it brews; also known as volcano juice

house cell, also known as crib or room

I.A.- Internal Affairs a unit that investigates major and/or questionable uses of force

inmate a prisoner who is locked up

jacking stealing

jag mag a pornographic magazine

jagging masturbation

jailhouse lawyer prisoner who studies the law and/or helps other prisoners with their cases; also known as legal beagle (works on appeals, seeks time cuts, etc.)

jewelry handcuffs, shackles

kangaroo court A prison disciplinary hearing that involves ranking correctional officers who decide whether a prisoner did or did not commit a disciplinary infraction against the rules.

keepers guards, correctional officers, screws, bosses, turn-keys

kicking it talking with someone else

kick-it-in give up your property

knock straight the fuck out to assault/knock a person out cold

lame story, idea, actions were limited, weak, see-through

Latin Kings a Hispanic prison gang with roots in the Chicago area

L-ball serving a life sentence (originated from eight-ball, which is serving an eight-year sentence)

legal beagle see jailhouse lawyer

lightweights prisoners who lack influence in prisoner society

list a written record of prisoners who owe payment for buying from an illegally run store

living large having money on the books to spend on commissary

lockdown everyone is told to go into their cells and are locked in

lock-n-sock a combination lock or a bar of soap placed in a sock to be used as a weapon

manhood pride, ego

man walking correctional officer approaching

mark someone to be conned; target; pigeon

maxin'-n-relaxin' chilling out, taking it easy

max mentality a way of violent thinking and behavior as a survival tactic that prisoners are forced into when doing time in older maximum security prisons; also known as Beirut mode

mean-mugging giving someone else an intimidating look

mission doing something; on a mission

moon cricket a derogatory term that people of other race/ethnic groups use for African Americans; coon, nigger, etc.

M.R. mandatory release date

mud packer gay man

new boot rookie correctional officer

nigga a friendly expression that African Americans use for another black friend: "that's my nigga."

nigger a derogatory term that people of other race/ethnic groups use for African Americans; moon cricket, coon

old con person locked up a long time

onion female, the lower part of a woman's body

only one life sentence a saying used when prisoners get tired of waiting

open up a can of whoop ass start fighting

O.P.P. other people's problem; other people's property

package a bundle of drugs smuggled into the prison

pat search when an officer searches the outer clothing of a prisoner by patting his body for contraband; also known as a shakedown or pat down

p-board   the Parole board; a committee that decides the optimal time for release

peckerwood   a derogatory term that people of other race/ethnic groups use for whites

perp   perpetrator; player; actions

player   play, played the game, conning

play-it-off   make it seem like you understand

pod   a living unit in a modern prison

police   correctional officer; fire in the hole; guard, etc.

pour salt on someone's back   gossip; talking bad behind someone's back

P.R.C.   program review committee; every prisoner sees this four-member board every six months on housing and job assignments

program   programming: state treatment; also known as "the plan"

program review   see P.R.C.

program segregation   temporary disciplinary housing that follows adjustment segregation, and allows prisoners limited property, but retains them in maximum security

punk   weak person, gay person; a mark

put your business out on the streets a person who talks too much

ratting   snitching, telling, informing (a rat is hated by other inmates inside prison)

real crime   murder and armed robbery perceived by prisoners as doing hard time (note that rape, pedophilia, and other violent crimes are not perceived by prisoners as real crime)

rec   indoor and outdoor recreation yard, weights, basketball, handball, track, etc.

reconstructive learning   permanent maximum security disciplinary housing; freedoms are similar to program segregation

redneck   a derogatory term that people of other race/ethnic groups use for whites; cracker

rep   a reputation

ribbing   joking

rib fest   a group of prisoners sitting around making jokes about one another or joking about current events.

riding the train   getting high or intoxicated

ringout   a buzzer that sounds to indicate that prisoners are leaving their cells for work

roll it   roll a cigarette; roll one

roll right   tobacco

roll the doors   a command from one officer to another to open or close the cell doors on a wing

rotunda   in some prisons this is the main hub of the complex

Royal   a white prison gang

rub   hand-rolled cigarette, "can I roll a rub?"

runner   a prisoner assigned to a job that allows him freedom of movement and participation in the prisoner economic system (e.g., laundry)

running wild   multiple sentences piled on top of one another

sandbox bandit   child molester

screw   guard

seg   segregation; the hole; see A.D.J.

send-out   sending money to someone outside of prison to buy drugs

senior   sergeant, private prison guard

shackles   leg irons that go around both ankles with a bar in the middle to prevent escape

shakedown   see pat search

shank   a homemade weapon used for cutting or stabbing

shit in the game   someone did something to negatively affect another's game

shitter   toilet

shuffle   the way an inmate on prescription drugs walks: medication shuffle

sissy   gay; acting feminine; weak

slick   wise crack, doing something slick

sloppy   see cave dweller

smashed   beat down, lost fight, got assaulted

smokes   cigarettes

snap   going nuts, crazy, can't take it anymore

snipes   cigarette butts

snitch   an informer; an inmate who is believed (whether true or not) to have passed information about one or more other prisoners or activities to the staff; a snitch is despised by other prisoners

spread your cheeks   during strip search: show guard your ass; submit to anal sex from another prisoner

spread your wings   fight; masturbate

square   cigarette; also short for "Square John"

square John   a label for most white prisoners who are not gang members; any person that is involved in positive programs and rehabilitation; lacks back-up friends

square ass shit   dumb ass shit; stupid

staff barber   a prisoner that has the job of cutting correctional officers' hair

stash   hide something

store   an entrepreneurial and illegal service where prisoners and/or gang members sell contraband or state supplies from their cell

straight   okay, telling the truth; not gay

streets   the society outside of prison; also known as bricks, freedom, free world, on the outside, outs, society

strip search   getting naked for inspection by a guard for contraband

strong-armed   assaulted and robbed

sucker punched   being hit without knowing or seeing it

sunshine   matches

sweat some tears   having a hard time, hard day

swipe   penis

take   rob; steal from someone else

take under his wing   guide another; mentor

taxation   robbed, paying dues, etc.

tender   tender-ronie: someone weak, soft, etc.

throw-down   fight

throwing dirt   talking bad about someone

ticket   disciplinary report for misbehavior committed while in prison; also called a "case" in other regions of the country

tier   upper level or levels of housing

time   sentence

tin mirror   shiny metal mirrors in the cells, instead of glass mirrors

tired   expression of dislike for someone else

TLU   temporary lock-up either for minor disciplinary infractions while in prison or while a major infraction is being investigated

together   multiple sentences being served all at the same time rather than consecutively

took his manhood   being raped or beat up

treejumper   rapist on the streets

treejumper school   an area of the prison or an entire prison unit that houses a large number of sex offenders; usually has a sex offender treatment program

turn-key   prison guard stationed at a hallway intersection whose job it is to open locked doors or gates

U.A.s   the analysis of one's urine to test for the presence of drugs in the body

Vice Lords   Black prison gang with roots in the Chicago area

volcano juice   see hootch

wack   used to describe something as good or bad: "that's wack"

walls   cement wall or fence surrounding the entire prison; the name of many maximum security units in the U.S.

wam-wams   junk food

wannabe   follower

wash your ass   shower

weak   soft, punk

wear the snitch label   someone who has been publicly called a snitch or is known for snitching behavior

weed wacker   child rapist

when the bars break   cell doors open

white-shirts   correctional officers of higher rank who wear white shirt as a uniform (Note: color of officer uniforms vary by state.)

wild wild West   violent place

wigger   white person who acts black

wing   a housing unit where all the cells are built in one long row

woods   see peckerwood

yo-yo   getting someone's attention

zine   thorazine; psychotropic medication used for a variety of mental illnesses

zoom-zooms   junk food